Francis Bacon

BACON'S ESSAYS

Francis Bacon

BACON'S ESSAYS

[Edited with Complete Introduction, Biography, Author's Background, Complete Text, Study Questions, Select Criticism and Bibliography]

Aditya Nandwani
B.A. English (Hons), Delhi University;
M.A. (English), IGNOU; Print Journalism (English) YMCA

ANMOL PUBLICATIONS PVT. LTD.
NEW DELHI - 110 002 (INDIA)

ANMOL PUBLICATIONS PVT. LTD.

H.O.: 4374/4B, Ansari Road, Darya Ganj,
New Delhi-110 002 (India)
Ph.: 23278000, 23261597

B.O.: No. 1015, Ist Main Road, BSK IIIrd Stage
IIIrd Phase, IIIrd Block
Bangalore - 560 085 (India)
Visit us at: www.anmolpublications.com

Bacon's Essays

First Published, 2009

PRINTED IN INDIA

Printed at Balaji Offset Press, Delhi.

Contents

Preface

Francis Bacon, 1st Viscount St Alban (22 January 1561 – 9 April 1626) was a popular essayist, statesman and philosopher. His birth place was the York House on the strand in London. His father was the Lord Keeper of the Great Seal under Elizabeth I, Sir Nicholas Bacon. Among his five sons, Francis Bacon was the youngest.

In the year 1603, Francis Bacon was knighted and followed by the creation of Baron Verulam in the year 1618 and Viscount St Alban in the year 1621. Because of Francis Bacon's ill health, his early education was at home. At the age of 15, he was enrolled at Trinity College, Cambridge. His major works comprise of Essays, as well as the Colours of Good and Evil and the Meditationes Sacrae, all published in the year 1597.

Chapter 1

Life and Works

Introduction

Bacon's real claim to fame is: not that he, as the lord chancellor, in 1621, was removed from office for accepting a litigant's bribe; nor, that he was the real writer of the Shakespearean plays (one of the controversies in English literature, the "Baconian controversy"); but rather Francis Bacon is known as a philosopher, one of the first order. Bacon delineated the principles of the inductive method, which constituted a breakthrough in the approach to science, even though philosophers and scientists of the day, - and seemingly today, yet - repudiated both his theories and methodology, alike. Bacon argued that the only knowledge of importance to man was empirically rooted in the natural world; and that a clear system of scientific inquiry would assure man's mastery over the world. He was the originator of the expression, "Knowledge is power." He was quite taken up by the "materialist" theories and the resultant discoveries of both Copernicus and Galileo. Bacon, along with Galileo are known in the literature as "the great anti-Aristotelians who created the 'modern scientific' view of Nature."

Francis Bacon was born at London. He entered Trinity College, Cambridge, at the age of twelve. He studied law and became a barrister in 1582; two years later he took a seat in the House of Commons. His opposition, in 1584, to Queen Elizabeth's tax programme retarded his political advancement. While in the earlier days he supported the earl of Essex, Bacon, in 1601, was involved in his prosecution. With the accession of James I (1566-1625) and thereafter, a number of honours were bestowed on Bacon: he was knighted in 1603, made Solicitor General in 1604, Attorney General in 1613, and Lord Chancellor in 1618. He had powerful enemies; foremost among them was Sir Edward Coke. "Bacon and Coke were bitter political rivals, in Parliament and the law courts." They even contended for the hand of the same woman, a widow, Lady Elizabeth Hatton, "beautiful, widowed, and rich."

Bacon, not having come from a rich family, and always pressed for money: accepted, and this is one of the great surprises of history, a litigant's bribe. This was in 1621; so, just four months after he was raised to the peerage, Bacon was evicted from office. ("I do plainly and ingenuously confess that I am guilty of corruption, and do renounce all defence.") Francis Bacon went into retirement and died in 1626; he was buried at Saint Michael's Church in St. Albans, just north of London, Hertfordshire.

The Elizabethan Times

If one is to get to know about another person's life and their work it will be necessary to take an historical look at the times during which that person lived; this is particularly so of Francis Bacon. Let us first start by looking to the principal actors of the age. Our leading lady is Elizabeth the First, the Queen of England. Elizabeth I, lived between the years 1533 and 1603. She was the daughter of Henry VIII and Anne Boleyn. She was, after her mother's execution, declared illegitimate, but in 1544 Parliament reestablished her in the succession. On her accession in 1558, (she reigned until 1603) England's low fortunes, included: religious strife, a huge government debt, and failure in wars with France.

Her reign took England through one of its greatest periods, a period that saw the country united to become a first-rate European power with a great navy; a period in which commerce and industry prospered and colonization began. Elizabeth followed in her father's footsteps and asserted the Tudor concept of strong rule. She reestablished Anglicanism, and measures against Catholics grew harsher. Although she had many favorites, Elizabeth never married, but she used the possibility of marriage as a diplomatic tool. Vain, fickle in bestowing favors, prejudiced, vacillating, and parsimonious, she was nonetheless considered to be a great monarch, highly aware of the responsibility of rule and immensely courageous.

Other personages of the time should be considered. There would be the 2nd earl of Essex, Robert Devereux (1566-1601) who quite literally lost his head over Elizabeth. Then there was the Earl of Leicester, Robert Dudley (1532-88), who received a number of favours from the queen. Dudley's wife Amy was reported to have committed suicide, but did she? Eventually, Dudley himself was found poisoned to death. Then there was James I (James VI of Scotland), son of Mary, Queen of Scots; and, indeed, Mary, herself. And a string of others, including: Sir William Cecil, Lord Burghley (1520-98), Sir Francis Walsingham (1530-90), Sir Francis Drake (1540-96), Sir Edmund Spencer (1552-1599), Walter Raleigh (1552-1618), Edward Coke (1552-1634), Sir Philip Sidney (1554-86), and Shakespeare (1564-1616). All of these historical figures should be looked up, I have no time but to only mention them at this place. I have yet to undertake an exhaustive examination of Bacon's life; it has been done many times before. The standard biography is that of James Spedding.

Before passing on to saying a few words about Bacon's philosophy it is worthwhile to make the comparison between Sir Thomas More and Francis Bacon, as Frederic R. White did:

"In many external respects, the life of Francis Bacon (1561-1626) was similar to that of Sir Thomas More [1478-1535], a century before. Both came from distinguished families, and both received excellent educations. Both studied law and both practiced that profession. Both entered public life at a comparatively early age, and both finally arrived, at the end of their political careers, at the Lord Chancellorship. Moreover, each fell into disfavor with his sovereign; each was accused of taking bribes; each was condemned and imprisoned in the Tower. Finally, each was the most distinguished writer and thinker of his time, and each was in a sense, a martyr to his faith. More died because of his steadfast devotion to his religion. Bacon, so the story goes, met his death through devotion to experimental science. While testing the preservation powers of snow, he contracted a chill and perished. This external similarity does not extend, however, to the characters of the two men. More was a man of the utmost integrity, sweetness, and generosity; Bacon was by no means admirable."

Bacon's Philosophy

Francis Bacon's major contribution to philosophy was his application of induction, the approach used by modern science, rather than the a priori method of medieval scholasticism. Up to and during Bacon's time there existed philosophies rooted not so much in reason but in pure faith; philosophies promoted by the church.

Bacon was "violently opposed to speculative philosophies and the syllogistic quibbling of the Schoolman..., Bacon argued that the only knowledge of importance to man was empirically rooted in the natural world." "There are and can be only two ways of searching into and discovering truth. The one flies from the senses and particulars to the most general axioms: this way is now in fashion.

The other derives axioms from the senses and particulars, rising by a gradual and unbroken ascent, so that it arrives at the most general axioms last of all. This is the true way, but as yet untried." Thus, Bacon delineated the principles of the inductive thinking method, which, while as a method goes back to the times of Aristotle, constituted a breakthrough in the approach to science. It was just these kind of materialist theories that brought about the great discoveries of Copernicus and Galileo. Bacon could see that the only knowledge of importance to man was empirically rooted in the natural world; and that a clear system of scientific inquiry would assure man's mastery over the world.

Bacon's Writings

"The style of Bacon has an idiosyncrasy which we might expect from his genius." Earlier, we referred to the comparison which Frederic R. White made between Sir Thomas More and Francis Bacon. Their lives were remarkably paralleled, but as White points out there was little similarity between their writings. "More was a classicist and a humanist; his Utopia is well-planned... Bacon... [was a] scientist; his New Atlantis is incomplete, ill-proportioned, somewhat heavy in style, and dogmatically devoted to the glorification of natural science."

Bacon's first work was The Advancement of Learning (1605). His second came along in 1620, Novum Organum; it was part of his larger philosophical work known as Instauratio Magna, of which he only completed two parts: this, Novum Organum, and De Augmentis Scientarum. De Augmentis Scientarum, which came out in 1623, was an expansion of his 1605 work. Apothegms came out in 1624. His aphoristic Essays were continually worked on between 1597 and 1625. Bacon's utopian fable about the island of "Bensalem," the New Atlantis, came out in 1627, appended to Sylva Sylvarum. And his final work, The World, came out three years after his death.

Bacon the Man

Carlyle thought Bacon was one of the few who could "converse with this universe, first hand." And Lord Macaulay thought that Bacon "had a wonderful talent for packing thought close, and rendering it portable... brilliant, expedient"; but, nonetheless, Bacon was to Macaulay a "thoroughly dishonest man." One who so dazzled others by his brilliant mind that he made them forget "the standards of ordinary decency and morality." Bacon acknowledged his weakness: "I will not question whether you... pass for a disinterested man or no; I freely confess myself that I am not, and so, I leave it there." "Francis Bacon's life, with its slow rise to political power and its sudden awful fall, is a drama on the heroic scale of the old Greek tragedies. The world knows the famous last will and testament, where Bacon left his "soul to God above, his body to be buried obscurely, his name to the next ages, and to foreign nations." The world knows his writings, or the titles of them, at least. But there is a composition of Bacon's which the world has lately forgotten or overlooked. In the fullness of his power and reputation as Lord Chancellor of England, Bacon was impeached by Parliament for taking bribes in office, convicted, and banished from London and the law courts....

We shrink from the evidence; it is painful to see genius stoop for a mean prize. Perhaps the times were to blame. To live in the shadow of a Queen's favor, to strive continually for a King's smile, is not pretty work. It drove Sir Walter Raleigh to fantastic plots, to despair, egregious lying and the executioner's block. Outside the circle of royal patronage there was no way for an ambitious man to rise in government, no way at all."

CHRONOLOGY

1558: Elizabeth, the 25-year-old daughter of Henry the VIII ascends to the throne.
1561: Born in London.
1564: Galileo is Born.
1582: Becomes a barrister.
1584: Becomes a member of parliament.
1588: Spanish Armada. Robert Dudley dies.
1601: Prosecutes Essex.
1603: Elizabeth I dies. Knighted. Nov 17th, 1603: the trial of Sir Walter Raleigh, as the Attorney General Coke prosecutes.
1604: Solicitor General.
1605: Publishes The Advancement of Learning.
1606: Coke is made Chief Justice of the Common Pleas on June 20th, 1606.
1613: Attorney General.
1618: Lord Chancellor.
1620: Publishes Novum Organum.
1621: Made a peer. Accepts a litigant's bribe.
1623: Publishes De Augmentis Scientarum.
1624: Publishes Apothegms.
1626: Dies.
1627: His work Apothegms comes out posthumously.
1629: His work The World comes out posthumously

BIOGRAPHY

Francis Bacon, 1st Viscount St Alban (22 January 1561- 9 April 1626) was an English philosopher, statesman, and essayist. He is also known as a proponent of the scientific revolution. Indeed, according to John Aubrey, his dedication may have brought him into a rare historical group of scientists who were killed by their own experiments.

His works established and popularized an inductive methodology for scientific inquiry, often called the Baconian method or simply, the scientific method. His demand for a planned procedure of investigating all things natural marked a new turn in the rhetorical and theoretical framework for science, much of which still informs conceptions of proper methodology today.

Bacon was knighted in 1603, created Baron Verulam in 1618, and created Viscount St Alban in 1621; without heirs, both peerages became extinct upon his death. He has been credited as the creator of the English essay.

Early life

Francis Bacon was born at York House in Strand, London. He was raised as an English gentleman. He was the youngest of five sons of Sir Nicholas Bacon, Lord Keeper of the Great Seal under Elizabeth I. His mother, Ann Cooke, was Sir Nicholas's second wife. She was a daughter of Sir Anthony Cooke and a member of the Reformed Puritan Church. His (maternal) aunt married William Cecil (Lord Burghley), the chief advisor of Queen Elizabeth I.

Biographers believe that Bacon received an education at home in his early years, and that his health during that time, as later, was delicate. He entered Trinity College, Cambridge, in 1573 at the age of twelve, living for three years there with his older brother Anthony. At Cambridge he first met the Queen, who was impressed by his precocious intellect, and was accustomed to calling him "the young Lord Keeper".

There also his studies brought him to the conclusion that the methods (and thus the results) of the science of his day were erroneous. His reverence for Aristotle conflicted with his dislike of Aristotelian philosophy, which seemed to him barren, disputatious, and wrong in its objectives. On 27 June 1576, he and Anthony were entered de societate magistrorum at Gray's Inn, and a few months later they went abroad with Sir Amias Paulet, the English ambassador at Paris. The disturbed state of government and society in France under Henry III afforded him valuable political instruction.

The sudden death of his father in February 1579 necessitated Bacon's return to England, and seriously influenced his fortunes. Sir Nicholas had laid up a considerable sum of money to purchase an estate for his youngest son, but he died before doing so, and Francis was left with only a fifth of that money. Having started with insufficient means, he borrowed money and became habitually in debt. To support himself, he took up his residence in law at Gray's Inn in 1579.

Career

Bacon's goals were threefold: discovery of truth, service to his country, and service to the church. Knowing that a prestigious post would aid him toward these ends, in 1580 he applied, through his uncle, Lord Burghley, for a post at court which might enable him to devote himself to a life of learning. His application failed, and for two years he worked quietly at Gray's Inn giving himself seriously to the study of law, until admitted as an outer barrister in 1582. In 1584 he took his seat in parliament for Melcombe in Dorset, and subsequently for Taunton (1586). He wrote on the condition of parties in the church, and he wrote down his thoughts on philosophical reform in the lost tract, Temporis Partus Maximus, but he failed to obtain a position of the kind he thought necessary for his own success.

In the Parliament of 1586 he took a prominent part in urging the execution of Mary Queen of Scots. About this time he seems again to have approached his powerful uncle, the result of which may possibly be traced in his rapid progress at the bar, and in his receiving, in 1589, the reversion to the Clerkship of the Star Chamber, a valuable appointment, the enjoyment of which, however, he did not enter into until 1608.

During this period Bacon became acquainted with Robert Devereux, 2nd Earl of Essex (1567â€"1601), Queen Elizabeth's favourite. By 1591 he was acting as the earl's confidential adviser. Bacon took his seat for Middlesex when in February 1593 Elizabeth called a Parliament to investigate a Roman Catholic plot against her. His opposition to a bill that would levy triple subsidies in half the usual time (he objected to the time span) offended many people; he was accused of seeking popularity, and was for a time excluded from the court. When the Attorney-Generalship fell vacant in 1594 and Bacon became a candidate for the office, Lord Essex's influence could not secure him the position; in fashion, Bacon failed to become solicitor in 1595. To console him for these disappointments, Essex presented him with a property at Twickenham, which he subsequently sold for Â£1800, the equivalent of around Â£240,000 today.

In 1596 he was made a Queen's Counsel, but missed the appointment of Master of the Rolls. During the next few years, his financial situation remained bad. His friends could find no public office for him, a scheme for retrieving his position by a marriage with the wealthy widow Lady Elizabeth Hatton failed, and in 1598 he was arrested for debt. His standing in the queen's eyes, however, was beginning to improve. He gradually acquired the standing of one of the learned counsel, though he had no commission or warrant and received no salary. His relationship with the queen also improved when he severed ties with Essex, a fortunate move considering that the latter was executed for treason in 1601 - Bacon was one of those appointed to investigate the charges against him, and examine witnesses, in connection with which he showed eagerness in pressing the case against his former friend and benefactor. This act Bacon endeavoured to justify in A Declaration of the Practices and Treasons, etc., of... the Earl of Essex, etc. He received a gift of a fine of Â£1200 on one of Essex's accomplices.

The accession of James I brought Bacon into greater favour; he was knighted in 1603, and endeavoured to set himself right with the new powers by writing his Apologie (defence) of his proceedings in the case of Essex, who had favoured the succession of James.

Bacon was present at the state opening of parliament in 1605, which would have all but certainly made him a victim of the Gunpowder Plot had it succeeded. The following year, during the course of the uneventful first parliament session Bacon married Alice Barnham.

In 1608, Bacon entered upon the Clerkship of the Star Chamber, and was in the enjoyment of a large income; but old debts and present extravagance kept him embarrassed, and he endeavoured to obtain further promotion and wealth by supporting the king in his arbitrary policy.

Bacon's services had been rewarded in June 1607 with the office of Solicitor. In 1610 the famous fourth parliament of James met. Despite Bacon's advice to him, James and the Commons found themselves frequently at odds over royal prerogatives and the king's embarrassing extravagance, and the House was dissolved in February 1611.

Through this Bacon managed in frequent debate to uphold the prerogative, while retaining the confidence of the Commons. In 1613, Bacon was finally able to become attorney general, by dint of advising the king to shuffle judicial appointments; and in this capacity he would prosecute Somerset in 1616. The parliament of April 1614 objected to Bacon's presence in the seat for Cambridge â€" he was allowed to stay, but a law was passed that forbade the attorney-general to sit in parliament â€" and to the various royal plans which Bacon had supported. His obvious influence over the king inspired resentment or apprehension in many of his peers. Bacon continued to receive the King's favour, and in 1618 was appointed by James to the position of Lord Chancellor. His public career ended in disgrace in 1621 when, after having fallen into debt, a Parliamentary Committee on the administration of the law charged him with corruption under twenty-three counts.

To the lords, who sent a committee to inquire whether the confession was really his, he replied, "My lords, it is my act, my hand, and my heart; I beseech your lordships to be merciful to a broken reed." He was sentenced to a fine of Â£40,000, remitted by the king, to be committed to the Tower of London during the king's pleasure (his imprisonment in fact lasted only a few days). More seriously, Lord St Alban (as he had been since earlier in 1621) was declared incapable of holding future office or sitting in parliament. He narrowly escaped being deprived of his titles. Thenceforth the disgraced viscount devoted himself to study and writing.

It has been argued by Nieves Mathews that Bacon was in fact innocent of the bribery charges; Bacon himself said that he was forced to plead guilty so as to save King James from a political scandal, stating:

I was the justest judge, that was in England these last fifty years. When the book of all hearts is opened, I trust I shall not be found to have the troubled fountain of a corrupt heart. I know I have clean hands and a clean heart. I am as innocent of bribes as any born on St Innocents Day.

Parentage theories

Various authors and scholars have written that Francis Bacon was the illegitimate son of Queen Elizabeth and Robert Dudley, Earl of Leicester[1][2] and that Elizabeth's other secret biological son was Robert Devereux, Earl of Essex (who the Queen forced Bacon to prosecute for treason). There is documented evidence that Elizabeth visited Nicholas Bacon's house at Gorhambury at least twice and was entertained by the eight or nine year old Francis.

It is claimed that by the age of fifteen he was frequently present at Queen Elizabeth's Court, and that it was there that he learned for the first time that he was her son. Robert Cecil, Lord Burleigh's son, whispered the secret of the parentage of Francis to the ladies of the Court. The Queen, overhearing one them, Lady Scales, repeating the story, seized the girl and beat her furiously. Francis, who supposedly walked into the room while the fracas was taking place, intervened. He learned the truth â€" and the cause of the incident â€" from the Queen's own lips, and, enraged that he should have taken the girl's part, she added: "Though you are my own child, I bar you from the Succession for withstanding your mother." That same evening, Anne Bacon confirmed the truth of the story, adding that the Queen was married to Robert Dudley in a secret ceremony on January 21, 1561 in the house of Lord Pembroke, and that Nicholas Bacon had been one of the witnesses.

Elizabeth promptly sent him off to France with the ambassador Amyas Paulet, arriving at Calais on the 25 September 1576, and with him went straight to the Court of Henry III. of France. Francis Bacon's trip to France under the care of Sir Amyas Paulet, with a personal send-off from the Queen herself, is a well-documented historical event. No other "commoner" ever received such royal treatment.

Pierre Ambroise, in writing the first biography of Francis Bacon in 1631, writes "And he saw himself destined to one day hold in his hands the helm of the Kingdom." He adds that Francis was "born in the purple" and "brought up in the expectation of a great career". This is another way of saying that he was of royal birth and an heir to the throne. Purple at this time was a colour reserved for royalty, and it would have been considered an insult to the monarch for a subject to clothe himself in robes of purple. Ambroise also mentions that Francis wished to study different peoples, and travelled extensively for some years in Europe, including France, Italy and Spain.

Chapter 2

Personal Relationships

Marriage

While in France, Francis mingled with the most exalted statesmen and wits of the period, and acquired knowledge of foreign courts and politics. For the next three years he visited Blois, Poitiers, Tours, also Italy and Spain. In Paris he allegedly met Marguerite de Valois, daughter of Henry II and Catherine de Medici, sister of the King of France and wife of Henry of Navarre. Marguerite was famous for her beauty, intelligence, and education. When Francis Bacon arrived at the French Court, a divorce was being arranged at Marguerite's instigation.

King Henry of Navarre, her legal husband, was passionately attached to the Baroness de Sauve who virtually lived with him as his mistress. Francis was 18 and Marguerite was 26. They immediately fell in love with each other "at first sight". They vowed that they were "eternally each other's". He remained in France three years, and was then suddenly ordered back to England upon the death of Nicholas Bacon, in February 1579. "Francis Bacon's love for Margueritte was the overmastering passion of his life, and dominated his mind for many years." The first of 7 Sonnets dedicated to his love for Marguerite was written the year he left France. The last ones were written after his public downfall, Sonnet XXX To Marguerite: And a Worthy Brother and Sonnet XXXI Found in Hiram's Grave... Resurrection

When he was 36, Francis engaged in the courtship of Elizabeth Hatton, a young widow of 20. She broke off their relationship upon accepting marriage to a wealthier man. Years later, Bacon still wrote of his regret that the marriage to Elizabeth had never taken place. At the age of forty five, Bacon married Alice Barnham (1592-1650), the fourteen year old daughter of a well-connected London alderman and M.P. Francis wrote 3 Sonnets proclaiming his love for Alice. The first Sonnet was written during his courtship and the second Sonnet on his wedding day 10 May 1606.

The third Sonnet was written years later "when by special Warrant of the King, Lady Bacon was given precedence over all other Court ladies" when Bacon was appointed "Regent of the Kingdom": Let not my Love be call'd Idolatry. Reports of increasing friction in his marriage to Alice Barnham appeared, with speculation that some of this may have been due to financial resources not being as readily available to Alice as she was accustomed to having in the past.

Alice was reportedly interested in fame and fortune, and when reserves of money were no longer available, there were complaints about where all the money was going. A. Chambers Bunten wrote in Life of Alice Barnham that, upon their descent into debt, she actually went on trips to ask for financial favours and assistance from their circle of friends. Francis disinherited her upon discovering her secret romantic relationship with John Underhill. He rewrote his will, which had previously been very generous to her (leaving her lands, goods, and income), to revoke it all.

Homosexuality

Several authors, such as A.L. Rowse, author of Homosexuals in History, believe that Bacon was homosexual. This conclusion has been disputed by others, such as Nieves Mathews, author of Francis Bacon: The History of a Character Assassination, who consider the sources to be questionable and the conclusions open to interpretation. John Aubrey in his Brief Lives says quite bluntly that Bacon 'was a pederast' and had 'ganimeds and favourites'; the puritan moralist Sir Simonds D'Ewes in his Autobiography and Correspondence discusses Bacon's love for his Welsh serving-men; in particular he says that when Bacon had to resign in 1621 he kept ' one Godrick, a verie effeminate faced youth, to bee his catamite and bedfellow, although heee had discharged the most oh his other household svants; which was the more to be admired, because men generallie after his fall begann to discourse of that his unnaturall crime, which hee had practiced manie yeares, destering the bedd of his Ladie ' (diary entry for 3 May 1621)

His mother, Lady Ann Bacon, complained especially about 'that bloody Percy' whom her son kept 'yea as a coach companion and a bed companion'. Many of the youths in his service were left legacies at his death[18]. Bacon's closest friend was Tobie Matthew, actor, spy and the inspiration for Bacon's famous essay 'On Friendship'. His brother, Anthony Bacon was also homosexual and was charged with sodomy in France in 1586.

Freemasonry

Francis Bacon frequently got together with the men at Gray's Inn to discuss politics and philosophy, and to try out various theatrical scenes that he admitted writing. He was frequently hosting banquets in which the leading men in the fields of science, the arts, literature, law, and politics were invited. Bacon's alleged connection to the Rosicrucians and the Freemasons has been widely discussed by authors and scholars in scores of books. Historian Frances Yates, in her books The Occult Philosophy in the Elizabethan Age and The Rosicrucian Enlightenment presents a great deal of evidence that he was involved in some of the more closed intellectual movements of his day - as were a whole host of other important individuals such as Elias Ashmole, Robert Fludd and several others.

On 22 January, 1621 in honour of Sir Francis Bacon's sixtieth birthday, a select group of men assembled without fanfare for a great Masonic banquet. This Masonic banquet was to pay tribute to their leader, Sir Francis Bacon. Only those of the Rosicrosse (Rosicrucians) and the Masons who were already aware of Bacon's leadership role were invited. The meeting was at the Great Hall at York Palace, England (now known as Whitehall). The tables were T-tables with gleaming white drapery and silver. Flowers decorated the Great Hall. A dear long-time friend of Bacon, the famous English Poet Ben Jonson gave a Masonic ode to Bacon that day. Jonson remarked about Bacon, "I love the man and do honour his memory above all others."

In March 1626, Sir Francis Bacon came to London. Continuing his scientific research, he was journeying to Highgate through the snow with the King's physician when, as John Aubrey recounts in Brief Lives, he was suddenly inspired by the possibility of using the snow to preserve meat. According to Aubrey "They were resolved they would try the experiment presently. They alighted out of the coach and went into a poor woman's house at the bottom of Highgate hill, and bought a fowl, and made the woman exenterate it". After stuffing the fowl with snow, he happened to contract a fatal case of pneumonia.

He then attempted to extend his fading lifespan by consuming the fowl that had caused his illness. Some people, including Aubrey, consider these two contiguous, possibly coincidental events as related and causative of his death: "The Snow so chilled him that he immediately fell so extremely ill, that he could not return to his Lodging... but went to the Earle of Arundel's house at Highgate, where they put him into... a damp bed that had not been layn-in... which gave him such a cold that in 2 or 3 days as I remember Mr Hobbes told me, he died of Suffocation." He died at Lord Arundel's home in Highgate on 9 April 1626, leaving assets of about Â£7,000 and debts to the amount of Â£22,000.

At his April 1626 funeral, over thirty great minds collected together their eulogies of him. It is clear from all these eulogies that he was not only loved deeply, but that there was something about his character which led men even of the stature of Ben Jonson to hold him in reverence and awe. A volume of the 32 eulogies was published in Latin in 1730. Bacon's peers refer to him as "a supreme poet" and "a concealed poet," and also link him with the theatre. There was a depth of love by a large body of men toward Bacon, similar to some degree in the manner that disciples love a Master. This is especially true when taking into account his membership (and some say leadership) of secret societies such as the Rosicrucians and Freemasons. Membership was restricted to males only, and secrecy as to the religious and philosophical activities that went on in those lodges was strictly enforced. In the inner esoteric membership, which included Francis Bacon, vows of celibacy (for spiritual reasons) were encouraged.

Works and Philosophy

Bacon's works include his Essays, as well as the Colours of Good and Evil and the Meditationes Sacrae, all published in 1597. His famous aphorism, "knowledge is power", is found in the Meditations. He published The Proficience and Advancement of Learning in 1605. Bacon also wrote In felicem memoriam Elizabethae, a eulogy for the queen written in 1609; and various philosophical works which constitute the fragmentary and incomplete Instauratio magna (Great Renewal), the most important part of which is the Novum Organum (New Instrument, published 1620); in this work he cites three world-changing inventions:

"Printing, gunpowder and the compass: These three have changed the whole face and state of things throughout the world; the first in literature, the second in warfare, the third in navigation; whence have followed innumerable changes, in so much that no empire, no sect, no star seems to have exerted greater power and influence in human affairs than these mechanical discoveries."

In 1623, Bacon expressed his aspirations and ideals in The New Atlantis. Released in 1627, this was his creation of an ideal land where "generosity and enlightenment, dignity and splendor, piety and public spirit" were the commonly held qualities of the inhabitants of Bensalem. In this work, he portrayed a vision of the future of human discovery and knowledge. The plan and organization of his ideal college, "Solomon's House", envisioned the modern research university in both applied and pure science. Peter Linebaugh and Marcus Rediker have argued that Bacon was not as idealistic as Atlantis might suggest. A year prior to the release of New Atlantis, Bacon published an essay that reveals a version of himself not often seen in history. This essay, a lesser-known work entitled, "An Advertisement Touching an Holy War," advocated the elimination of detrimental societal elements by the English and compared this to the endeavors of Hercules while establishing civilized society in ancient Greece. He saw the "extirpation and debellating of giants, monsters, and foreign tyrants, not only as lawful, but as meritorious, even divine honour..." Laurence Lampert wrote that Bacon dared to suggest that a revolution in thinking and acting was necessary because European intellectual and spiritual life as well as European politics had been captured by religious fanaticism that threatened to plunge Renaissance Europe into another dark age.

Bacon chose the old literary device of dialogue to present his argument for wholesale change indirectly. In the conversation of his characters, he allows readers to see the reasons for kindling spiritual warfare against the spiritual rulers of European civilization. Bacon did not propose an actual philosophy, but rather a method of developing philosophy; he wrote that, whilst philosophy at the time used the deductive syllogism to interpret nature, the philosopher should instead proceed through inductive reasoning from fact to axiom to law. Before beginning this induction, the inquirer is to free his mind from certain false notions or tendencies which distort the truth.

These are called "Idols" (idola), and are of four kinds: "Idols of the Tribe" (idola tribus), which are common to the race; "Idols of the Den" (idola specus), which are peculiar to the individual; "Idols of the Marketplace" (idola fori), coming from the misuse of language; and "Idols of the Theatre" (idola theatri), which result from an abuse of authority. The end of induction is the discovery of forms, the ways in which natural phenomena occur, the causes from which they proceed.

Bacon's somewhat fragmentary ethical system, derived through use of his methods, is explicated in the seventh and eighth books of his De augmentis scientiarum (1623). He distinguishes between duty to the community, an ethical matter, and duty to God, a purely religious matter. Any moral action is the action of the human will, which is governed by reason and spurred on by the passions; habit is what aids men in directing their will toward the good. No universal rules can be made, as both situations and men's characters differ.

Bacon distinctly separated religion and philosophy, though the two can coexist. Where philosophy is based on reason, faith is based on revelation, and therefore irrational (or perhaps super-rational) â€" in De augmentis he writes that "the more discordant, therefore, and incredible, the divine mystery is, the more honour is shown to God in believing it, and the nobler is the victory of faith."

And yet he writes in "The Essays: Of Atheism" that "a little philosophy inclineth mans mind to atheism; but depth in philosophy bringeth mens minds about to religion", suggesting he continued to employ inductive reasoning in all areas of his life, including his own spiritual beliefs.

Bacon contrasted the new approach of the development of science, with that of the Middle Ages. He once said, to top it all off: "Men have sought to make a world from their own conception and to draw from their own minds all the material which they employed, but if, instead of doing so, they had consulted experience and observation, they would have the facts and not opinions to reason about, and might have ultimately arrived at the knowledge of the laws which govern the material world."

Bacon and Shakespeare

The Shakespeare authorship question, which ascribes the famous plays to various contemporaries instead of Shakespeare of Stratford, has produced a large number of candidates, of whom Bacon is one of the most popular. An 1888 two-volume book, "The Great Cryptogram", by American journalist and adventurer Ignatius Donnely, had much to do with this. Donnely developed complex numerical schemes for working out hidden messages within the plays, but his methods "were so flexible that one could literally use them to obtain any desired text." Donnely himself used them to discover that Bacon had written not only Shakespeare, but Montaigne and Marlowe as well. After Donnely, the Baconian Theory became extremely popular and gave birth to many further studies of Bacon's cipher.

Edward Clark's late 19th century "The Tale of the Shakespeare Epitaph by Francis Bacon" referred to an inscription on a bust of Shakespeare which he asserted concealed the sentence, "FRA BA WRT EAR AY", an abbreviation of "Francis Bacon wrote Shakespeare's plays." Another author, Francis Carr, has suggested that Bacon wrote not only Shakespeare's plays but Don Quixote as well, while Dr Orville Owen, in his monumental (5 volumes) "Francis Bacon's Cipher Story" (1893-95), recounted his success in using a special machine to prove Bacon the true author of Shakespeare and the son of the Earl of Leicester and Elizabeth I. Even Mark Twain was a Baconian arguing vigorously for Bacon and ridiculing the "Stratfordolators" and the "Shakespearoids" in "Is Shakespeare Dead?" (New York: Harper and Brothers, 1909). Friedrich Nietzsche, in his Ecce Homo (II, 4), also opined that Bacon was the true author of Shakespeare's plays, despite mockingly referring to Donnely as a "muddlehead and blockhead."

Influences Up to the Present

Bacon's ideas about the improvement of the human lot were influential in the 1630s and 1650s among a number of Parliamentarian scholars. During the Restoration, Bacon was commonly invoked as a guiding spirit of the Royal Society founded under Charles II in 1660. In the nineteenth century his emphasis on induction was revived and developed by William Whewell, among others. Various authors have written that there were indications that Francis Bacon had gone into debt while secretly funding the publishing of materials for the Freemasons, Rosicrucians, "Spear-Shakers", "Knights of the Helmet", as well as publishing, with the assistance of Ben Jonson, a selection of the plays that they believe he had written under the pen name of "Shake-Speare" in a "First Folio" in

1623. Furthermore, they allege that Bacon faked his own death, crossed the English Channel, and secretly traveled in disguise after 1626 through France, Germany, Poland, Hungary, and other areas utilizing the secret network of Freemasons and Rosicrucians that he was associated with.

It is alleged that he continued to write under pseudonyms, as he had done before 1626, continuing to write as late as 1670 (using the pseudonym "Comte De Gabalis"). Elinor Von Le Coq, wife of Professor Von Le Coq in Berlin, stated that she had found evidence in the German Archives that Francis Bacon stayed after 1626 with the Andrea family in Germany.

There are some scholars who believe that Bacon's vision for a Utopian New World in North America was laid out in his novel The New Atlantis. He envisioned a land where there would be greater rights for women, the abolishing of slavery, elimination of "debtors prisons", separation of church and state, and freedom of religious and political expression. Francis Bacon played a leading role in creating the British colonies, especially in Virginia, the Carolinas and Newfoundland. His government report on The Virginia Colony was made in 1609. Francis Bacon and his associates formed the Newfoundland Colonization Company and in 1610 sent John Guy to found a colony in Newfoundland. In 1910 Newfoundland issued a stamp to commemorate Francis Bacon's role in establishing Newfoundland. The stamp states about Bacon, "the guiding spirit in Colonization Schemes in 1610."

Francis Bacon's influence can also be seen on a variety of religious and spiritual authors, and on groups that have utilized his writings in their own belief systems. Beginning early in the 20th century in the U.S.A., a number of Ascended Master Teachings organizations began making the claim that Francis Bacon had never died. They believed that soon after completing the "Shake-Speare" plays, he had feigned his own death on Easter Sunday 1626 and then travelled extensively outside of England, eventually attaining his physical Ascension on May 1, 1684 in the region of the Carpathian Mountains. Their belief is that Bacon took on the name "Saint Germain" as an Ascended Master.

Chapter 3

Introduction to Bacon's Essays

Bacon's virtue consists in his style and sagacity, which is all the more penetrating because confined to a certain range of ideas. In the edition of 1597, he had refrained from the ornaments of diction to be found in his earlier works, apparently because the essays were intended only as private notes for the perusal of a few friends. But, by 1612, the popularity of the genre and his own reputation as the inventor 101 induced him to revise the first series and add twenty-eight new essays in a smoother, less jejune style. By 1625, his final edition was complete. This collection contains fifty-eight essays, written with a perfect mastery of language in a spirit of superb confidence.

The true importance of his style is to be found in its pregnancy. In an age of complicated and superficial verbiage, he turns the licence of imaginative and allusive expression into an instrument of accurate and chastened thought. Character writers had introduced their portraits with a pointed or fanciful definition. Bacon does the same, but so as to express an abstract idea in the commonest objects of sight and experience.

Thus, "Men in great place are thrice servants," "Fortune is like the market," "Virtue is like a rich stone, best plain set," "Praise is the reflection of virtue," "He that hath wife and children hath given hostages to fortune." These appeals for confirmation to everyday facts run all through his essays. Selfish statesmen are compared to ants in an orchard; men are bettered by believing in a God, as a dog when he owns a master. Again, though he never condescends to convince, his oracular utterances are the fruit of minute calculation; and this scientific process appears in the almost judicial balancing of pros and contras, as in the essay, "Of Usury," or in the methodical and detailed directions which he gives, as in the essay "Of Travel." His logical habit of mind has transformed even the materials of pedantry. The numerous quotations and illustrations drawn from the Bible, the classics and Machiavelli, seem necessary to his argument, and his unacknowledged appropriations from Montaigne strike one as mere coincidences of thought. All forms of knowledge are subjected to the elucidation of his views on life.

The primum mobile of astronomy illustrates "the motions of the greatest persons in a government," and the legend of Briareus is interpreted as an emblem of the people's power. These excellencies were largely due to the fact that Bacon regarded the popularity of the Essays as ephemeral and was not posing for posterity. He wrote down simply the things which interested himself. This spontaneity carried its own limitations. Many of the essays are made up of extracts, compiled from his other works, and woven together into a new whole.

He frequently misquotes or misrepresents his quoted authors; and, sometimes, he does not adhere closely to the title of his essay. Besides, Bacon led two lives, and in his views on worldly matters we have only half the man: the side of him engaged in a struggle for advancement. 106 Hence, he regards life as a stage, and his meditations almost always recur to the rôle which men play in the eyes of the world. Adversity is discussed as a means of evoking the practice of virtue; friendship is viewed as a condition in which a man's judgment may become clearer and his happiness more complete. Even love and marriage are considered chiefly as an impediment to the serious pursuits of life.

But the greater number of his "Dispersed Meditations" deal with the immediate problem of success; how far secrecy in dissembling will substitute an inborn gift of discretion; whether boldness will counteract a reputation for failure; in what way a knowledge of men rather than of books can be turned to account in the intrigues of court life. These speculations lead him into higher circles of government and diplomacy, where, to penetrate the problems of statecraft, he dispels the illusions of greatness. He fathoms the "inscrutable hearts of kings" and pictures their pitiable isolation and toilsome existence.

His book is destined for the commons of the realm: so the advice which he professes to give their rulers is really an exposure (perhaps not intentional) of the machinery of government. We have glimpses of the monarch seated at the council-board, preparing his public utterances or choosing his favourites. The same interest leads him to raise questions of public policy.

In the essay "On Superstition," he marshals the chief accusations against the Roman Catholic church; and, in treating of the greatness of kingdoms, he does not ignore the bitter quarrel between the peasantry and the gentry. Through every discussion, whether on death and religion, or on gardens and masques, there runs that subconscious ideal of versatile liberal culture out of which the essay sprang.

Chapter 4

Civil and Moral Essays or Counsels

Of Truth

WHAT is truth? said jesting Pilate, and would not stay for an answer. Certainly there be, that delight in giddiness, and count it a bondage to fix a belief; affecting free will in thinking, as well as in acting. Though the sects of philosophers of that kind be gone, yet there remain certain discoursing wits, which are of the same veins, though there be not so much blood in them, as was in those of the ancients. But it is not only the difficulty and labour, which men take in finding out of truth, nor again, that when it is found, it imposeth upon men's thoughts, that doth bring lies in favor; but a natural though corrupt love, of the lie itself.

One of the later school of the Grecians, examineth the matter, and is at a stand, to think what should be in it, that men should love lies; where neither they make for pleasure, as with poets, nor for advantage, as with the merchant; but for the lie's sake. But I cannot tell; this same truth, is a naked, and open day-light, that doth not show the masks, and mummeries, and triumphs, of the world, half so stately and daintily as candle-lights.

Truth may perhaps come to the price of a pearl, that showeth best by day; but it will not rise to the price of a diamond, or carbuncle, that showeth best in varied lights. A mixture of a lie doth ever add pleasure. Doth any man doubt, that if there were taken out of men's minds, vain opinions, flattering hopes, false valuations, imaginations as one would, and the like, but it would leave the minds, of a number of men, poor shrunken things, full of melancholy and indisposition, and unpleasing to themselves? One of the fathers, in great severity, called poesy vinum doemonum, because it filleth the imagination; and yet, it is but with the shadow of a lie. But it is not the lie that passeth through the mind, but the lie that sinketh in, and settleth in it, that doth the hurt; such as we spake of before.

But, howsoever these things are thus in men's depraved judgments, and affections, yet truth, which only doth judge itself, teacheth that the inquiry of truth, which is the love-making, or wooing of it, the knowledge of truth, which is the presence of it, and the belief of truth, which is the enjoying of it, is the sovereign good of human nature. The first creature of God, in the works of the days, was the light of the sense; the last, was the light of reason; and his sabbath work ever since, is the illumination of his Spirit. First he breathed light, upon the face of the matter or chaos; then he breathed light, into the face of man; and still he breatheth and inspireth light, into the face of his chosen.

The poet, that beautified the sect, that was otherwise inferior to the rest, saith yet excellently well: It is a pleasure, to stand upon the shore, and to see ships tossed upon the sea; a pleasure, to stand in the window of a castle, and to see a battle, and the adventures thereof below: but no pleasure is comparable to the standing upon the vantage ground of truth (a hill not to be commanded, and where the air is always clear and serene), and to see the errors, and wanderings, and mists, and tempests, in the vale below: so always that this prospect be with pity, and not with swelling, or pride. Certainly, it is heaven upon earth, to have a man's mind move in charity, rest in providence, and turn upon the poles of truth.

To pass from theological, and philosophical truth, to the truth of civil business; it will be acknowledged, even by those that practice it not, that clear, and round dealing, is the honor of man's nature; and that mixture of falsehoods, is like alloy in coin of gold and silver, which may make the metal work the better, but it embaseth it. For these winding, and crooked courses, are the goings of the serpent; which goeth basely upon the belly, and not upon the feet.

There is no vice, that doth so cover a man with shame, as to be found false and perfidious. And therefore Montaigny saith prettily, when he inquired the reason, why the word of the lie should be such a disgrace, and such an odious charge? Saith he, If it be well weighed, to say that a man lieth, is as much to say, as that he is brave towards God, and a coward towards men. For a lie faces God, and shrinks from man. Surely the wickedness of falsehood, and breach of faith, cannot possibly be so highly expressed, as in that it shall be the last peal, to call the judgments of God upon the generations of men; it being foretold, that when Christ cometh, he shall not find faith upon the earth.

Of Death

MEN fear death, as children fear to go in the dark; and as that natural fear in children, is increased with tales, so is the other. Certainly, the contemplation of death, as the wages of sin, and passage to another world, is holy and religious; but the fear of it, as a tribute due unto nature, is weak. Yet in religious meditations, there is sometimes mixture of vanity, and of superstition.

You shall read, in some of the friars' books of mortification, that a man should think with himself, what the pain is, if he have but his finger's end pressed, or tortured, and thereby imagine, what the pains of death are, when the whole body is corrupted, and dissolved; when many times death passeth, with less pain than the torture of a limb; for the most vital parts, are not the quickest of sense. And by him that spake only as a philosopher, and natural man, it was well said, Pompa mortis magis terret, quam mors ipsa. Groans, and convulsions, and a discolored face, and friends weeping, and blacks, and obsequies, and the like, show death terrible.

It is worthy the observing, that there is no passion in the mind of man, so weak, but it mates, and masters, the fear of death; and therefore, death is no such terrible enemy, when a man hath so many attendants about him, that can win the combat of him. Revenge triumphs over death; love slights it; honor aspireth to it; grief flieth to it; fear preoccupateth it; nay, we read, after Otho the emperor had slain himself, pity (which is the tenderest of affections) provoked many to die, out of mere compassion to their sovereign, and as the truest sort of followers. Nay, Seneca adds niceness and satiety: Cogita quamdiu eadem feceris; mori velle, non tantum fortis aut miser, sed etiam fastidiosus potest. A man would die, though he were neither valiant, nor miserable, only upon a weariness to do the same thing so oft, over and over. It is no less worthy, to observe, how little alteration in good spirits, the approaches of death make; for they appear to be the same men, till the last instant. Augustus CÃ¦sar died in a compliment; Livia, conjugii nostri memor, vive et vale.

Tiberius in dissimulation; as Tacitus saith of him, Jam Tiberium vires et corpus, non dissimulatio, deserebant. Vespasian in a jest, sitting upon the stool; Ut puto deus fio. Galba with a sentence; Feri, si ex re sit populi Romani, holding forth his neck. Septimius Severus in despatch: Adeste si quid mihi restat agendum. And the like. Certainly the Stoics bestowed too much cost upon death, and by their great preparations, made it appear more fearful. Better saith he, Qui finem vitÃ¦ extremum inter munera ponat naturÃ¦. It is as natural to die, as to be born; and to a little infant, perhaps, the one is as painful, as the other. He that dies in an earnest pursuit, is like one that is wounded in hot blood; who, for the time, scarce feels the hurt; and therefore a mind fixed, and bent upon somewhat that is good, doth avert the dolors of death. But, above all, believe it, the sweetest canticle is Nunc dimittis; when a man hath obtained worthy ends, and expectations. Death hath this also; that it openeth the gate to good fame, and extinguisheth envy. —Extinctus amabitur idem.

Of Unity in Religion

Religion being the chief band of human society, is a happy thing, when itself is well contained within the true band of unity. The quarrels, and divisions about religion, were evils unknown to the heathen. The reason was, because the religion of the heathen, consisted rather in rites and ceremonies, than in any constant belief. For you may imagine, what kind of faith theirs was, when the chief doctors, and fathers of their church, were the poets. But the true God hath this attribute, that he is a jealous God; and therefore, his worship and religion, will endure no mixture, nor partner. We shall therefore speak a few words, concerning the unity of the church; what are the fruits thereof; what the bounds; and what the means.

The fruits of unity (next unto the well pleasing of God, which is all in all) are two: the one, towards those that are without the church, the other, towards those that are within. For the former; it is certain, that heresies, and schisms, are of all others the greatest scandals; yea, more than corruption of manners. For as in the natural body, a wound, or solution of continuity, is worse than a corrupt humour; so in the spiritual. So that nothing, doth so much keep men out of the church and drive men out of the church, as breach of unity. And therefore, when so ever it cometh to that pass, that one saith, Ecce in deserto, another saith, Ecce in penetralibus; that is, when some men seek Christ in the conventicles of heretics, and others, in an outward face of a church, that voice had need continually to sound in men's ears, Nolite exire, —Go not out.

The doctor of the Gentiles (the propriety of whose vocation, drew him to have a special care of those without) saith, If an heathen come in, and hear you speak with several tongues, will he not say that you are mad? And certainly it is little better, when atheists, and profane persons, do hear of so many discordant, and contrary opinions in religion; it doth avert them from the church, and made them, to sit down in the chair of the scorners. It is but a light thing, to be vouched in so serious a matter, but yet it expresseth well the deformity.

There is a master of scoffing, that in his catalogue of books of a feigned library, sets down this title of a book, The morris-dance of heretics. For indeed, every sect of them, hath a diverse posture, or cringe by themselves, which cannot but move derision in worldlings, and depraved politics, who are apt to contemn holy things. As for the fruit towards those that are within; it is peace; which containeth infinite blessings. It establisheth faith; it kindleth charity; the outward peace of the church, distilleth into peace of conscience; and it turneth the labors of writing, and reading of controversies, into treaties of mortification and devotion. Concerning the bounds of unity; the true placing of them, importeth exceedingly.

There appear to be two extremes. For to certain zealants, all speech of pacification is odious. Is it peace, Jehu? What hast thou to do with peace? turn thee behind me. Peace is not the matter, but following, and party. Contrariwise, certain Laodiceans, and lukewarm persons, think they may accommodate points of religion, by middle way, and taking part of both, and witty reconcilements; as if they would make an arbitrament between God and man. Both these extremes are to be avoided; which will be done, if the league of Christians, penned by our Savior himself, were in two cross clauses thereof, soundly and plainly expounded: He that is not with us, is against us; and again, He that is not against us, is with us; that is, if the points fundamental and of substance in religion, were truly discerned and distinguished, from points not merely of faith, but of opinion, order, or good intention. This is a thing may seem to many a matter trivial, and done already. But if it were done less partially, it would be embraced more generally.

Of this I may give only this advice, according to my small model. Men ought to take heed, of rending God's church, by two kinds of controversies. The one is, when the matter of the point controverted, is too small and light, not worth the heat and strife about it, kindled only by contradiction. For, as it is noted, by one of the fathers, Christ's coat indeed had no seam, but the church's vesture was of divers colors; whereupon he saith, In veste varietas sit, scissura non sit: they be two things, unity and uniformity. The other is, when the matter of the point controverted, is great, but it is driven to an over-great subtilty, and obscurity; so that it becometh a thing rather ingenious, than substantial.

A man that is of judgment and understanding, shall sometimes hear ignorant men differ, and know well within himself, that those which so differ, mean one thing, and yet they themselves would never agree. And if it come so to pass, in that distance of judgment, which is between man and man, shall we not think that God above, that knows the heart, doth not discern that frail men, in some of their contradictions, intend the same thing; and accepteth of both?

The nature of such controversies is excellently expressed, by St. Paul, in the warning and precept, that he giveth concerning the same, Devita profanas vocum novitates, et oppositiones falsi nominis scientiÃ¦. Men create oppositions, which are not; and put them into new terms, so fixed, as whereas the meaning ought to govern the term, the term in effect governeth the meaning. There be also two false peaces, or unities: the one, when the peace is grounded, but upon an implicit ignorance; for all colors will agree in the dark: the other, when it is pieced up, upon a direct admission of contraries, in fundamental points. For truth and falsehood, in such things, are like the iron and clay, in the toes of Nebuchadnezzar's image; they may cleave, but they will not incorporate.

Concerning the means of procuring unity; men must beware, that in the procuring, or muniting, of religious unity, they do not dissolve and deface the laws of charity, and of human society. There be two swords amongst Christians, the spiritual and temporal; and both have their due office and place, in the maintenance of religion. But we may not take up the third sword, which is Mahomet's sword, or like unto it; that is, to propagate religion by wars, or by sanguinary persecutions to force consciences; except it be in cases of overt scandal, blasphemy, or intermixture of practice against the state; much less to nourish seditions; to authorize conspiracies and rebellions; to put the sword into the people's hands; and the like; tending to the subversion of all government, which is the ordinance of God. For this is but to dash the first table against the second; and so to consider men as Christians, as we forget that they are men. Lucretius the poet, when he beheld the act of Agamemnon, that could endure the sacrificing of his own daughter, exclaimed: Tantum religio potuit suadere malorum. What would he have said, if he had known of the massacre in France, or the powder treason of England? He would have been seven times more Epicure, and atheist, than he was. For as the temporal sword is to be drawn with great circumspection in cases of religion; so it is a thing monstrous, to put it into the hands of the common people. Let that be left unto the Anabaptists, and other furies.

It was great blasphemy, when the devil said, I will ascend and be like the Highest; but it is greater blasphemy, to personate God, and bring him in saying, I will descend, and be like the prince of darkness; and what is it better, to make the cause of religion to descend, to the cruel and execrable actions of murthering princes, butchery of people, and subversion of states and governments? Surely this is to bring down the Holy Ghost, instead of the likeness of a dove, in the shape of a vulture or raven; and set, out of the bark of a Christian church, a flag of a bark of pirates, and assassins.

Therefore it is most necessary, that the church, by doctrine and decree, princes by their sword, and all learnings, both Christian and moral, as by their Mercury rod, do damn and send to hell for ever, those facts and opinions tending to the support of the same; as hath been already in good part done. Surely in counsels concerning religion, that counsel of the apostle would be prefixed, Ira hominis non implet justitiam Dei. And it was a notable observation of a wise father, and no less ingenuously confessed: That those which held and persuaded pressure of consciences, were commonly interessed therein themselves for their own ends.

Of Revenge

REVENGE is a kind of wild justice; which the more man's nature runs to, the more ought law to weed it out. For as for the first wrong, it doth but offend the law; but the revenge of that wrong, putteth the law out of office. Certainly, in taking revenge, a man is but even with his enemy; but in passing it over, he is superior; for it is a prince's part to pardon. And Salomon, I am sure, saith, It is the glory of a man to pass by an offence. That which is past is gone, and irrevocable; and wise men have enough to do, with things present and to come; therefore they do but trifle with themselves, that labour in past matters. There is no man doth a wrong, for the wrong's sake; but thereby to purchase himself profit, or pleasure, or honor, or the like. Therefore why should I be angry with a man, for loving himself better than me? And if any man should do wrong, merely out of ill-nature, why, yet it is but like the thorn or briar, which prick and scratch, because they can do no other.

The most tolerable sort of revenge, is for those wrongs which there is no law to remedy; but then let a man take heed, the revenge be such as there is no law to punish; else a man's enemy is still before hand, and it is two for one. Some, when they take revenge, are desirous, the party should know, whence it cometh. This is the more generous. For the delight seemeth to be, not so much in doing the hurt, as in making the party repent. But base and crafty cowards, are like the arrow that flieth in the dark. Cosmus, duke of Florence, had a desperate saying against perfidious or neglecting friends, as if those wrongs were unpardonable; You shall read (saith he) that we are commanded to forgive our enemies; but you never read, that we are commanded to forgive our friends. But yet the spirit of Job was in a better tune: Shall we (saith he) take good at God's hands, and not be content to take evil also? And so of friends in a proportion.

This is certain, that a man that studieth revenge, keeps his own wounds green, which otherwise would heal, and do well. Public revenges are for the most part fortunate; as that for the death of CÃ¦sar; for the death of Pertinax; for the death of Henry the Third of France; and many more. But in private revenges, it is not so. Nay rather, vindictive persons live the life of witches; who, as they are mischievous, so end they infortunate.

Of Adversity

It was a high speech of Seneca (after the manner of the Stoics): That the good things, which belong to prosperity, are to be wished; but the good things, that belong to adversity, are to be admired. Bona rerum secundarum optabilia;

adversarum mirabilia. Certainly if miracles be the command over nature, they appear most in adversity. It is yet a higher speech of his, than the other (much too high for a heathen), It is true greatness, to have in one the frailty of a man, and the security of a God. Vere magnum habere fragilitatem hominis, securitatem dei. This would have done better in poesy, where transcendences are more allowed. And the poets indeed have been busy with it; for it is in effect the thing, which figured in that strange fiction of the ancient poets, which seemeth not to be without mystery; nay, and to have some approach to the state of a Christian; that Hercules, when he went to unbind Prometheus (by whom human nature is represented), sailed the length of the great ocean, in an earthen pot or pitcher: lively describing Christian resolution, that saileth in the frail bark of the flesh, through the waves of the world.

But to speak in a mean. The virtue of prosperity, is temperance; the virtue of adversity, is fortitude; which in morals is the more heroical virtue. Prosperity is the blessing of the Old Testament; adversity is the blessing of the New; which carrieth the greater benediction, and the clearer revelation of God's favor. Yet even in the Old Testament, if you listen to David's harp, you shall hear as many hearse-like airs as carols; and the pencil of the Holy Ghost hath labored more in describing the afflictions of Job, than the felicities of Salomon. Prosperity is not without many fears and distastes; and adversity is not without comforts and hopes. We see in needle-works and embroideries, it is more pleasing to have a lively work, upon a sad and solemn ground, than to have a dark and melancholy work, upon a lightsome ground: judge therefore of the pleasure of the heart, by the pleasure of the eye. Certainly virtue is like precious odors, most fragrant when they are incensed, or crushed: for prosperity doth best discover vice, but adversity doth best discover virtue.

Of Simulation and Dissimulation

Dissimulation is but a faint kind of policy, or wisdom; for it asketh a strong wit, and a strong heart, to know when to tell truth, and to do it. Therefore it is the weaker sort of politics, that are the great dissemblers. Tacitus saith, Livia sorted well with the arts of her husband, and dissimulation of her son; attributing arts or policy to Augustus, and dissimulation to Tiberius. And again, when Mucianus encourageth Vespasian, to take arms against Vitellius, he saith, We rise not against the piercing judgment of Augustus, nor the extreme caution or closeness of Tiberius. These properties, of arts or policy, and dissimulation or closeness, are indeed habits and faculties several, and to be distinguished.

For if a man have that penetration of judgment, as he can discern what things are to be laid open, and what to be secreted, and what to be showed at half lights, and to whom and when (which indeed are arts of state, and arts of life, as Tacitus well calleth them), to him, a habit of dissimulation is a hinderance and a poorness. But if a man cannot obtain to that judgment, then it is left to him generally, to be close, and a dissembler. For where a man cannot choose, or vary in particulars, there it is good to take the safest, and wariest way, in general; like the going softly, by one that cannot well see. Certainly the ablest men that ever were, have had all an openness, and frankness, of dealing; and a name of certainty and veracity; but then they were like horses well managed; for they could tell passing well, when to stop or turn; and at such times, when they thought the case indeed required dissimulation, if then they used it, it came to pass that the former opinion, spread abroad, of their good faith and clearness of dealing, made them almost invisible.

There be three degrees of this hiding and veiling of a man's self. The first, closeness, reservation, and secrecy; when a man leaveth himself without observation, or without hold to be taken, what he is. The second, dissimulation, in the negative; when a man lets fall signs and arguments, that he is not, that he is. And the third, simulation, in the affirmative; when a man industriously and expressly feigns and pretends to be, that he is not.

For the first of these, secrecy; it is indeed the virtue of a confessor. And assuredly, the secret man heareth many confessions. For who will open himself, to a blab or a babbler?

But if a man be thought secret, it invited discovery; as the more close air sockets in the more open; and as in confession, the revealing is not for worldly use, but for the ease of a man's heart, so secret men come to the knowledge of many things in that kind; while men rather discharge their minds, than impart their minds. In few words, mysteries are due to secrecy. Besides (to say truth) nakedness is uncomely, as well in mind as body; and it added no small reverence, to men's manners and actions, if they be not altogether open.

As for talkers and futile persons, they are commonly vain and credulous withal. For he that talked what he know, will also talk what he know not. Therefore set it down, that an habit of secrecy, is both politic and moral. And in this part, it is good that a man's face give his tongue leave to speak. For the discovery of a man's self, by the tracts of his countenance, is a great weakness and betraying; by how much it is many times more marked, and believed, than a man's words.

For the second, which is dissimulation; it followed many times upon secrecy, by a necessity; so that he that will be secret, must be a dissembler in some degree. For men are too cunning, to suffer a man to keep an indifferent carriage between both, and to be secret, without swaying the balance on either side. They will so beset a man with questions, and draw him on, and pick it out of him, that, without an absurd silence, he must show an inclination one way; or if he do not, they will gather as much by his silence, as by his speech. As for equivocations, or oraculous speeches, they cannot hold out long. So that no man can be secret, except he give himself a little scope of dissimulation; which is, as it were, but the skirts or train of secrecy.

But for the third degree, which is simulation, and false profession; that I hold more culpable, and less politic; except it be in great and rare matters: And therefore a general custom of simulation (which is this last degree) is a vice, rising either of a natural falseness or fearfulness, or of a mind that hath some main faults, which because a man must needs disguise, it make him practice simulation in other things, lest his hand should be out of use.

The great advantages of simulation and dissimulation are three. First, to lay asleep opposition, and to surprise. For where a man's intentions are published, it is an alarum, to call up all that are against them. The second is, to reserve to a man's self a fair retreat. For if a man engage himself by a manifest declaration, he must go through or take a fall. The third is, the better to discover the mind of another. For to him that opens himself, men will hardly show themselves adverse; but will fair let him go on, and turn their freedom of speech, to freedom of thought. And therefore it is a good shrewd proverb of the Spaniard, Tell a lie and find a troth; as if there were no way of discovery, but by simulation.

There be also three disadvantages, to set it even. The first, that simulation and dissimulation commonly carry with them a show of fearfulness, which in any business, doth spoil the feathers, of round flying up to the mark. The second, that it puzzled and perplexed the conceits of many, that perhaps would otherwise co-operate with him; and makes a man walk almost alone, to his own ends. The third and greatest is, that it deprived a man of one of the most principal instruments for action; which is trust and belief. The best composition and temperature, is to have openness in fame and opinion; secrecy in habit; dissimulation in seasonable use; and a power to feign, if there be no remedy.

Of Parents and Children

The joys of parents are secret; and so are their grief's and fears. They cannot utter the one; nor they will not utter the other. Children sweeten labors; but they make misfortunes more bitter. They increase the cares of life; but they mitigate the remembrance of death. The perpetuity by generation is common to beasts; but memory, merit, and noble works, are proper to men. And surely a man shall see the noblest works and foundations have proceeded from childless men, which have sought to express the images of their minds, where those of their bodies have failed. So the care of posterity is most in them, that have no posterity. They that are the first raisers of their houses, are most indulgent towards their children;

beholding them as the continuance, not only of their kind, but of their work; and so both children and creatures. The difference in affection, of parents towards their several children, is many times unequal; and sometimes unworthy; especially in the mothers; as Salomon saith, A wise son rejoiceth the father, but an ungracious son shames the mother. A man shall see, where there is a house full of children, one or two of the eldest respected, and the youngest made wantons; but in the midst, some that are as it were forgotten, who many times, nevertheless, prove the best. The illiberality of parents, in allowance towards their children, is an harmful error; makes them base; acquaints them with shifts; makes them sort with mean company; and makes them surfeit more when they come to plenty. And therefore the proof is best, when men keep their authority towards the children, but not their purse.

Men have a foolish manner (both parents and schoolmasters and servants) in creating and breeding an emulation between brothers, during childhood, which many times sorteth to discord when they are men, and disturbeth families. The Italians make little difference between children, and nephews or near kinsfolks; but so they be of the lump, they care not though they pass not through their own body. And, to say truth, in nature it is much a like matter; insomuch that we see a nephew sometimes resembled an uncle, or a kinsman, more than his own parent; as the blood happens. Let parents choose betimes, the vocations and courses they mean their children should take; for then they are most flexible; and let them not too much apply themselves to the disposition of their children, as thinking they will take best to that, which they have most mind to. It is true, that if the affection or aptness of the children be extraordinary, then it is good not to cross it; but generally the precept is good, Optimum elige, suave et facile illud faciet consuetudo. Younger brothers are commonly fortunate, but seldom or never where the elder are disinherited.

Of Marriage and Single Life

He that hath wife and children hath given hostages to

fortune; for they are impediments to great enterprises, either of virtue or of mischief. Certainly the best works, and of greatest merit for the public, have proceeded from the unmarried or childless men; which both in affection and means, have married and endowed the public. Yet it was great reason that those that have children should have greatest care of future times; unto which they know they must transmit their dearest pledges. Some there are, who though they lead a single life, yet their thoughts do end with themselves, and account future times impertinences.

Nay, there are some other, that account wife and children, but as bills of charges. Nay more, there are some foolish rich covetous men that take a pride, in having no children, because they may be thought so much the richer. For perhaps they have heard some talk, Such an one is a great rich man, and another except to it, Yea, but he hath a great charge of children; as if it were an abatement to his riches. But the most ordinary cause of a single life, is liberty, especially in certain self-pleasing and humorous minds, which are so sensible of every restraint, as they will go near to think their girdles and garters, to be bonds and shackles. Unmarried men are best friends, best masters, best servants; but not always best subjects; for they are light to run away; and almost all fugitives, are of that condition. A single life doth well with churchmen; for charity will hardly water the ground, where it must first fill a pool. It is indifferent for judges and magistrates; for if they be facile and corrupt, you shall have a servant, five times worse than a wife.

For soldiers, I find the generals commonly in their hortative, put men in mind of their wives and children; and I think the despising of marriage amongst the Turks, make the vulgar soldier more base. Certainly wife and children are a kind of discipline of humanity; and single men, though they may be many times more charitable, because their means are less exhaust, yet, on the other side, they are more cruel and hardhearted (good to make severe inquisitors), because their tenderness is not so oft called upon.

Grave natures, led by custom, and therefore constant, are commonly loving husbands, as was said of Ulysses, Vetulam suam prÃ¦tulit immortalitati. Chaste women are often proud and froward, as presuming upon the merit of their chastity. It is one of the best bonds, both of chastity and obedience, in the wife, if she think her husband wise; which she will never do, if she find him jealous. Wives are young men's mistresses; companions for middle age; and old men's nurses. So as a man may have a quarrel to marry, when he will. But yet he was reputed one of the wise men, that made answer to the question, when a man should marry? A young man not yet, an elder man not at all. It is often seen that bad husbands, have very good wives; whether it be, that it raiseth the price of their husband's kindness, when it comes; or that the wives take a pride in their patience. But this never fails, if the bad husbands were of their own choosing, against their friends' consent; for then they will be sure to make good their own folly.

Of Envy

There be none of the affections, which have been noted to fascinate or bewitch, but love and envy. They both have vehement wishes; they frame themselves readily into imaginations and suggestions; and they come easily into the eye, especially upon the present of the objects; which are the points that conduce to fascination, if any such thing there be. see likewise, the Scripture called envy an evil eye; and the astrologers, call the evil influences of the stars, evil aspects; so that still there seemed to be acknowledged, in the act of envy, an ejaculation or irradiation of the eye.

Nay, some have been so curious, as to note, that the times when the stroke or percussion of an envious eye doth most hurt, are when the party envied is beheld in glory or triumph; for that sets an edge upon envy: and besides, at such times the spirits of the person envied, do come forth most into the outward parts, and so meet the blow. But leaving these curiosities (though not unworthy to be thought on, in fit place), we will handle, what persons are apt to envy others; what persons are most subject to be envied themselves; and what is the difference between public and private envy. A man that hath no virtue in himself, ever envied virtue in others. For men's minds, will either feed upon their own good, or upon others' evil; and who wanted the one, will prey upon the other; and whoso is out of hope, to attain to another's virtue, will seek to come at even hand, by depressing another's fortune.

A man that is busy, and inquisitive, is commonly envious. For to know much of other men's matters, cannot be because all that ado may concern his own estate; therefore it must needs be, that he take a kind of play-pleasure, in looking upon the fortunes of others. Neither can he that minded but his own business find much matter for envy. For envy is a gadding passion, and walked the streets, and doth not keep home: Non est curiosus, quin idem sit malevolus.

Men of noble birth, are noted to be envious towards new men, when they rise. For the distance is altered, and it is like a deceit of the eye, that when others come on, they think themselves, go back. Deformed persons, and eunuchs, and old men, and bastards, are envious. For he that cannot possibly mend his own case, will do what he can, to impair another's; except these defects light upon a very brave, and heroical nature, which thinketh to make his natural wants part of his honor; in that it should be said, that an eunuch, or a lame man, did such great matters; affecting the honor of a miracle; as it was in Narses the eunuch, and Agesilaus and Tamberlanes, that were lame men.

The same is the case of men that rise after calamities and misfortunes. For they are as men fallen out with the times; and think other men's harms, a redemption of their own sufferings. They that desire to excel in too many matters, out of levity and vain glory, are ever envious. For they cannot want work; it being impossible, but many, in some one of those things, should surpass them. Which was the character of Adrian the Emperor; that mortally envied poets, and painters, and artificers, in works wherein he had a vein to excel. Lastly, near kinsfolk, and fellows in office, and those that have been bred together, are more apt to envy their equals, when they are raised. For it doth upbraid unto them their own fortunes, and pointed at them, and cometh oftener into their remembrance, and incurred likewise more into the note of others; and envy ever redoubled from speech and fame. Cain's envy was the more vile and malignant, towards his brother Abel, because when his sacrifice was better accepted, there was no body to look on. Thus much for those, that are apt to envy.

Concerning those that are more or less subject to envy: First, persons of eminent virtue, when they are advanced, are less envied. For their fortune seemed, but due unto them; and no man envied the payment of a debt, but rewards and liberality rather. Again, envy is ever joined with the comparing of a man's self; and where there is no comparison, no envy; and therefore kings are not envied, but by kings. Nevertheless it is to be noted, that unworthy persons are most envied, at their first coming in, and afterwards overcome it better; whereas contrariwise, persons of worth and merit are most envied, when their fortune continued long. For by that time, though their virtue be the same, yet it hath not the same luster; for fresh men grow up that darken it.

Persons of noble blood, are less envied in their rising. For it seemed but right done to their birth. Besides, there seemed not much added to their fortune; and envy is as the sunbeams, that beat hotter upon a bank, or steep rising ground, than upon a flat. And for the same reason, those that are advanced by degrees, are less envied than those that are advanced suddenly and per saltum.

Those that have joined with their honor great travels, cares, or perils, are less subject to envy. For men think that they earn their honors hardly, and pity them sometimes; and pity ever healeth envy. Wherefore you shall observe, that the more deep and sobre sort of politic persons, in their greatness, are ever bemoaning themselves, what a life they lead; chanting a quanta patimur. Not that they feel it so, but only to abate the edge of envy. But this is to be understood, of business that is laid upon men, and not such, as they call unto themselves. For nothing increaseth envy more, than an unnecessary and ambitious engrossing of business. And nothing doth extinguish envy than for a great person to preserve all other inferior officers, in their full rights and pre-eminences of their places. For by that means, there be so many screens between him and envy. Above all, those are most subject to envy, which carry the greatness of their fortunes, in an insolent and proud manner; being never well, but while they are showing how great they are, either by outward pomp, or by triumphing over all opposition or competition; whereas wise men will rather do sacrifice to envy, in suffering themselves sometimes of purpose to be crossed, and overborne in things that do not much concern them.

Notwithstanding, so much is true, that the carriage of greatness, in a plain and open manner (so it be without arrogance and vain glory) doth draw less envy, than if it be in a more crafty and cunning fashion. For in that course, a man doth but disavow fortune; and seemed to be conscious of his own want in worth; and doth but teach others, to envy him.

Lastly, to conclude this part; as we said in the beginning, that the act of envy had somewhat in it of witchcraft, so there is no other cure of envy, but the cure of witchcraft; and that is to remove the lot (as they call it) and to lay it upon another. For which purpose, the wiser sort of great persons, bring in ever upon the stage somebody upon whom to derive the envy, that would come upon themselves; sometimes upon ministers and servants; sometimes upon colleagues and associates; and the like; and for that turn there are never wanting, some persons of violent and undertaking natures, who, so they may have power and business, will take it at any cost.

Now, to speak of public envy. There is yet some good in public envy, whereas in private, there is none. For public envy, is as an ostracism, that eclipsed men, when they grow too great. And therefore it is a bridle also to great ones, to keep them within bounds. This envy, being in the Latin word invidia, goeth in the modern language, by the name of discontentment: of which we shall speak, in handling sedition. It is a disease, in a state, like to infection. For as infection spread upon that which is sound, and tainted it; so when envy is gotten once into a state, it traduced even the best actions thereof, and turned them into an ill odor. And therefore there is little won, by intermingling of plausible actions. For that doth argue but a weakness, and fear of envy, which hurtled so much the more, as it is likewise usual in infections; which if you fear them, you call them upon you. This public envy, seemed to beat chiefly upon principal officers or ministers, rather than upon kings, and estates themselves. But this is a sure rule, that if the envy upon the minister be great, when the cause of it in him is small; or if the envy be general, in a manner upon all the ministers of an estate; then the envy (though hidden) is truly upon the state itself. And so much of public envy or discontentment, and the difference thereof from private envy, which was handled in the first place.

We will add this in general, touching the affection of envy; that of all other affections, it is the most importune and continual. For of other affections, there is occasion given, but now and then; and therefore it was well said, Invidia festos dies non agit. For it is ever working upon some or other.

And it is also noted, that love and envy do make a man pine, which other affections do not, because they are not so continual. It is also the vilest affection, and the most depraved; for which cause it is the proper attribute of the devil, who is called The envious man, that soweth tares amongst the wheat by night: as it always cometh to pass, that envy worketh subtilly, and in the dark, and to the prejudice of good things, such as is the wheat.

Of Love

The stage is more beholding to love, than the life of man. For as to the stage, love is ever matter of comedies, and now and then of tragedies; but in life it doth much mischief; sometimes like a siren, sometimes like a fury. You may observe, that amongst all the great and worthy persons (whereof the memory remaineth, either ancient or recent) there is not one, that hath been transported to the mad degree of love: which shows that great spirits, and great business, do keep out this weak passion.

You must except, nevertheless, Marcus Antonius, the half partner of the empire of Rome, and Appius Claudius, the decemvir and lawgiver; whereof the former was indeed a voluptuous man, and inordinate; but the latter was an austere and wise man: and therefore it seems (though rarely) that love can find entrance, not only into an open heart, but also into a heart well fortified, if watch be not well kept. It is a poor saying of Epicurus, Satis magnum alter alteri theatrum sumus: as if man, made for the contemplation of heaven, and all noble objects, should do nothing but kneel before a little idol and make himself a subject, though not of the mouth (as beasts are), yet of the eye; which was given him for higher purposes.

It is a strange thing, to note the excess of this passion, and how it braves the nature, and value of things, by this; that the speaking in a perpetual hyperbole, is comely in nothing but in love. Neither is it merely in the phrase; for whereas it hath been well said, that the arch-flatterer, with whom all the petty flatterers have intelligence, is a man's self; certainly the lover is more. For there was never proud man thought so absurdly well of himself, as the lover doth of the person loved; and therefore it was well said, That it is impossible to love and to be wise.

Neither doth this weakness appear to others only, and not to the party loved; but to the loved most of all, except the love be reciproque. For it is a true rule, that love is ever rewarded, either with the reciproque, or with an inward and secret contempt. By how much the more, men ought to beware of this passion, which loseth not only other things, but itself! As for the other losses, the poet's relation doth well figure them: that he that preferred Helena, quitted the gifts of Juno and Pallas. For whosoever esteemeth too much of amorous affection, quitteth both riches and wisdom.

This passion hath his floods, in very times of weakness; which are great prosperity, and great adversity; though this latter hath been less observed: both which times kindle love, and make it more fervent, and therefore show it to be the child of folly. They do best, who if they cannot but admit love, yet make it keep quarters; and sever it wholly from their serious affairs, and actions, of life; for if it check once with business, it troubleth men's fortunes, and made men, that they can no ways be true to their own ends. I know not how, but martial men are given to love: I think, it is but as they are given to wine; for perils commonly ask to be paid in pleasures. There is in man's nature, a secret inclination and motion, towards love of others, which if it be not spent upon some one or a few, doth naturally spread itself towards many, and made men become humane and charitable; as it is seen sometime in friars. Nuptial love made mankind; friendly love perfecteth it; but wanton love corrupteth, and embaseth it.

Of Great Place

Men in great place are thrice servants: servants of the sovereign or state; servants of fame; and servants of business. So as they have no freedom; neither in their persons, nor in their actions, nor in their times. It is a strange desire, to seek power and to lose liberty: or to seek power over others, and to lose power over a man's self. The rising unto place is laborious; and by pains, men come to greater pains; and it is sometimes base; and by indignities, men come to dignities. The standing is slippery, and the regress is either a downfall, or at least an eclipse, which is a melancholy thing.

Cum non sis qui fueris, non esse cur velis vivere. Nay, retire men cannot when they would, neither will they, when it were reason; but are impatient of privateness, even in age and sickness, which require the shadow; like old townsmen, that will be still sitting at their street door, though thereby they offer age to scorn.

Certainly great persons had need to borrow other men's opinions, to think themselves happy; for if they judge by their own feeling, they cannot find it; but if they think with themselves, what other men think of them, and that other men would fain be, as they are, then they are happy, as it were, by report; when perhaps they find the contrary within.

For they are the first, that find their own griefs, though they be the last, that find their own faults. Certainly men in great fortunes are strangers to themselves, and while they are in the puzzle of business, they have no time to tend their health, either of body or mind.

Illi mors gravis incubat, qui notus nimis omnibus, ignotus moritur sibi. In place, there is license to do good, and evil;

whereof the latter is a curse: for in evil the best condition is not to will; the second, not to can. But power to do good, is the true and lawful end of aspiring. For good thoughts (though God accept them) yet, towards men, are little better than good dreams, except they be put in act; and that cannot be, without power and place, as the vantage, and commanding ground.

Merit and good works, is the end of man's motion; and conscience of the same is the accomplishment of man's rest. For if a man can be partaker of God's theatre, he shall likewise be partaker of God's rest. Et conversus Deus, ut aspiceret opera quÃ¦ fecerunt manus suÃ¦, vidit quod omnia essent bona nimis; and then the sabbath. In the discharge of thy place, set before thee the best examples; for imitation is a globe of precepts. And after a time, set before thee thine own example; and examine thyself strictly, whether thou didst not best at first. Neglect not also the examples, of those that have carried themselves ill, in the same place; not to set off thyself, by taxing their memory, but to direct thyself, what to avoid.

Reform therefore, without bravery, or scandal of former times and persons; but yet set it down to thyself, as well to create good precedents, as to follow them. Reduce things to the first institution, and observe wherein, and how, they have degenerate; but yet ask counsel of both times; of the ancient time, what is best; and of the latter time, what is fittest. Seek to make thy course regular, that men may know beforehand, what they may expect; but be not too positive and peremptory; and express thyself well, when thou digressest from thy rule. Preserve the right of thy place; but stir not questions of jurisdiction; and rather assume thy right, in silence and de facto, than voice it with claims, and challenges.

Preserve likewise the rights of inferior places; and think it more honor, to direct in chief, than to be busy in all. Embrace and invite helps, and advices, touching the execution of thy place; and do not drive away such, as bring thee information, as meddlers; but accept of them in good part. The vices of authority are chiefly four: delays, corruption, roughness, and facility. For delays: give easy access; keep times appointed; go through with that which is in hand, and interlace not business, but of necessity. For corruption: do not only bind thine own hands, or, thy servants' hands, from taking, but bind the hands of suitors also, from offering. For integrity used doth the one; but integrity professed, and with a manifest detestation of bribery, doth the other. And avoid not only the fault, but the suspicion. Whosoever is found variable, and changeth manifestly without manifest cause, giveth suspicion of corruption.

Therefore always, when thou changest thine opinion or course, profess it plainly, and declare it, together with the reasons that move thee to change; and do not think to steal it. A servant or a favourite, if he be inward, and no other apparent cause of esteem, is commonly thought, but a by-way to close corruption. For roughness: it is a needless cause of discontent: severity breedeth fear, but roughness breedeth hate. Even reproofs from authority, ought to be grave, and not taunting. As for facility: it is worse than bribery. For bribes come but now and then; but if importunity, or idle respects, lead a man, he shall never be without. As Salomon saith, To respect persons is not good; for such a man will transgress for a piece of bread.

It is most true, that was anciently spoken, A place showeth the man: and it showeth some to the better, and some to the worse. Omnium consensu capax imperii, nisi imperasset, saith Tacitus of Galba; but of Vespasian he saith, Solus imperantium, Vespasianus mutatus in melius: though the one was meant of sufficiency, the other of manners, and affection. It is an assured sign of a worthy and generous spirit, whom honor amends. For honor is, or should be, the place of virtue and as in nature, things move violently to their place, and calmly in their place, so virtue in ambition is violent, in authority settled and calm.

All rising to great place is by a winding star; and if there be factions, it is good to side a man's self, whilst he is in the rising, and to balance himself when he is placed. Use the memory of thy predecessor, fairly and tenderly; for if thou dost not, it is a debt will sure be paid when thou art gone. If thou have colleagues, respect them, and rather call them, when they look not for it, than exclude them, when they have reason to look to be called. Be not too sensible, or too remembering, of thy place in conversation, and private answers to suitors; but let it rather be said, When he sits in place, he is another man.

Of Boldness

It is a trivial grammar-school text, but yet worthy a wise man's consideration. Question was asked of Demosthenes, what was the chief part of an orator? he answered, action: what next? action: what next again? action. He said it, that knew it best, and had, by nature, himself no advantage in that he commended. A strange thing, that that of an orator, which is but superficial and rather the virtue of a player, should be placed so high, above those other noble parts, of invention, elocution, and the rest; nay, almost alone, as if it were all in all. But the reason is plain.

There is in human nature generally, more of the fool than of the wise; and therefore those faculties, by which the foolish part of men's minds is taken, are most potent. Wonderful like is the case of boldness in civil business: what first? boldness: what second and third? boldness. And yet boldness is a child of ignorance and baseness, far inferior to other parts. But nevertheless it doth fascinate, and bind hand and foot, those that are either shallow in judgment, or weak in courage, which are the greatest part; yea and prevaileth with wise men at weak times. Therefore we see it hath done wonders, in popular states; but with senates, and princes less; and more ever upon the first entrance of bold persons into action, than soon after; for boldness is an ill keeper of promise. Surely, as there are mountebanks for the natural body, so are there mountebanks for the politic body; men that undertake great cures, and perhaps have been lucky, in two or three experiments, but want the grounds of science, and therefore cannot hold out. Nay, you shall see a bold fellow many times do Mahomet's miracle. Mahomet made the people believe that he would call an hill to him, and from the top of it offer up his prayers, for the observers of his law.

The people assembled; Mahomet called the hill to come to him, again and again; and when the hill stood still, he was never a whit abashed, but said, If the hill will not come to

Mahomet, Mahomet, will go to the hill. So these men, when they have promised great matters, and failed most shamefully, yet (if they have the perfection of boldness) they will but slight it over, and make a turn, and no more ado. Certainly to men of great judgment, bold persons are a sport to behold; nay, and to the vulgar also, boldness has somewhat of the ridiculous.

For if absurdity be the subject of laughter, doubt you not but great boldness is seldom without some absurdity. Especially it is a sport to see, when a bold fellow is out of countenance; for that puts his face into a most shrunken, and wooden posture; as needs it must; for in bashfulness, the spirits do a little go and come; but with bold men, upon like occasion, they stand at a stay; like a stale at chess, where it is no mate, but yet the game cannot stir.

But this last were fitter for a satire than for a serious observation. This is well to be weighed; that boldness is ever blind; for it seeth not danger, and inconveniences. Therefore it is ill in counsel, good in execution; so that the right use of bold persons is, that they never command in chief, but be seconds, and under the direction of others. For in counsel, it is good to see dangers; and in execution, not to see them, except they be very great.

Of Goodness & Goodness Of Nature

I take goodness in this sense, the affecting of the weal of men, which is that the Grecians call philanthropia; and the word humanity (as it is used) is a little too light to express it. Goodness I call the habit, and goodness of nature, the inclination. This of all virtues, and dignities of the mind, is the greatest; being the character of the Deity: and without it, man is a busy, mischievous, wretched thing; no better than a kind of vermin. Goodness answers to the theological virtue, charity, and admits no excess, but error.

The desire of power in excess, caused the angels to fall; the desire of knowledge in excess, caused man to fall: but in charity there is no excess; neither can angel, nor man, come in danger by it. The inclination to goodness, is imprinted deeply in the nature of man; insomuch, that if it issue not towards men, it will take unto other living creatures; as it is seen in the Turks, a cruel people, who nevertheless are kind to beasts, and give alms, to dogs and birds; insomuch, as Busbechius reporteth, a Christian boy, in Constantinople, had like to have been stoned, for gagging in a waggishness a long-billed fowl.

Errors indeed in this virtue of goodness, or charity, may be committed. The Italians have an ungracious proverb, Tanto buon che val niente: So good, that he is good for nothing. And one of the doctors of Italy, Nicholas Machiavel, had the confidence to put in writing, almost in plain terms, That the Christian faith, had given up good men in prey to those that are tyrannical and unjust. Which he spake, because indeed there was never law, or sect, or opinion, did so much magnify goodness, as the Christian religion doth.

Therefore, to avoid the scandal and the danger both, it is good, to take knowledge of the errors of an habit so excellent. Seek the good of other men, but be not in bondage to their faces or fancies; for that is but facility, or softness; which taketh an honest mind prisoner. Neither give thou Ã†sop's cock a gem, who would be better pleased, and happier, if he had had barley-corn. The example of God, teacheth the lesson truly: He sendeth his rain, and made his sun to shine, upon the just and unjust; but he doth not rain wealth, nor shine honor and virtues, upon men equally. Common benefits, are to be communicate with all; but peculiar benefits, with choice.

And beware how in making the portraiture, thou breakest the pattern. For divinity, made the love of ourselves the pattern; the love of our neighbors, but the portraiture. Sell all thou hast, and give it to the poor, and follow me: but, sell not all thou hast, except thou come and follow me; that is, except thou have a vocation, wherein thou mayest do as much good, with little means as with great; for otherwise, in feeding the streams, thou driest the fountain. Neither is there only a habit of goodness, directed by right reason; but there is in some men, even in nature, a disposition towards it; as on the other side, there is a natural malignity. For there be that in their nature do not affect the good of others.

The lighter sort of malignity, turneth but to a crossness, or frowardness, or aptness to oppose, or difficulties, or the like; but the deeper sort, to envy and mere mischief. Such men, in other men's calamities, are, as it were, in season, and are ever on the loading part: not so good as the dogs, that licked Lazarus' sores; but like Ries, that are still buzzing upon any thing that is raw; misanthropi, that make it their practice, to bring men to the bough, and yet never a tree for the purpose in their gardens, as Timon had.

Such dispositions, are the very errors of human nature; and yet they are the fittest timber, to make great pontics of; like to knee timber, that is good for ships, that are ordained to be tossed; but not for building houses, that shall stand firm. The parts and signs of goodness, are many.

If a man be gracious and courteous to strangers, it shows he is a citizen of the world, and that his heart is no island, cut off from other lands, but a continent, that joins to them. If he be compassionate towards the afflictions of others, it shows that his heart is like the noble tree, that is wounded itself, when it gives the balm. If he easily pardons, and remits offences, it shows that his mind is planted above injuries; so that he cannot be shot. If he be thankful for small benefits, it shows that he weighs men's minds, and not their trash.

But above all if he have St. Paul's perfection, that he would wish to be anathema from Christ, for the salvation of his brethren, it shows much of a divine nature, and a kind of conformity with Christ himself.

Of Nobility

We will speak of nobility, first as a portion of an estate, then as a condition of particular persons. A monarchy, where there is no nobility at all, is ever a pure and absolute tyranny; as that of the Turks. For nobility attempts sovereignty, and draws the eyes of the people, somewhat aside from the line royal. But for democracies, they need it not; and they are commonly more quiet, and less subject to sedition, than where there are stirs of nobles. For men's eyes are upon the business, and not upon the persons; or if upon the persons, it is for the business' sake, as fittest, and not for flags and pedigree. We see the Switzers last well, notwithstanding their diversity of religion, and of cantons. For utility is their bond, and not respects. The united provinces of the Low Countries, in their government, excel; for where there is an equality, the consultations are more indifferent, and the payments and tributes, more cheerful. A great and potent nobility, addeth majesty to a monarch, but diminisheth power; and putteth life and spirit into the people, but presseth their fortune.

It is well, when nobles are not too great for sovereignty nor for justice; and yet maintained in that height, as the insolency of inferiors may be broken upon them, before it come on too fast upon the majesty of kings. A numerous nobility causeth poverty, and inconvenience in a state; for it is a surcharge of expense; and besides, it being of necessity, that many of the nobility fall, in time, to be weak in fortune, it made a kind of disproportion, between honor and means. As for nobility in particular persons; it is a reverend thing, to see an ancient castle or building, not in decay; or to see a fair timber tree, sound and perfect. How much more, to behold an ancient noble family, which has stood against the waves and weathers of time! For new nobility is but the act of power, but ancient nobility is the act of time.

Those that are first raised to nobility, are commonly more virtuous, but less innocent, than their descendants; for there is rarely any rising, but by a commixture of good and evil arts. But it is reason, the memory of their virtues remain to their posterity, and their faults die with themselves. Nobility of birth commonly abateth industry; and he that is not industrious, envieth him that is.

Besides, noble persons cannot go much higher; and he that standeth at a stay, when others rise, can hardly avoid motions of envy. On the other side, nobility extinguisheth the passive envy from others, towards them; because they are in possession of honor. Certainly, kings that have able men of their nobility, shall find ease in employing them, and a better slide into their business; for people naturally bend to them, as born in some sort to command.

Of Seditions and Troubles

Shepherds of people, had need know the calendars of tempests in state; which are commonly greatest, when things grow to equality; as natural tempests are greatest about the Ã†quinoctia. And as there are certain hollow blasts of wind, and secret swellings of seas before a tempest, so are there in states:

—Ille etiam cÃ¦cos instare tumultus
SÃ¦pe monet, fraudesque et operta tumescere bella.

Libels and licentious discourses against the state, when they are frequent and open; and in like sort, false news often running up and down, to the disadvantage of the state, and hastily embraced; are amongst the signs of troubles. Virgil, giving the pedigree of Fame, saith she was sister to the Giants:

Illam Terra parens, ira irritata deorum,
Extremam (ut perhibent) Coeo Enceladoque sororem
Progenuit.—

As if fames were the relics of seditions past; but they are no less, indeed, the preludes of seditions to come. Howsoever he noteth it right, that seditious tumults, and seditious fames, differ no more but as brother and sister, masculine and feminine; especially if it come to that, that the best actions of a state, and the most plausible, and which ought to give greatest contentment, are taken in ill sense, and traduced: for that shows the envy great, as Tacitus saith, Conflata magna invidia, seu bene seu male gesta premunt.

Neither doth it follow, that because these fames are a sign of troubles, that the suppressing of them with too much severity, should be a remedy of troubles. For the despising of them, many times checks them best; and the going about to stop them, doth but make a wonder long-lived. Also that kind of obedience, which Tacitus speaketh of, is to be held suspected: Erant in officio, sed tamen qui mallent mandata imperantium interpretari quam exequi: disputing, excusing, cavilling upon mandates and directions, is a kind of shaking off the yoke, and assay of disobedience; especially if in those disputings, they which are for the direction, speak fearfully and tenderly, and those that are against it, audaciously. Also, as Machiavel noteth well, when princes, that ought to be common parents, make themselves as a party, and lean to a side, it is as a boat, that is overthrown by uneven weight on the one side; as was well seen, in the time of Henry the Third of France; for first, himself entered league for the extirpation of the Protestants; and presently after, the same league was turned upon himself. For when the authority of princes, is made but an accessory to a cause, and that there be other bands, that tie faster than the band of sovereignty, kings begin to be put almost out of possession.

Also, when discords, and quarrels, and factions are carried openly and audaciously, it is a sign the reverence of government is lost. For the motions of the greatest persons in a government, ought to be as the motions of the planets under primum mobile, according to the old opinion: which is, that every of them, is carried swiftly by the highest motion, and softly in their own motion.

And therefore, when great ones in their own particular motion, move violently, and, as Tacitus expresseth it well, liberius quam ut imperantium meminissent, it is a sign the orbs are out of frame. For reverence is that? Where with princes are girt from God; who threateneth the dissolving thereof: Solvam cingula regum.

So when any of the four pillars of government, are mainly shaken, or weakened (which are religion, justice, counsel, and treasure), men had need to pray for fair weather. But let us pass from this part of predictions (concerning which, nevertheless, more light may be taken from that which followeth); and let us speak first, of the materials of seditions; then of the motives of them; and thirdly of the remedies.

Concerning the materials of seditions. It is a thing well to be considered; for the surest way to prevent seditions (if the times do bear it) is to take away the matter of them. For if there be fuel prepared, it is hard to tell, whence the spark shall come, that shall set it on fire. The matter of seditions is of two kinds: much poverty, and much discontentment. It is certain, so many overthrown estates, so many votes for troubles. Lucan noteth well the state of Rome before the Civil War,

Hinc usura vorax, rapidumque in tempore foenus,
Hinc concussa fides, et multis utile bellum.

This same multis utile bellum, is an assured and infallible sign, of a state disposed to seditions and troubles. And if this poverty and broken estate in the better sort, be joined with a want and necessity in the mean people, the danger is imminent and great. For the rebellions of the belly are the worst. As for discontentments, they are, in the politic body, like to humors in the natural, which are apt to gather a preternatural heat, and to inflame.

And let no prince measure the danger of them by this, whether they be just or unjust: for that were to imagine people, to be too reasonable; who do often spurn at their own good: nor yet by this, whether the griefs whereupon they rise, be in fact great or small: for they are the most dangerous discontentments, where the fear is greater than the feeling. Dolendi modus, timendi non item. Besides, in great oppressions, the same things that provoke the patience, do withal mate the courage; but in fears it is not so. Neither let any prince, or state, be secure concerning discontentments, because they have been often, or have been long, and yet no peril hath ensued: for as it is true, that every vapor or fume doth not turn into a storm; so it is nevertheless true, that storms, though they blow over divers times, yet may fall at last; and, as the Spanish proverb noteth well, The cord breaketh at the last by the weakest pull.

The causes and motives of seditions are, innovation in religion; taxes; alteration of laws and customs; breaking of privileges; general oppression; advancement of unworthy persons; strangers; dearths; disbanded soldiers; factions grown desperate; and what soever, in offending people, joineth and knitteth them in a common cause.

For the remedies; there may be some general preservatives, whereof we will speak: as for the just cure, it must answer to the particular disease; and so be left to counsel, rather than rule. The first remedy or prevention is to remove, by all means possible, that material cause of sedition whereof we spake; which is, want and poverty in the estate. To which purpose serveth the opening, and well-balancing of trade; the cherishing of manufactures; the banishing of idleness; the repressing of waste, and excess, by sumptuary laws; the improvement and husbanding of the soil; the regulating of prices of things vendible; the moderating of taxes and tributes; and the like. Generally, it is to be foreseen that the population of a kingdom (especially if it be not mown down by wars) do not exceed the stock of the kingdom, which should maintain them. Neither is the population to be reckoned only by number; for a smaller number, that spend more and earn less, do wear out an estate sooner, than a greater number that live lower, and gather more. Therefore the multiplying of nobility, and other degrees of quality, in an over proportion to the common people, doth speedily bring a state to necessity; and so doth likewise an overgrown clergy; for they bring nothing to the stock; and in like manner, when more are bred scholars, than preferments can take off.

It is likewise to be remembered, that forasmuch as the increase of any estate must be upon the foreigner (for whatsoever is somewhere gotten, is somewhere lost), there be but three things, which one nation selleth unto another; the commodity as nature yieldeth it; the manufacture; and the vecture, or carriage. So that if these three wheels go, wealth will flow as in a spring tide. And it cometh many times to pass, that materiam superabit opus; that the work and carriage is more worth than the material, and enricheth a state more; as is notably seen in the Low-Countrymen, who have the best mines above ground, in the world.

Above all things, good policy is to be used, that the treasure and moneys, in a state, be not gathered into few hands. For otherwise a state may have a great stock, and yet starve. And money is like muck, not good except it be spread. This is done, chiefly by suppressing, or at least keeping a strait hand, upon the devouring trades of usury, ingrossing great pasturages, and the like. For removing discontentments, or at least the danger of them; there is in every state (as we know) two portions of subjects; the noblesse and the commonalty. When one of these is discontent, the danger is not great; for common people are of slow motion, if they be not excited by the greater sort; and the greater sort are of small strength, except the multitude be apt, and ready to move of themselves. Then is the danger, when the greater sort, do but wait for the troubling of the waters amongst the meaner, that then they may declare themselves.

The poets feign, that the rest of the gods would have bound Jupiter; which he hearing of, by the counsel of Pallas, sent for Briareus, with his hundred hands, to come in to his aid. An emblem, no doubt, to show how safe it is for monarchs, to make sure of the good will of common people. To give moderate liberty for griefs and discontentments to evaporate (so it be without too great insolency or bravery), is a safe way. For he that turneth the humors back, and made the wound bleed inwards, endangereth malign ulcers, and pernicious imposthumations.

The part of Epimetheus mought well become Prometheus, in the case of discontentments: for there is not a better provision against them. Epimetheus, when griefs and evils flew abroad, at last shut the lid, and kept hope in the bottom of the vessel. Certainly, the politic and artificial nourishing, and entertaining of hopes, and carrying men from hopes to hopes, is one of the best antidotes against the poison of discontentments.

And it is a certain sign of a wise government and proceeding, when it can hold men's hearts by hopes, when it cannot by satisfaction; and when it can handle things, in such manner, as no evil shall appear so peremptory, but that it hath some outlet of hope; which is the less hard to do, because both particular persons and factions, are apt enough to flatter themselves, or at least to brave that, which they believe not.

Also the foresight and prevention, that there be no likely or fit head, whereunto discontented persons may resort, and under whom they may join, is a known, but an excellent point of caution. I understand a fit head, to be one that hath greatness and reputation; that hath confidence with the discontented party, and upon whom they turn their eyes; and that is thought discontented, in his own particular: which kind of persons, are either to be won, and reconciled to the state, and that in a fast and true manner; or to be fronted with some other, of the same party, that may oppose them, and so divide the reputation. Generally, the dividing and breaking, of all factions and combinations that are adverse to the state, and setting them at distance, or at least distrust, amongst themselves, is not one of the worst remedies. For it is a desperate case, if those that hold with the proceeding of the state, be full of discord and faction, and those that are against it, be entire and united.

I have noted that some witty and sharp speeches which have fallen from princes have given fire to seditions. CÃ¦sar did himself infinite hurt in that speech, Sylla nescivit literas, non potuit dictare; for it did utterly cut off that hope, which men had entertained, that he would at one time or other give over his dictatorship. Galba undid himself by that speech, Legi a se militem, non emi; for it put the soldiers out of hope of the donative. Probus likewise, by that speech, Si vixero, non opus erit amplius Romano imperio militibus: a speech of great despair for the soldiers.

And many the like. Surely princes had need, in tender matters and ticklish times, to beware what they say; especially in these short speeches, which fly abroad like darts, and are thought to be shot out of their secret intentions. For as for large discourses, they are flat things, and not so much noted. Lastly, let princes, against all events, not be without some great person, one or rather more, of military valor, near unto them, for the repressing of seditions in their beginnings. For without that, there useth to be more trepidation in court upon the first breaking out of troubles, than were fit. And the state runneth the danger of that which Tacitus saith; Atque is habitus animorum fuit, ut pessimum facinus auderent pauci, plures vellent, omnes paterentur. But let such military persons be assured, and well reputed of, rather than factious and popular; holding also good correspondence with the other great men in the state; or else the remedy, is worse than the disease.

Of Atheism

I had rather believe all the fables in the Legend, and the

Talmud, and the Alcoran, than that this universal frame is without a mind. And therefore, God never wrought miracle, to convince atheism, because his ordinary works convince it. It is true, that a little philosophy inclineth man's mind to atheism; but depth in philosophy bringeth men's minds about to religion. For while the mind of man looketh upon second causes scattered, it may sometimes rest in them, and go no further; but when it beholdeth the chain of them, confederate and linked together, it must needs fly to Providence and Deity. Nay, even that school which is most accused of atheism doth most demonstrate religion; that is, the school of Leucippus and Democritus and Epicurus.

For it is a thousand times more credible, that four mutable elements, and one immutable fifth essence, duly and eternally placed, need no God, than that an army of infinite small portions, or seeds unplaced, should have produced this order and beauty, without a divine marshal. The Scripture saith, The fool hath said in his heart, there is no God: it is not said, The fool hath thought in his heart; so as he rather saith it, by rote to himself, as that he would have, than that he can thoroughly believe it, or be persuaded of it. For none deny, there is a God, but those, for whom it made that there were no God. It appeareth in nothing more, that atheism is rather in the lip, than in the heart of man, than by this; that atheists will ever be talking of that their opinion, as if they fainted in it, within themselves, and would be glad to be strengthened, by the consent of others.

Nay more, you shall have atheists strive to get disciples, as it fareth with other sects. And, which is most of all, you shall have of them, that will suffer for atheism, and not recant; whereas if they did truly think, that there were no such thing as God, why should they trouble themselves? Epicurus is charged, that he did but dissemble for his credit's sake, when he affirmed there were blessed natures, but such as enjoyed themselves, without having respect to the government of the world. Wherein they say he did temporize; though in secret, he thought there was no God. But certainly he is traduced; for his words are noble and divine: Non deos vulgi negare profanum; sed vulgi opiniones diis applicare profanum. Plato could have said no more. And although he had the confidence, to deny the administration, he had not the power, to deny the nature.

The Indians of the West, have names for their particular gods, though they have no name for God: as if the heathens should have had the names Jupiter, Apollo, Mars, etc., but not the word Deus; which shows that even those barbarous people have the notion, though they have not the latitude and extent of it. So that against atheists, the very savages take part, with the very subtlest philosophers. The contemplative atheist is rare: a Diagoras, a Bion, a Lucian perhaps, and some others; and yet they seem to be more than they are; for that all that impugn a received religion, or superstition, are by the adverse part branded with the name of atheists.

But the great atheists, indeed are hypocrites; which are ever handling holy things, but without feeling; so as they must needs be cauterized in the end. The causes of atheism are: divisions in religion, if they be many; for any one main division, addeth zeal to both sides; but many divisions introduce atheism. Another is, scandal of priests; when it is come to that which St. Bernard saith: Non est jam dicere, ut populus sic sacerdos; quia nec sic populus ut sacerdos. A third is, custom of profane scoffing in holy matters; which doth, by little and little, deface the reverence of religion. And lastly, learned times, specially with peace and prosperity; for troubles and adversities do more bow men's minds to religion.

They that deny a God, destroy man's nobility; for certainly man is of kin to the beasts, by his body; and, if he be not of kin to God, by his spirit, he is a base and ignoble creature. It destroys likewise magnanimity, and the raising of human nature; for take an example of a dog, and mark what a generosity and courage he will put on, when he finds himself maintained by a man; who to him is instead of a God, or melior natura; which courage is manifestly such, as that creature, without that confidence of a better nature than his own, could never attain. So man, when he resteth and assureth himself, upon divine protection and favor, gathered a force and faith, which human nature in itself could not obtain. Therefore, as atheism is in all respects hateful, so in this, that it depriveth human nature of the means to exalt itself, above human frailty.

As it is in particular persons, so it is in nations. Never was there such a state for magnanimity as Rome. Of this state hear what Cicero saith: Quam volumus licet, patres conscripti, nos amemus, tamen nec numero Hispanos, nec robore Gallos, nec calliditate Poenos, nec artibus GrÃ¦cos, nec denique hoc ipso hujus gentis et terrÃ¦ domestico nativoque sensu Italos ipsos et Latinos; sed pietate, ad religione, atque hac una sapientia, quod deorum immortalium numine omnia regi gubernarique perspeximus, omnes gentes nationesque superavimus.

Of Superstition

It were better to have no opinion of God at all, than such an opinion, as is unworthy of him. For the one is unbelief, the other is contumely; and certainly superstition is the reproach of the Deity. Plutarch saith well to that purpose: Surely (saith he) I had rather a great deal, men should say, there was no such man at all as Plutarch, than that they should say, that there was one Plutarch that would eat his children as soon as they were born; as the poets speak of Saturn. And as the contumely is greater towards God, so the danger is greater towards men.

Atheism leaves a man to sense, to philosophy, to natural piety, to laws, to reputation all which may be guides to an outward moral virtue, though religion were not; but superstition dismounts all these, and erecteth an absolute monarchy, in the minds of men. Therefore atheism did never perturb states; for it makes men wary of themselves, as looking no further: and we see the times inclined to atheism (as the time of Augustus CÃ¦sar) were civil times. But superstition hath been the confusion of many states, and bringeth in a new primum mobile, that ravisheth all the spheres of government.

The master of superstition, is the people; and in all superstition, wise men follow fools; and arguments are fitted to practice, in a reversed order. It was gravely said by some of the prelates in the Council of Trent, where the doctrine of the

Schoolmen bare great sway, that the schoolmen were like astronomers, which did feign eccentrics and epicycles, and such engines of orbs, to save the phenomena; though they knew there were no such things; and in like manner, that the Schoolmen had framed a number of subtle and intricate axioms, and theorems, to save the practice of the church.

The causes of superstition are: pleasing and sensual rites and ceremonies; excess of outward and pharisaical holiness; overgreat reverence of traditions, which cannot but load the church; the stratagems of prelates, for their own ambition and lucre; the favoring too much of good intentions, which openeth the gate to conceits and novelties; the taking an aim at divine matters, by human, which cannot but breed mixture of imaginations: and, lastly, barbarous times, especially joined with calamities and disasters.

Superstition, without a veil, is a deformed thing; for, as it addeth deformity to an ape, to be so like a man, so the similitude of superstition to religion, makes it the more deformed. And as wholesome meat corrupteth to little worms, so good forms and orders corrupt, into a number of petty observances. There is a superstition in avoiding superstition, when men think to do best, if they go furthest from the superstition, formerly received; therefore care would be had that (as it fareth in ill purgings) the good be not taken away with the bad; which commonly is done, when the people is the reformer.

Of Travel

Travel, in the younger sort, is a part of education, in the elder, a part of experience. He that travelleth into a country, before he hath some entrance into the language, goeth to school, and not to travel.

That young men travel under some tutor, or grave servant, I allow well; so that he be such a one that hath the language, and hath been in the country before; whereby he may be able to tell them what things are worthy to be seen, in the country where they go; what acquaintances they are to seek; what exercises, or discipline, the place yieldeth. For else, young men shall go hooded, and look abroad little. It is a strange thing, that in sea voyages, where there is nothing to be seen, but sky and sea, men should make diaries; but in land-travel, wherein so much is to be observed, for the most part they omit it; as if chance were fitter to be registered, than observation.

Let diaries, therefore, be brought in use. The things to be seen and observed are: the courts of princes, especially when they give audience to ambassadors; the courts of justice, while they sit and hear causes; and so of consistories ecclesiastic; the churches and monasteries, with the monuments which are therein extant; the walls and fortifications of cities, and towns, and so the heavens and harbors; antiquities and ruins; libraries; colleges, disputations, and lectures, where any are; shipping and navies; houses and gardens of state and pleasure, near great cities; armories; arsenals; magazines; exchanges; burses; warehouses; exercises of horsemanship, fencing, training of soldiers, and the like; comedies, such whereunto the better sort of persons do resort; treasuries of jewels and robes; cabinets and rarities; and, to conclude, whatsoever is memorable, in the places where they go. After all which, the tutors, or servants, ought to make diligent inquiry.

As for triumphs, masks, feasts, weddings, funerals, capital executions, and such shows, men need not to be put in mind of them; yet are they not to be neglected. If you will have a young man to put his travel into a little room, and in short time to gather much, this you must do. First, as was said, he must have some entrance into the language before he goeth. Then he must have such a servant, or tutor, as knoweth the country, as was likewise said. Let him carry with him also, some card or book, describing the country where he travelleth; which will be a good key to his inquiry.

Let him keep also a diary. Let him not stay long, in one city or town; more or less as the place deserveth, but not long; nay, when he stayeth in one city or town, let him change his lodging from one end and part of the town, to another; which is a great adamant of acquaintance. Let him sequester himself, from the company of his countrymen, and diet in such places, where there is good company of the nation where he traveled.

Let him, upon his removes from one place to another, procure recommendation to some person of quality, residing in the place whither he removed; that he may use his favor, in those things he desired to see or know. Thus he may abridge his travel, with much profit. As for the acquaintance, which is to be sought in travel; that which is most of all profitable, is acquaintance with the secretaries and employed men of ambassadors: for so in traveling in one country, he shall suck the experience of many. Let him also see, and visit, eminent persons in all kinds, which are of great name abroad; that he may be able to tell, how the life agreed with the fame. For quarrels, they are with care and discretion to be avoided.

They are commonly for mistresses, healths, place, and words. And let a man beware, how he keepeth company with choleric and quarrelsome persons; for they will engage him into their own quarrels. When a traveller returneth home, let him not leave the countries, where he hath travelled, altogether behind him; but maintain a correspondence by letters, with those of his acquaintance. which are of most worth. And let his travel appear rather in his discourse, than his apparel or gesture; and in his discourse, let him be rather advised in his answers, than forward to tell stories; and let it appear that he doth not change his country manners, for those of foreign parts; but only prick in some flowers, of that he hath learned abroad, into the customs of his own country.

Of Empire

It is a miserable state of mind, to have few things to desire, and many things to fear; and yet that commonly is the case of kings; who, being at the highest, want matter of desire, which makes their minds more languishing; and have many representations of perils and shadows, which makes their minds the less clear. And this is one reason also, of that effect which the Scripture speaketh of, That the king's heart is inscrutable.

For multitude of jealousies, and lack of some predominant desire, that should marshal and put in order all the rest, made any man's heart, hard to find or sound. Hence it comes likewise, that princes many times make themselves desires, and set their hearts upon toys; sometimes upon a building; sometimes upon erecting of an order; sometimes upon the advancing of a person; sometimes upon obtaining excellency in some art, or feat of the hand; as Nero for playing on the harp, Domitian for certainty of the hand with the arrow, Commodus for playing at fence, Caracalla for driving chariots, and the like.

This seemeth incredible, unto those that know not the principle, that the mind of man is more cheered and refreshed by profiting in small things, than by standing at a stay in great. We see also that kings that have been fortunate conquerors, in their first years, it being not possible for them to go forward infinitely, but that they must have some check, or arrest in their fortunes, turn in their latter years to be superstitious, and melancholy; as did Alexander the Great; Diocletian; and in our memory, Charles the Fifth; and others: for he that is used to go forward, and findeth a stop, falleth out of his own favor, and is not the thing he was.

To speak now of the true temper of empire, it is a thing rare and hard to keep; for both temper, and distemper, consist of contraries. But it is one thing, to mingle contraries, another to interchange them. The answer of Apollonius to Vespasian, is full of excellent instruction. Vespasian asked him, What was Nero's overthrow? He answered, Nero could touch and tune the harp well; but in government, sometimes he used to wind the pins too high, sometimes to let them down too low. And certain it is, that nothing destroyeth authority so much, as the unequal and untimely interchange of power pressed too far, and relaxed too much. This is true, that the wisdom of all these latter times, in princes' affairs, is rather fine deliveries, and shiftings of dangers and mischiefs, when they are near, than solid and grounded courses to keep them aloof. But this is but to try masteries with fortune. And let men beware, how they neglect and suffer matter of trouble to be prepared for no man can forbid the spark, nor tell whence it may come.

The difficulties in princes' business are many and great; but the greatest difficulty, is often in their own mind. For it is common with princes (saith Tacitus) to will contradictories, Sunt plerumque regum voluntates vehementes, et inter se contrariÃ¦. For it is the solecism of power, to think to command the end, and yet not to endure the mean.

Kings have to deal with their neighbors, their wives, their children, their prelates or clergy, their nobles, their second-nobles or gentlemen, their merchants, their commons, and their men of war; and from all these arise dangers, if care and circumspection be not used.

First for their neighbors; there can no general rule be given (for occasions are so variable), save one, which ever holdeth, which is, that princes do keep due sentinel, that none of their neighbors do ever grow so (by increase of territory, by embracing of trade, by approaches, or the like), as they become more able to annoy them, than they were. And this is generally the work of standing counsels, to foresee and to hinder it. During that triumvirate of kings, King Henry the Eighth of England, Francis the First King of France, and Charles the Fifth Emperor, there was such a watch kept, that none of the three could win a palm of ground, but the other two would straightways balance it, either by confederation, or, if need were, by a war; and would not in any wise take up peace at interest. And the like was done by that league (which Guicciardini saith was the security of Italy) made between Ferdinando King of Naples, Lorenzius Medici, and Ludovicus Sforza, potentates, the one of Florence, the other of Milan.

Neither is the opinion of some of the Schoolmen, to be received, that a war cannot justly be made, but upon a precedent injury, or provocation. For there is no question, but a just fear of an imminent danger, though there be no blow given, is a lawful cause of a war.

For their wives; there are cruel examples of them. Livia is infamed, for the poisoning of her husband; Roxalana, Solyman's wife, was the destruction of that renowned prince, Sultan Mustapha, and otherwise troubled his house and succession; Edward the Second of England, his queen, had the principal hand in the deposing and murder of her husband. This kind of danger, is then to be feared chiefly, when the wives have plots, for the raising of their own children; or else that they be advoutresses. For their children; the tragedies likewise of dangers from them, have been many. And generally, the entering of fathers into suspicion of their children, hath been ever unfortunate. The destruction of Mustapha (that we named before) was so fatal to Solyman's line, as the succession of the Turks, from Solyman until this day, is suspected to be untrue, and of strange blood; for that Selymus the Second, was thought to be suppositious. The destruction of Crispus, a young prince of rare towardness, by Constantinus the Great, his father, was in like manner fatal to his house; for both Constantinus and Constance, his sons, died violent deaths; and Constantius, his other son, did little better; who died indeed of sickness, but after that Julianus had taken arms against him.

The destruction of Demetrius, son to Philip the Second of Macedon, turned upon the father, who died of repentance. And many like examples there are; but few or none, where the fathers had good by such distrust; except it were, where the sons were up in open arms against them; as was Selymus the First against Bajazet; and the three sons of Henry the Second, King of England.

For their prelates; when they are proud and great, there is also danger from them; as it was in the times of Anselmus, and Thomas Becket, Archbishops of Canterbury; who, with their croziers, did almost try it with the king's sword; and yet they had to deal with stout and haughty kings, William Rufus, Henry the First, and Henry the Second. The danger is not from that state, but where it hath a dependence of foreign authority; or where the churchmen come in and are elected, not by the collation of the king, or particular patrons, but by the people.

For their nobles; to keep them at a distance, it is not amiss; but to depress them, may make a king more absolute, but less safe; and less able to perform, any thing that he desires. I have noted it, in my History of King Henry the Seventh of England, who depressed his nobility; whereupon it came to pass, that his times were full of difficulties and troubles; for the nobility, though they continued loyal unto him, yet did they not co-operate with him in his business. So that in effect, he was fain to do all things himself. For their second-nobles; there is not much danger from them, being a body dispersed. They may sometimes discourse high, but that doth little hurt; besides, they are a counterpoise to the higher nobility, that they grow not too potent; and, lastly, being the most immediate in authority, with the common people, they do best temper popular commotions. For their merchants; they are vena porta; and if they flourish not, a kingdom may have good limbs, but will have empty veins, and nourish little. Taxes and imposts upon them, do seldom good to the king's revenue; for that that wins in the hundred, he leeseth in the shire; the particular rates being increased, but the total bulk of trading, rather decreased. For their commons; there is little danger from them, except it be, where they have great and potent heads; or where you meddle with the point of religion, or their customs, or means of life. For their men of war; it is a dangerous state, where they live and remain in a body, and are used to donatives; whereof we see examples in the janizaries, and pretorian bands of Rome; but trainings of men, and arming them in several places, and under several commanders, and without donatives, are things of defence, and no danger.

Princes are like to heavenly bodies, which cause good or evil times; and which have much veneration, but no rest. All precepts concerning kings, are in effect comprehended in those two remembrances: memento quod es homo; and memento quod es Deus, or vice Dei: the one bridleth their power, and the other their will.

Of Counsel

The greatest trust, between man and man, is the trust of giving counsel. For in other confidences, men commit the parts of life; their lands, their goods, their children, their credit, some particular affair; but to such as they make their counsellors, they commit the whole: by how much the more, they are obliged to all faith and integrity.

The wisest princes need not think it any diminution to their greatness, or derogation to their sufficiency, to rely upon counsel. God himself is not without, but hath made it one of the great names of his blessed Son; The Counsellor. Salomon hath pronounced, that in counsel is stability. Things will have their first, or second agitation: if they be not tossed upon the arguments of counsel, they will be tossed upon the waves of fortune; and be full of inconstancy, doing and undoing, like the reeling of a drunken man.

Salomon's son found the force of counsel, as his father saw the necessity of it. For the beloved kingdom of God, was first rent, and broken, by ill counsel; upon which counsel, there are set for our instruction, the two marks whereby bad counsel is for ever best discerned; that it was young counsel, for the person; and violent counsel, for the matter. The ancient times, do set forth in figure, both the incorporation, and inseparable conjunction, of counsel with kings, and the wise and politic use of counsel by kings: the one, in that they say Jupiter did marry Metis, which signifieth counsel; whereby they intend that Sovereignty, is manied to Counsel: the other in that which followeth, which was thus: They say, after Jupiter was married to Metis, she conceived by him, and was with child, but Jupiter suffered her not to stay, till she brought forth, but eat her up; whereby he became himself with child, and was delivered of Pallas armed, out of his head.

Which monstrous fable containeth a secret of empire; how kings are to make use of their counsel of state. That first, they ought to refer matters unto them, which is the first begetting, or impregnation; but when they are elaborate, moulded, and shaped in the womb of their counsel, and grow ripe, and ready to be brought forth, that then they suffer not their counsel, to go through with the resolution and direction, as if it depended on them; but take the matter back into their own hands, and make it appear to the world, that the decrees and final directions (which, because they come forth, with prudence and power, are resembled to Pallas armed) proceeded from themselves; and not only from their authority, but (the more to add reputation to themselves) from their head and device.

Let us now speak of the inconveniences of counsel, and of the remedies. The inconveniences that have been noted, in calling and using counsel, are three. First, the revealing of affairs, whereby they become less secret. Secondly, the weakening of the authority of princes, as if they were less of themselves. Thirdly, the danger of being unfaithfully counselled, and more for the good of them that counsel, than of him that is counselled.

For which inconveniences, the doctrine of Italy, and practice of France, in some kings' times, hath introduced cabinet counsels; a remedy worse than the disease. As to secrecy; princes are not bound to communicate all matters, with all counsellors; but may extract and select. Neither is it necessary, that he that consulteth what he should do, should declare what he will do. But let princes beware, that the unsecreting of their affairs, comes not from themselves. And as for cabinet counsels, it may be their motto, plenus rimarum sum: one futile person, that made it his glory to tell, will do more hurt than many, that know it their duty to conceal. It is true there be some affairs, which require extreme secrecy, which will hardly go beyond one or two persons, besides the king: neither are those counsels unprosperous; for, besides the secrecy, they commonly go on constantly, in one spirit of direction, without distraction.

But then it must be a prudent king, such as is able to grind with a handmill; and those inward counsellors had need also be wise men, and especially true and trusty to the king's ends; as it was with King Henry the Seventh of England, who, in his great business, imparted himself to none, except it were to Morton and Fox. For weakening of authority; the fable showeth the remedy. Nay, the majesty of kings, is rather exalted than diminished, when they are in the chair of counsel; neither was there ever prince, bereaved of his dependences, by his counsel, except where there hath been, either an over-greatness in one counsellor, or an over-strict combination in divers; which are things soon found, and holpen.

For the last inconvenience, that men will counsel, with an eye to themselves; certainly, non inveniet fidem super terram is meant, of the nature of times, and not of all particular persons. There be, that are in nature faithful, and sincere, and plain, and direct; not crafty and involved; let princes, above all, draw to themselves such natures. Besides, counsellors are not commonly so united, but that one counsellor, keepeth sentinel over another; so that if any do counsel out of faction or private ends, it commonly comes to the king's ear. But the best remedy is, if princes know their counsellors, as well as their counsellors know them:

Principis est virtus maxima nosse suos.

And on the other side, counsellors should not be too speculative into their sovereign's person. The true composition of a counsellor, is rather to be skilful in their master's business than in his nature; for then he is like to advise him, and not feed his humour. It is of singular use to princes, if they take the opinions of their counsel, both separately and together. For private opinion is more free; but opinion before others, is more reverent. In private, men are more bold in their own humors; and in consort, men are more obnoxious to others' humors; therefore it is good to take both; and of the inferior sort, rather in private, to preserve freedom; of the greater, rather in consort, to preserve respect.

It is in vain for princes, to take counsel concerning matters, if they take no counsel likewise concerning persons; for all matters are as dead images; and the life of the execution of affairs, resteth in the good choice of persons. Neither is it enough, to consult concerning persons secundum genera, as in an idea, or mathematical description, what the kind and character of the person should be; for the greatest errors are committed, and the most judgment is shown, in the choice of individuals. It was truly said, Optimi consiliarii mortui: books will speak plain, when counsellors blanch. Therefore it is good to be conversant in them, specially the books of such as themselves have been actors upon the stage.

The counsels at this day, in most places, are but familiar meetings, where matters are rather talked on, than debated. And they run too swift, to the order, or act, of counsel. It were better that in causes of weight, the matter were propounded one day, and not spoken to till the next day; in nocte consilium. So was it done in the Commission of Union, between England and Scotland; which was a grave and orderly assembly.

I commend set days for petitions; for both it gives the suitors more certainty for their attendance, and it frees the meetings for matters of estate, that they may hoc agere. In choice of committees; for ripening business for the counsel, it is better to choose indifferent persons, than to make an indifferency, by putting in those, that are strong on both sides. I commend also standing commissions; as for trade, for treasure, for war, for suits, for some provinces; for where there be divers particular counsels, and but one counsel of estate (as it is in Spain), they are, in effect, no more than standing commissions: save that they have greater authority.

Let such as are to inform counsels, out of their particular professions (as lawyers, seamen, mint men, and the like) be first heard before committees; and then, as occasion serves, before the counsel. And let them not come in multitudes, or in a tribunitious manner; for that is to clamor counsels, not to inform them. A long table and a square table, or seats about the walls, seem things of form, but are things of substance; for at a long table a few at the upper end, in effect, sway all the business; but in the other form, there is more use of the counselors' opinions, that sit lower. A king, when he presides in counsel, let him beware how he opens his own inclination too much, in that which he propounded; for else counselors will but take the wind of him, and instead of giving free counsel, sing him a song of placebo.

Of Delays

Fortune is like the market; where many times if you can stay a little, the price will fall. Again, it is sometimes like Sibylla's offer; which at first, offereth the commodity at full, then consumeth part and part, and still holdeth up the price. For Occasion (as it is in the common verse) turneth a bald noddle, after she hath presented her locks in front, and no hold taken; or at least turneth the handle of the bottle, first to be received, and after the belly, which is hard to clasp. There is surely no greater wisdom, than well to time the beginnings, and onsets, of things.

Dangers are no more light, if they once seem light; and

more dangers have deceived men, than forced them. Nay, it were better, to meet some dangers half way, though they come nothing near, than to keep too long a watch upon their approaches; for if a man watch too long, it is odds he will fall asleep. On the other side, to be deceived with too long shadows (as some have been, when the moon was low, and shone on their enemies' back), and so to shoot off before the time; or to teach dangers to come on, by over early buckling towards them; is another extreme. The ripeness, or unripeness, of the occasion (as we said) must ever be well weighed; and generally it is good, to commit the beginnings of an great actions to Argus, with his hundred eyes, and the ends to Briareus, with his hundred hands; first to watch, and then to speed.

For the helmet of Pluto, which make the politic man go invisible, is secrecy in the counsel, and celerity in the execution. For when things are once come to the execution, there is no secrecy, comparable to celerity; like the motion of a bullet in the air, which flieth so swift, as it outruns the eye.

Of Cunning

We take cunning for a sinister or crooked wisdom. And certainly there is a great difference, between a cunning man, and a wise man; not only in point of honesty, but in point of ability. There be, that can pack the cards, and yet cannot play well; so there are some that are good in canvasses and factions, that are otherwise weak men. Again, it is one thing to understand persons, and another thing to understand matters; for many are perfect in men's humors, that are not greatly capable of the real part of business; which is the constitution of one that hath studied men, more than books. Such men are fitter for practice, than for counsel; and they are good, but in their own alley: turn them to new men, and they have lost their aim; so as the old rule, to know a fool from a wise man, Mitte ambos nudos ad ignotos, et videbis, doth scarce hold for them. And because these cunning men, are like haberdashers of small wares, it is not amiss to set forth their shop. It is a point of cunning, to wait upon him with whom you speak, with your eye; as the Jesuits give it in precept: for there be many wise men, that have secret hearts, and transparent countenances. Yet this would be done with a demure abasing of your eye, sometimes, as the Jesuits also do use. Another is, that when you have anything to obtain, of present dispatch, you entertain and amuse the party, with whom you deal, with some other discourse; that he be not too much awake to make objections. I knew a counselor and secretary, that never came to Queen Elizabeth of England, with bills to sign, but he would always first put her into some discourse of estate, that she mought the less mind the bills.

The like surprise may be made by moving things, when the party is in haste, and cannot stay to consider advisedly of that is moved. If a man would cross a business, that he doubts some other would handsomely and effectually move, let him pretend to wish it well, and move it himself in such sort as may foil it. The breaking off, in the midst of that one was about to say, as if he took himself up, breeds a greater appetite in him with whom you confer, to know more. And because it works better, when anything seemed to be gotten from you by question, than if you offer it of yourself, you may lay a bait for a question, by showing another visage, and countenance, than you are wont; to the end to give occasion, for the party to ask, what the matter is of the change? As Nehemias did: And I had not before that time, been sad before the king.

In things that are tender and unpleasing, it is good to break the ice, by some whose words are of less weight, and to reserve the more weighty voice, to come in as by chance, so that he may be asked the question upon the other's speech: as Narcissus did, relating to Claudius the marriage of Messalina and Silius. In things that a man would not be seen in himself, it is a point of cunning, to borrow the name of the world; as to say, The world says, or, There is a speech abroad.

I knew one that, when he wrote a letter, he would put that, which was most material, in the postscript, as if it had been a by-matter. I knew another that, when he came to have speech, he would pass over that, that he intended most; and go forth, and come back again, and speak of it as of a thing, that he had almost forgot.

Some procure themselves, to be surprised, at such times as it is like the party that they work upon, will suddenly come upon them; and to be found with a letter in their hand or doing somewhat which they are not accustomed; to the end, they may be apposed of those things, which of themselves they are desirous to utter.

It is a point of cunning, to let fall those words in a man's own name, which he would have another man learn, and use, and thereupon take advantage. I knew two, that were competitors for the secretary's place in Queen Elizabeth's time, and yet kept good quarter between themselves; and would confer, one with another, upon the business; and the one of them said, That to be a secretary in the declination of a monarchy was a ticklish thing, and that he did not affect it: the other straight caught up those words, and discoursed with divers of his friends, that he had no reason to desire to be secretary, in the declination of a monarchy. The first man took hold of it, and found means it was told the Queen; who, hearing of a declination of a monarchy, took it so ill, as she would never after hear of the other's suit.

There is a cunning, which we in England can, the turning of the cat in the pan; which is, when that which a man says to another, he lays it as if another had said it to him. And to say truth, it is not easy, when such a matter passed between two, to make it appear from which of them it first moved and began.

It is a way that some men have, to glance and dart at others, by justifying themselves by negatives; as to say, This I do not: as Tigellinus did towards Burrhus; Se non diversas spes, sed incolumitatem imperatoris simpliciter spectare.

Some have in readiness so many tales and stories, as there is nothing they would insinuate, but they can wrap it into a tale; which serveth both to keep themselves more in guard, and to make others carry it with more pleasure. It is a good point of cunning, for a man to shape the answer he would have, in his own words and propositions; for it makes the other party stick the less. It is strange how long some men will lie in wait to speak somewhat they desire to say; and how far about they will fetch; and how many other matters they will beat over, to come near it. It is a thing of great patience, but yet of much use. A sudden, bold, and unexpected question doth many times surprise a man, and lay him open. Like to him that, having changed his name, and walking in Paul's, another suddenly came behind him, and called him by his true name whereat straightways he looked back.

But these small wares, and petty points, of cunning, are infinite; and it were a good deed to make a list of them; for that nothing doth more hurt in a state, than that cunning men pass for wise. But certainly some there are that know the resorts and fans of business, that cannot sink into the main of it; like a house that hath convenient stairs and entries, but never a fair room. Therefore you shall see them find out pretty looses in the conclusion, but are no ways able to examine or debate matters. And yet commonly they take advantage of their inability, and would be thought wits of direction. Some build rather upon the abusing of others, and (as we now say) putting tricks upon them, than upon soundness of their own proceedings. But Salomon saith: Prudens advertit ad gressus suos; stultus divertit ad dolos.

Of Wisdom for a Man's Self

An ant is a wise creature for itself, but it is a shrewd thing, in an orchard or garden. And certainly, men that are great lovers of themselves, waste the public. Divide with reason; between self love and society; and be so true to thyself, as thou be not false to others; specially to thy king and country. It is a poor centre of a man's actions, himself. It is right earth. For that only stands fast upon his own centre; whereas all things, that have affinity with the heavens, move upon the centre of another, which they benefit.

The referring of all to a man's self, is more tolerable in a sovereign prince; because themselves are not only themselves, but their good and evil is at the peril of the public fortune. But it is a desperate evil, in a servant to a prince, or a citizen in a republic. For whatsoever affairs pass such a man's hands, he crooketh them to his own ends; which must needs be often eccentric to the ends of his master, or state. Therefore, let princes, or states, choose such servants, as have not this mark; except they mean their service should be made but the accessory. That which made the effect more pernicious, is that all proportion is lost. It were disproportion enough, for the servant's good to be preferred before the master's; but yet it is a greater extreme, when a little good of the servant, shall carry things against a great good of the master's.

And yet that is the case of bad officers, treasurers, ambassadors, generals, and other false and corrupt servants; which set a bias upon their bowl, of their own petty ends and envies, to the overthrow of their master's great and important affairs. And for the most part, the good such servants receive, is after the model of their own fortune; but the hurt they sell for that good, is after the model of their master's fortune. And certainly it is the nature of extreme self-lovers, as they will set an house on fire, and it were but to roast their eggs; and yet these men many times hold credit with their masters, because their study is but to please them, and profit themselves; and for either respect, they will abandon the good of their affairs.

Wisdom for a man's self is, in many branches thereof, a depraved thing. It is the wisdom of rats, that will be sure to leave a house, somewhat before it fall. It is the wisdom of the fox, that thrusts out the badger, who digged and made room for him. It is the wisdom of crocodiles, that shed tears when they would devour. But that which is specially to be noted is, that those which (as Cicero says of Pompey) are sui amantes sine rivali, are many times unfortunate. And whereas they have, all their times, sacrificed to themselves, they become in the end, themselves sacrifices to the inconstancy of fortune, whose wings they thought, by their self-wisdom, to have pinioned.

Of Innovations

As the births of living creatures, at first are ill-shapen so are all innovations, which are the births of time. Yet notwithstanding, as those that first bring honor into their family, are commonly more worthy than most that succeed, so the first precedent (if it be good) is seldom attained by imitation. For ill, to man's nature, as it stands perverted, hath a natural motion, strongest in continuance; but good, as a forced motion, strongest at first. Surely every medicine is an innovation; and he that will not apply new remedies, must expect new evils; for time is the greatest innovator; and if time of course alter things to the worse, and wisdom and counsel shall not alter them to the better, what shall be the end? It is true, that what is settled by custom, though it be not good, yet at least it is fit; and those things which have long gone together, are, as it were, confederate within themselves; whereas new things piece not so well; but though they help by their utility, yet they trouble by their inconformity. Besides, they are like strangers; more admired, and less favored.

All this is true, if time stood still; which contrariwise moveth so round, that a froward retention of custom, is as turbulent a thing as an innovation; and they that reverence too much old times, are but a scorn to the new. It were good, therefore, that men in their innovations would follow the example of time itself; which indeed innovateth greatly, but quietly, by degrees scarce to be perceived.

For otherwise, whatsoever is new is unlooked for; and ever it mends some, and pairs others; and he that holpen, takes it for a fortune, and thanks the time; and he that is hurt, for a wrong, and imputeth it to the author. It is good also, not to try experiments in states, except the necessity be urgent, or the utility evident; and well to beware, that it be the reformation, that draweth on the change, and not the desire of change, that pretendeth the reformation. And lastly, that the novelty, though it be not rejected, yet be held for a suspect; and, as the Scripture saith, that we make a stand upon the ancient way, and then look about us, and discover what is the straight and right way, and so to walk in it.

Of Dispatch

Affected dispatch is one of the most dangerous things to business that can be. It is like that, which the physicians call predigestion or hasty digestion; which is sure to fill the body full of crudities, and secret seeds of diseases. Therefore, measure not dispatch, by the times of sitting, but by the advancement of the business. And as in races it is not the large stride or high lift that makes the speed; so in business, the keeping close to the matter, and not taking of it too much at once, procureth dispatch.

It is the care of some, only to come off speedily for the time; or to contrive some false periods of business, because they may seem men of dispatch. But it is one thing, to abbreviate by contracting, another by cutting off. And business so handled, at several sittings or meetings, goeth commonly backward and forward in an unsteady manner. I knew a wise man that had it for a byword, when he saw men hasten to a conclusion, Stay a little, that we may make an end the sooner.

On the other side, true dispatch is a rich thing. For time is the measure of business, as money is of wares; and business is bought at a dear hand, where there is small dispatch. The Spartans and Spaniards have been noted to be of small dispatch; Mi venga la muerte de Spagna; Let my death come from Spain; for then it will be sure to be long in coming.

Give good hearing to those, that give the first information in business; and rather direct them in the beginning, than interrupt them in the continuance of their speeches; for he that is put out of his own order, will go forward and backward, and be more tedious, while he waits upon his memory, than he could have been, if he had gone on in his own course. But sometimes it is seen, that the moderator is more troublesome, than the actor. Iterations are commonly loss of time. But there is no such gain of time, as to iterate often the state of the question; for it chaseth away many a frivolous speech, as it is coming forth. Long and curious speeches, are as fit for dispatch, as a robe or mantle, with a long train, is for race. Prefaces and passages, and excusations, and other speeches of reference to the person, are great wastes of time; and though they seem to proceed of modesty, they are bravery. Yet beware of being too material, when there is any impediment or obstruction in men's wills; for pre-occupation of mind ever requireth preface of speech; like a fomentation to make the unguent enter. Above all things, order, and distribution, and singling out of parts, is the life of dispatch; so as the distribution be not too subtle: for he that doth not divide, will never enter well into business; and he that divideth too much, will never come out of it clearly.

To choose time, is to save time; and an unseasonable motion, is but beating the air. There be three parts of business; the preparation, the debate or examination, and the perfection. Whereof, if you look for dispatch, let the middle only be the work of many, and the first and last the work of few. The proceeding upon somewhat conceived in writing, doth for the most part facilitate dispatch: for though it should be wholly rejected, yet that negative is more pregnant of direction, than an indefinite; as ashes are more generative than dust.

Of Seeming Wise

It hath been an opinion that the French are wiser than they seem, and the Spaniards seem wiser than they are. But howsoever it be between nations, certainly it is so between man and man. For as the Apostle saith of godliness, Having a show of godliness, but denying the power thereof; so certainly there are, in point of wisdom and sufficiently, that do nothing or little very solemnly: magno conatu nugas.

It is a ridiculous thing, and fit for a satire to persons of judgment, to see what shifts these formalists have, and what prospectives to make superficies to seem body, that hath depth and bulk. Some are so close and reserved, as they will not show their wares, but by a dark light; and seem always to keep back somewhat; and when they know within themselves, they speak of that they do not well know, would nevertheless seem to others, to know of that which they may not well speak. Some help themselves with countenance and gesture, and are wise by signs; as Cicero saith of Piso, that when he answered him he fetched one of his brows up to his forehead, and bent the other down to his chin; Respondes, altero ad frontem sublato, altero ad mentum depresso supercilio, crudelitatem tibi non placere.

Some think to bear it by speaking a great word, and being peremptory; and go on, and take by admittance, that which they cannot make good. Some, whatsoever is beyond their reach, will seem to despise, or make light of it, as impertinent or curious; and so would have their ignorance seem judgment. Some are never without a difference, and commonly by amusing men with a subtilty, blanch the matter; of whom A. Gellius saith, Hominem delirum, qui verborum minutiis rerum frangit pondera.

Of which kind also, Plato, in his Protagoras, bringeth in Prodius in scorn, and made him make a speech, that consisteth of distinction from the beginning to the end. Generally, such men in all deliberations find ease to be of the negative side, and affect a credit to object and foretell difficulties; for when propositions are denied, there is an end of them; but if they be allowed, it requireth a new work; which false point of wisdom is the bane of business.

To conclude, there is no decaying merchant, or inward beggar, hath so many tricks to uphold the credit of their wealth, as these empty persons have, to maintain the credit of their sufficiency. Seeming wise men may make shift to get opinion; but let no man choose them for employment; for certainly you were better take for business, a man somewhat absurd, than over-formal.

Of Friendship

It had been hard for him that spake it to have put more truth and untruth together in few words, than in that speech, Whosoever is delighted in solitude, is either a wild beast or a god. For it is most true, that a natural and secret hatred, and aversation towards society, in any man, hath somewhat of the savage beast; but it is most untrue, that it should have any character at all, of the divine nature; except it proceed, not out of a pleasure in solitude, but out of a love and desire to sequester a man's self, for a higher conversation: such as is found to have been falsely and feignedly in some of the heathen; as Epimenides the Candian, Numa the Roman, Empedocles the Sicilian, and Apollonius of Tyana; and truly and really, in divers of the ancient hermits and holy fathers of the church. But little do men perceive what solitude is, and how far it extendeth. For a crowd is not company; and faces are but a gallery of pictures; and talk but a tinkling cymbal, where there is no love. The Latin adage meeteth with it a little: Magna civitas, magna solitudo; because in a great town friends are scattered; so that there is not that fellowship, for the most part, which is in less neighborhoods. But we may go further, and affirm most truly, that it is a mere and miserable solitude to want true friends; without which the world is but a wilderness; and even in this sense also of solitude, whosoever in the frame of his nature and affections, is unfit for friendship, he taketh it of the beast, and not from humanity.

A principal fruit of friendship, is the ease and discharge of the fulness and swellings of the heart, which passions of all kinds do cause and induce. We know diseases of stoppings, and suffocations, are the most dangerous in the body; and it is not much otherwise in the mind; you may take sarza to open the liver, steel to open the spleen, flowers of sulphur for the lungs, castoreum for the brain; but no receipt openeth the heart, but a true friend; to whom you may impart griefs, joys, fears, hopes, suspicions, counsels, and whatsoever lieth upon the heart to oppress it, in a kind of civil shrift or confession.

It is a strange thing to observe, how high a rate great kings and monarchs do set upon this fruit of friendship, whereof we speak: so great, as they purchase it, many times, at the hazard of their own safety and greatness. For princes, in regard of the distance of their fortune from that of their subjects and servants, cannot gather this fruit, except (to make themselves capable thereof) they raise some persons to be, as it were, companions and almost equals to themselves, which many times sorteth to inconvenience. The modern languages give unto such persons the name of favorites, or privadoes; as if it were matter of grace, or conversation.

But the Roman name attaineth the true use and cause thereof, naming them participes curarum; for it is that which tieth the knot. And we see plainly that this hath been done, not by weak and passionate princes only, but by the wisest and most politic that ever reigned; who have oftentimes joined to themselves some of their servants; whom both themselves have called friends, and allowed other likewise to call them in the same manner; using the word which is received between private men.

L. Sylla, when he commanded Rome, raised Pompey (after surnamed the Great) to that height, that Pompey vaunted himself for Sylla's overmatch. For when he had carried the consulship for a friend of his, against the pursuit of Sylla, and that Sylla did a little resent thereat, and began to speak great, Pompey turned upon him again, and in effect bade him be quiet; for that more men adored the sun rising than the sun setting. With Julius CÃ¦sar, Decimus Brutus had obtained that interest, as he set him down, in his testament, for heir in remainder, after his nephew.

And this was the man that had power with him, to draw him forth to his death. For when CÃ¦sar would have discharged the senate, in regard of some ill presages, and specially a dream of Calpurnia; this man lifted him gently by the arm out of his chair, telling him he hoped he would not dismiss the senate, till his wife had dreamt a better dream.

And it seemeth his favor was so great, as Antonius, in a letter which is recited verbatim in one of Cicero's Philippics, calleth him venefica, witch; as if he had enchanted CÃ¦sar. Augustus raised Agrippa (though of mean birth) to that height, as when he consulted with MÃ¦cenas, about the marriage of his daughter Julia, MÃ¦cenas took the liberty to tell him, that he must either marry his daughter to Agrippa, or take away his life; there was no third way, he had made him so great. With Tiberius CÃ¦sar, Sejanus had ascended to that height, as they two were termed, and reckoned, as a pair of friends. Tiberius in a letter to him saith, HÃ¦c pro amicitia nostra non occultavi; and the whole senate dedicated an altar to Friendship, as to a goddess, in respect of the great dearness of friendship, between them two.

The like, or more, was between Septimius Severus and Plautianus. For he forced his eldest son to marry the daughter of Plautianus; and would often maintain Plautianus, in doing affronts to his son; and did write also in a letter to the senate, by these words: I love the man so well, as I wish he may overlive me. Now if these princes had been as a Trajan, or a Marcus Aurelius, a man might have thought that this had proceeded of an abundant goodness of nature; but being men so wise, of such strength and severity of mind, and so extreme lovers of themselves, as all these were, it proveth most plainly that they found their own felicity (though as great as ever happened to mortal men) but as an half piece, except they mought have a friend, to make it entire; and yet, which is more, they were princes that had wives, sons, nephews; and yet all these could not supply the comfort of friendship.

It is not to be forgotten, what Comineus observeth of his first master, Duke Charles the Hardy, namely, that he would communicate his secrets with none; and least of all, those secrets which troubled him most. Whereupon he goeth on, and saith that towards his latter time, that closeness did impair, and a little perish his understanding. Surely Comineus mought have made the same judgment also, if it had pleased him, of his second master, Lewis the Eleventh, whose closeness was indeed his tormentor.

The parable of Pythagoras is dark, but true; Cor ne edito, 'Eat not the heart.' Certainly if a man would give it a hard phrase, those that want friends, to open themselves unto are cannibals of their own hearts. But one thing is most admirable (wherewith I will conclude this first fruit of friendship), which is, that this communicating of a man's self to his friend, works two contrary effects; for it redoubleth joys, and cutteth griefs in halves. For there is no man, that imparteth his joys to his friend, but he joyeth the more; and no man that imparteth his griefs to his friend, but he grieveth the less. So that it is in truth, of operation upon a man's mind, of like virtue as the alchemists use to attribute to their stone, for man's body; that it worketh all contrary effects, but still to the good and benefit of nature.

But yet without praying in aid of alchemists, there is a manifest image of this, in the ordinary course of nature. For in bodies, union strengtheneth and cherisheth any natural action; and on the other side, weakeneth and dulleth any violent impression: and even so it is of minds.

The second fruit of friendship, is healthful and sovereign

for the understanding, as the first is for the affections. For friendship made indeed a fair day in the affections, from storm and tempests; but it made daylight in the understanding, out of darkness, and confusion of thoughts.

Neither is this to be understood only of faithful counsel, which a man receiveth from his friend; but before you come to that, certain it is, that whosoever hath his mind fraught with many thoughts, his wits and understanding do clarify and break up, in the communicating and discoursing with another; he tosseth his thoughts more easily; he marshalleth them more orderly, he seeth how they look when they are turned into words: finally, he waxeth wiser than himself; and that more by an hour's discourse, than by a day's meditation.

It was well said by Themistocles, to the king of Persia, that speech was like cloth of Arras, opened and put abroad; whereby the imagery doth appear in figure; whereas in thoughts they lie but as in packs. Neither is this second fruit of friendship, in opening the understanding, restrained only to such friends as are able to give a man counsel; (they indeed are best;) but even without that, a man learneth of himself, and bringeth his own thoughts to light, and whetteth his wits as against a stone, which itself cuts not. In a word, a man were better relate himself to a statua, or picture, than to suffer his thoughts to pass in smother.

Add now, to make this second fruit of friendship complete, that other point, which lieth more open, and falleth within vulgar observation; which is faithful counsel from a friend. Heraclitus saith well in one of his enigmas, Dry light is ever the best. And certain it is, that the light that a man receiveth by counsel from another, is drier and purer, than that which cometh from his own understanding and judgment; which is ever infused, and drenched, in his affections and customs. So as there is as much difference between the counsel, that a friend giveth, and that a man giveth himself, as there is between the counsel of a friend, and of a flatterer. For there is no such flatterer as is a man's self; and there is no such remedy against flattery of a man's self, as the liberty of a friend. Counsel is of two sorts: the one concerning manners, the other concerning business. For the first, the best preservative to keep the mind in health, is the faithful admonition of a friend. The calling of a man's self to a strict account, is a medicine, sometime too piercing and corrosive.

Reading good books of morality, is a little flat and dead. Observing our faults in others, is sometimes improper for our case. But the best receipt (best, I say, to work, and best to take) is the admonition of a friend. It is a strange thing to behold, what gross errors and extreme absurdities many (especially of the greater sort) do commit, for want of a friend to tell them of them; to the great damage both of their fame and fortune: for, as St. James saith, they are as men, that look sometimes into a glass, and presently forget their own shape and favour.

As for business, a man may think, if he will, that two eyes see no more than one; or that a gamester seeth always more than a looker-on; or that a man in anger, is as wise as he that hath said over the four and twenty letters; or that a musket may be shot off as well upon the arm, as upon a rest; and such other fond and high imaginations, to think himself all in all. But when all is done, the help of good counsel is that which setteth business straight.

And if any man think that he will take counsel, but it shall be by pieces; asking counsel in one business, of one man, and in another business, of another man; it is well (that is to say, better, perhaps, than if he asked none at all); but he runneth two dangers: one, that he shall not be faithfully counselled; for it is a rare thing, except it be from a perfect and entire friend, to have counsel given, but such as shall be bowed and crooked to some ends, which he hath, that giveth it.

The other, that he shall have counsel given, hurtful and unsafe (though with good meaning), and mixed partly of mischief and partly of remedy; even as if you would call a physician, that is thought good for the cure of the disease you complain of, but is unacquainted with your body; and therefore may put you in way for a present cure, but overthroweth your health in some other kind; and so cure the disease, and kill the patient. But a friend that is wholly acquainted with a man's estate, will beware, by furthering any present business, how he dasheth upon other inconvenience. And therefore rest not upon scattered counsels; they will rather distract and mislead, than settle and direct.

After these two noble fruits of friendship (peace in the affections, and support of the judgment), followeth the last fruit; which is like the pomegranate, full of many kernels; I mean aid, and bearing a part, in all actions and occasions. Here the best way to represent to life the manifold use of friendship, is to cast and see how many things there are, which a man cannot do himself; and then it will appear, that it was a sparing speech of the ancients, to say, that a friend is another himself; for that a friend is far more than himself. Men have their time, and die many times, in desire of some things which they principally take to heart; the bestowing of a child, the finishing of a work, or the like.

If a man have a true friend, he may rest almost secure that the care of those things will continue after him. So that a man hath, as it were, two lives in his desires. A man hath a body, and that body is confined to a place; but where friendship is, all offices of life are as it were granted to him, and his deputy. For he may exercise them by his friend. How many things are there which a man cannot, with any face or comeliness, say or do himself? A man can scarce allege his own merits with modesty, much less extol them; a man cannot sometimes brook to supplicate or beg; and a number of the like. But all these things are graceful, in a friend's mouth, which are blushing in a man's own. So again, a man's person hath many proper relations, which he cannot put off. A man cannot speak to his son but as a father; to his wife but as a husband; to his enemy but upon terms: whereas a friend may speak as the case requires, and not as it sorteth with the person. But to enumerate these things were endless; I have given the rule, where a man cannot fitly play his own part; if he have not a friend, he may quit the stage.

Of Expense

Riches are for spending, and spending for honor and good actions. Therefore extraordinary expense must be limited by the worth of the occasion; for voluntary undoing, may be as well for a man's country, as for the kingdom of heaven. But ordinary expense, ought to be limited by a man's estate; and governed with such regard, as it be within his compass; and not subject to deceit and abuse of servants; and ordered to the best show, that the bills may be less than the estimation abroad. Certainly, if a man will keep but of even hand, his ordinary expenses ought to be but to the half of his receipts; and if he think to wax rich, but to the third part. It is no baseness, for the greatest to descend and look into their own estate.

Some forbear it, not upon negligence alone, but doubting to bring themselves into melancholy, in respect they shall find it broken. But wounds cannot be cured without searching. He that cannot look into his own estate at all, had need both choose well those whom he employeth, and change them often; for new are more timorous and less subtle. He that can look into his estate but seldom, it behooveth him to turn all to certainties. A man had need, if he be plentiful in some kind of expense, to be as saving again in some other. As if he be plentiful in diet, to be saving in apparel; if he be plentiful in the hall, to be saving in the stable; and the like. For he that is plentiful in expenses of all kinds, will hardly be preserved from decay. In clearing of a man's estate, he may as well hurt himself in being too sudden, as in letting it run on too long. For hasty selling, is commonly as disadvantageable as interest. Besides, he that clears at once will relapse; for finding himself out of straits, he will revert to his custom: but he that cleareth by degrees, induceth a habit of frugality, and gaineth as well upon his mind, as upon his estate. Certainly, who hath a state to repair, may not despise small things; and commonly it is less dishonorable, to abridge petty charges, than to stoop to petty gettings. A man ought warily to begin charges which once begun will continue; but in matters that return not, he may be more magnificent.

Of The True Greatness Of Kingdoms And Estates

The speech of Themistocles the Athenian, which was haughty and arrogant, in taking so much to himself, had been a grave and wise observation and censure, applied at large to others. Desired at a feast to touch a lute, he said, He could not fiddle, but yet he could make a small town a great city. These words (holpen a little with a metaphor) may express two differing abilities, in those that deal in business of estate.

For if a true survey be taken of counsellors and statesmen, there may be found (though rarely) those which can make a small state great, and yet cannot fiddle; as on the other side, there will be found a great many, that can fiddle very cunningly, but yet are so far from being able to make a small state great, as their gift lieth the other way; to bring a great and flourishing estate, to ruin and decay. And certainly whose degenerate arts and shifts, whereby many counsellors and governors gain both favor with their masters, and estimation with the vulgar, deserve no better name than fiddling; being things rather pleasing for the time, and graceful to themselves only, than tending to the weal and advancement of the state which they serve.

There are also (no doubt) counsellors and governors which may be held sufficient (negotiis pares), able to manage affairs, and to keep them from precipices and manifest inconveniences; which nevertheless are far from the ability to raise and amplify an estate in power, means, and fortune. But be the workmen what they may be, let us speak of the work; that is, the true greatness of kingdoms and estates, and the means thereof. An argument fit for great and mighty princes to have in their hand; to the end that neither by over-measuring their forces, they leese themselves in vain enterprises; nor on the other side, by undervaluing them, they descend to fearful and pusillanimous counsels.zzz The greatness of an estate, in bulk and territory, doth fall under measure; and the greatness of finances and revenue, doth fall under computation.

The population may appear by musters; and the number and greatness of cities and towns by cards and maps. But yet there is not any thing amongst civil affairs more subject to error, than the right valuation and true judgment concerning the power and forces of an estate. The kingdom of heaven is compared, not to any great kernel or nut, but to a grain of mustard-seed: which is one of the least grains, but hath in it a property and spirit hastily to get up and spread.

So are there states, great in territory, and yet not apt to enlarge or command; and some that have but a small dimension of stem, and yet apt to be the foundations of great monarchies.zzz Walled towns, stored arsenals and armoiies, goodly races of horse, chariots of war, elephants, ordnance, artillery, and the like; all this is but a sheep in a lion's skin, except the breed and disposition of the people, be stout and warlike.

Nay, number (itself) in armies importeth not much, where the people is of weak courage; for (as Virgil saith) It never troubles a wolf, how many the sheep be. The army of the Persians, in the plains of Arbela, was such a vast sea of people, as it did somewhat astonish the commanders in Alexander's army; who came to him therefore, and wished him to set upon them by night; and he answered, He would not pilfer the victory. And the defeat was easy. When Tigranes the Armenian, being encamped upon a hill with four hundred thousand men, discovered the army of the Romans, being not above fourteen thousand, marching towards him, he made himself merry with it, and said, Yonder men are too many for an embassage, and too few for a fight. But before the sun set, he found them enow to give him the chase with infinite slaughter. Many are the examples of the great odds, between number and courage; so that a man may truly make a judgment, that the principal point of greatness in any state, is to have a race of military men. Neither is money the sinews of war (as it is trivially said), where the sinews of men's arms, in base and effeminate people, are failing. For Solon said well to Croesus (when in ostentation he showed him his gold), Sir, if any other come, that hath better iron than you, he will be master of all this gold.

Therefore let any prince or state think solely of his forces, except his militia of natives be of good and valiant soldiers. And let princes, on the other side, that have subjects of martial disposition, know their own strength; unless they be otherwise wanting unto themselves. As for mercenary forces (which is the help in this case), all examples show, that whatsoever estate or prince doth rest upon them, he may spread his feathers for a time, but he will mew them soon after.

The blessing of Judah and Issachar will never meet; that the same people, or nation, should be both the lion's whelp and the ass between burthens; neither will it be, that a people overlaid with taxes, should ever become valiant and martial. It is true that taxes levied by consent of the estate, do abate men's courage less: as it hath been seen notably, in the excises of the Low Countries; and, in some degree, in the subsidies of England. For you must note, that we speak now of the heart, and not of the purse. So that although the same tribute and tax, laid by consent or by imposing, be all one to the purse, yet it works diversely upon the courage. So that you may conclude, that no people over-charged with tribute, is fit for empire.

Let states that aim at greatness, take heed how their nobility and gentlemen do multiply too fast. For that made the common subject, grow to be a peasant and base swain, driven out of heart, and in effect but the gentleman's laborer. Even as you may see in coppice woods; if you leave your staddles too thick, you shall never have clean underwood, but shrubs and bushes. So in countries, if the gentlemen be too many, commons will be base; and you will bring it to that, that not the hundred poll, will be fit for an helmet; especially as to the infantry, which is the nerve of an army; and so there will be great population, and little strength. This which I speak of, hath been nowhere better seen, than by comparing of England and France; whereof England, though far less in territory and population, hath been (nevertheless) an overmatch; in regard the middle people of England make good soldiers, which the peasants of France do not. And herein the device of king Henry the Seventh (whereof I have spoken largely in the History of his Life) was profound and admirable; in making farms and houses of husbandry of a standard; that is, maintained with such a proportion of land unto them, as may breed a subject to live in convenient plenty and no servile condition; and to keep the plough in the hands of the owners, and not mere hirelings. And thus indeed you shall attain to Virgil's character which he gives to ancient Italy:

Terra potens armis atque ubere glebÃ¦.

Neither is that state (which, for any thing I know, is almost peculiar to England, and hardly to be found anywhere else, except it be perhaps in Poland) to be passed over; I mean the state of free servants, and attendants upon noblemen and gentlemen; which are no ways inferior unto the yeomanry for arms. And therefore out of all questions, the splendor and magnificence, and great retinues and hospitality, of noblemen and gentlemen, received into custom, doth much conduce unto martial greatness. Whereas, contrariwise, the close and reserved living of noblemen and gentlemen, causeth a penury of military forces.

By all means it is to be procured, that the trunk of Nebuchadnezzar's tree of monarchy, be great enough to bear the branches and the boughs; that is, that the natural subjects of the crown or state, bear a sufficient proportion to the stranger subjects, that they govern. Therefore all states that are liberal of naturalization towards strangers, are fit for empire. For to think that an handful of people can, with the greatest courage and policy in the world, embrace too large extent of dominion, it may hold for a time, but it will fail suddenly. The Spartans were a nice people in point of naturalization; whereby, while they kept their compass, they stood firm; but when they did spread, and their boughs were becomen too great for their stem, they became a windfall, upon the sudden. Never any state was in this point so open to receive strangers into their body, as were the Romans. Therefore it sorted with them accordingly; for they grew to the greatest monarchy.

Their manner was to grant naturalization (which they called jus civitatis), and to grant it in the highest degree; that is, not only jus commercii, jus connubii, jus hÃ¦reditatis; but also jus suffragii, and jus honorum. And this not to singular persons alone, but likewise to whole families; yea to cities, and sometimes to nations. Add to this their custom of plantation of colonies; whereby the Roman plant was removed into the soil of other nations. And putting both constitutions together, you will say that it was not the Romans that spread upon the world, but it was the world that spread upon the Romans; and that was the sure way of greatness.

I have marvelled, sometimes, at Spain, how they clasp and contain so large dominions, with so few natural Spaniards; but sure the whole compass of Spain, is a very great body of a tree; far above Rome and Sparta at the first. And besides, though they have not had that usage, to naturalize liberally, yet they have that which is next to it; that is, to employ, almost indifferently, all nations in their militia of ordinary soldiers; yea, and sometimes in their highest commands. Nay, it seemeth at this instant they are sensible, of this want of natives; as by the Pragmatical Sanction, now published, appeareth.

It is certain that sedentary, and within-door arts, and delicate manufactures (that require rather the finger than the arm), have, in their nature, a contrariety to a military disposition. And generally, all warlike people are a little idle, and love danger better than travail. Neither must they be too much broken of it, if they shall be preserved in vigour. Therefore it was great advantage, in the ancient states of Sparta, Athens, Rome, and others, that they had the use of slaves, which commonly did rid those manufactures. But that is abolished in greatest part, by the Christian law. That which cometh nearest to it, is to leave those arts chiefly to strangers (which, for that purpose, are the more easily to be received), and to contain the principal bulk of the vulgar natives, within those three kinds,-tillers of the ground; free servants; and handicraftsmen of strong and manly arts, as smiths, masons, carpenters, etc.; not reckoning professed soldiers.

But above all, for empire and greatness, it importeth most, that a nation do profess arms, as their principal honor, study, and occupation. For the things which we formerly have spoken of, are but habilitations towards arms; and what is habilitation without intention and act? Romulus, after his death (as they report or feign), sent a present to the Romans, that above all, they should intend arms; and then they should prove the greatest empire of the world. The fabric of the state of Sparta was wholly (though not wisely) framed and composed, to that scope and end.

The Persians and Macedonians had it for a flash. The Gauls, Germans, Goths, Saxons, Normans, and others, had it for a time. The Turks have it at this day, though in great declination. Of Christian Europe, they that have it are, in effect, only the Spaniards. But it is so plain, that every man profiteth in that, he most intendeth, that it needeth not to be stood upon. It is enough to point at it; that no nation which doth not directly profess arms, may look to have greatness fall into their mouths. And on the other side, it is a most certain oracle of time, that those states that continue long in that profession (as the Romans and Turks principally have done) do wonders. And those that have professed arms but for an age, have, notwithstanding, commonly attained that greatness, in that age, which maintained them long after, when their profession and exercise of arms hath grown to decay.

Incident to this point is, for a state to have those laws or customs, which may reach forth unto them just occasions (as may be pretended) of war. For there is that justice, imprinted in the nature of men, that they enter not upon wars (whereof so many calamities do ensue) but upon some, at the least specious, grounds and quarrels. The Turk hath at hand, for cause of war, the propagation of his law or sect; a quarrel that he may always command.

The Romans, though they esteemed the extending the limits of their empire, to be great honor to their generals, when it was done, yet they never rested upon that alone, to begin a war. First, therefore, let nations that pretend to greatness have this; that they be sensible of wrongs, either upon borderers, merchants, or politic ministers; and that they sit not too long upon a provocation. Secondly, let them be prest, and ready to give aids and succors, to their confederates; as it ever was with the Romans; insomuch, as if the confederate had leagues defensive, with divers other states, and, upon invasion offered, did implore their aids severally, yet the Romans would ever be the foremost, and leave it to none other to have the honor.

As for the wars which were anciently made, on the behalf

of a kind of party, or tacit conformity of estate, I do not see how they may be well justified: as when the Romans made a war, for the liberty of Grecia; or when the LacedÃ¦monians and Athenians, made wars to set up or pull down democracies and oligarchies; or when wars were made by foreigners, under the pretence of justice or protection, to deliver the subjects of others, from tyranny and oppression; and the like. Let it suffice, that no estate expect to be great, that is not awake upon any just occasion of arming.

No body can be healthful without exercise, neither natural body nor politic; and certainly to a kingdom or estate, a just and honorable war, is the true exercise. A civil war, indeed, is like the heat of a fever; but a foreign war is like the heat of exercise, and serveth to keep the body in health; for in a slothful peace, both courages will effeminate, and manners corrupt. But howsoever it be for happiness, without all question, for greatness, it made to be still for the most part in arms; and the strength of a veteran army (though it be a chargeable business) always on foot, is that which commonly giveth the law, or at least the reputation, amongst all neighbor states; as may well be seen in Spain, which hath had, in one part or other, a veteran army almost continually, now by the space of six score years.

To be master of the sea is an abridgment of a monarchy. Cicero, writing to Atticus of Pompey his preparation against CÃ¦sar, saith, Consilium Pompeii plane Themistocleum est; putat enim, qui mari potitur, eum rerum potiri. And, without doubt, Pompey had tired out CÃ¦sar, if upon vain confidence, he had not left that way. We see the great effects of battles by sea. The battle of Actium, decided the empire of the world. The battle of Lepanto, arrested the greatness of the Turk.

There be many examples, where sea-fights have been final to the war; but this is when princes or states have set up their rest, upon the battles. But thus much is certain, that he that commands the seal is at great liberty, and may take as much, and as little, of the war as he will. Whereas those that be strongest by land, are many times nevertheless in great straits. Surely, at this day, with us of Europe, the vantage of strength at sea (which is one of the principal dowries of this kingdom of Great Britain) is great; both because most of the kingdoms of Europe, are not merely inland, but girt with the sea most part of their compass; and because the wealth of both Indies seems in great part, but an accessory to the command of the seas. The wars of latter ages seem to be made in the dark, in respect of the glory, and honor, which reflected upon men from the wars, in ancient time. There be now, for martial encouragement, some degrees and orders of chivalry; which nevertheless are conferred promiscuously, upon soldiers and no soldiers; and some remembrance perhaps, upon the scutcheon; and some hospitals for maimed soldiers; and such like things. But in ancient times, the trophies erected upon the place of the victory; the funeral laudatives and monuments for those that died in the wars; the crowns and garlands personal; the style of emperor, which the great kings of the world after borrowed; the triumphs of the generals, upon their return; the great donatives and largesses, upon the disbanding of the armies; were things able to inflame all men's courages. But above all, that of the triumph, amongst the Romans, was not pageants or gaudery, but one of the wisest and noblest institutions, that ever was.

For it contained three things: honor to the general; riches to the treasury out of the spoils; and donatives to the army. But that honor, perhaps were not fit for monarchies; except it be in the person of the monarch himself, or his sons; as it came to pass in the times of the Roman emperors, who did impropriate the actual triumphs to themselves, and their sons, for such wars as they did achieve in person; and left only, for wars achieved by subjects, some triumphal garments and ensigns to the general. To conclude: no man can by care taking (as the Scripture saith) add a cubit to his stature, in this little model of a man's body; but in the great frame of kingdoms and commonwealths, it is in the power of princes or estates, to add amplitude and greatness to their kingdoms; for by introducing such ordinances, constitutions, and customs, as we have now touched, they may sow greatness to their posterity and succession. But these things are commonly not observed, but left to take their chance.

Of Regiment of Health

There is a wisdom in this; beyond the rules of physic: a man's own observation, what he finds good of, and what he finds hurt of, is the best physic to preserve health. But it is a safer conclusion to say, This agreeth not well with me, therefore, I will not continue it; than this, I find no offence of this, therefore I may use it. For strength of nature in youth, passeth over many excesses, which are owing a man till his age. Discern of the coming on of years, and think not to do the same things still; for age will not be defied. Beware of sudden change, in any great point of diet, and, if necessity inforce it, fit the rest to it.

For it is a secret both in nature and state, that it is safer to change many things, than one. Examine thy customs of diet, sleep, exercise, apparel, and the like; and try, in any thing thou shalt judge hurtful, to discontinue it, by little and little; but so, as if thou dost find any inconvenience by the change, thou come back to it again: for it is hard to distinguish that which is generally held good and wholesome, from that which is good particularly, and fit for thine own body.

To be free-minded and cheerfully disposed, at hours of meat, and of sleep, and of exercise, is one of the best precepts of long lasting. As for the passions, and studies of the mind; avoid envy, anxious fears; anger fretting inwards; subtle and knotty inquisitions; joys and exhilarations in excess; sadness not communicated. Entertain hopes; mirth rather than joy; variety of delights, rather than surfeit of them; wonder and admiration, and therefore novelties; studies that fill the mind with splendid and illustrious objects, as histories, fables, and contemplations of nature.

If you fly physic in health altogether, it will be too strange for your body, when you shall need it. If you make it too familiar, it will work no extraordinary effect, when sickness cometh. I commend rather some diet for certain seasons, than frequent use of physic, except it be grown into a custom. For those diets alter the body more, and trouble it less. Despise no new accident in your body, but ask opinion of it. In sickness, respect health principally; and in health, action. For those that put their bodies to endure in health, may in most sicknesses, which are not very sharp, be cured only with diet, and tendering. Celsus could never have spoken it as a physician, had he not been a wise man withal, when he giveth it for one of the great precepts of health and lasting, that a man do vary, and interchange contraries, but with an inclination to the more benign extreme: use fasting and full eating, but rather full eating; watching and sleep, but rather sleep; sitting and exercise, but rather exercise; and the like. So shall nature be cherished, and yet taught masteries.

Physicians are, some of them, so pleasing and conformable to the humour of the patient, as they press not the true cure of the disease; and some other are so regular, in proceeding according to art for the disease, as they respect not sufficiently the condition of the patient. Take one of a middle temper; or if it may not be found in one man, combine two of either sort; and forget not to call as well, the best acquainted with your body, as the best reputed of for his faculty.

Of Suspicion

Suspicions amongst thoughts are like bats amongst birds, they ever fly by twilight. Certainly, they are to be repressed, or at least well guarded: for they cloud the mind; they leese friends; and they check with business, whereby business cannot go on currently and constantly. They dispose kings to tyranny, husbands to jealousy, wise men to irresolution and melancholy. They are defects, not in the heart, but in the brain; for they take place in the stoutest natures; as in the example of Henry the Seventh of England.

There was not a more suspicious man, nor a more stout. And in such a composition they do small hurt. For commonly they are not admitted, but with examination, whether they be likely or no. But in fearful natures they gain ground too fast. There is nothing makes a man suspect much, more than to know little; and therefore men should remedy suspicion, by procuring to know more, and not to keep their suspicions in smother. What would men have? Do they think, those they employ and deal with, are saints? Do they not think, they will have their own ends, and be truer to themselves, than to them? Therefore there is no better way, to moderate suspicions, than to account upon such suspicions as true, and yet to bridle them as false. For so far a man ought to make use of suspicions, as to provide, as if that should be true, that he suspects, yet it may do him no hurt. Suspicions that the mind of itself gathers, are but buzzes; but suspicions that are artificially nourished, and put into men's heads, by the tales and whisperings of others, have stings.

Certainly, the best mean, to clear the way in this same wood of suspicions, is frankly to communicate them with the party, that he suspects; for thereby he shall be sure to know more of the truth of them, than he did before; and withal shall make that party more circumspect, not to give further cause of suspicion. But this would not be done to men of base natures; for they, if they find themselves once suspected, will never be true. The Italian says, Sospetto licentia fede; as if suspicion, did give a passport to faith; but it ought, rather, to kindle it to discharge itself.

Of Discourse

Some in their discourse, desire rather commendation of wit, in being able to hold all arguments, than of judgment, in discerning what is true; as if it were a praise, to know what might be said, and not, what should be thought. Some have certain common places, and themes, wherein they are good, and want variety; which kind of poverty is for the most part tedious, and when it is once perceived, ridiculous. The honorablest part of talk, is to give the occasion; and again to moderate, and pass to somewhat else; for then a man leads the dance. It is good, in discourse and speech of conversation, to vary and intermingle speech of the present occasion, with arguments, tales with reasons, asking of questions, with telling of opinions, and jest with earnest: for it is a dull thing to tire, and, as we say now, to jade, any thing too far. As for jest, there be certain things, which ought to be privileged from it; namely, religion, matters of state, great persons, any man's present business of importance, and any case that deserveth pity. Yet there be some, that think their wits have been asleep, except they dart out somewhat that is piquant, and to the quick. That is a vein which would be bridled: Parce, puer, stimulis, et fortius utere loris.

And generally, men ought to find the difference, between saltness and bitterness. Certainly, he that hath a satirical vein, as he made others afraid of his wit, so he had need be afraid of others' memory. He that questioneth much, shall learn much, and content much; but especially, if he apply his questions to the skill of the persons whom he asketh; for he shall give them occasion, to please themselves in speaking, and himself shall continually gather knowledge. But let his questions not be troublesome; for that is fit for a poser. And let him be sure to leave other men, their turns to speak. Nay, if there be any, that would reign and take up all the time, let him find means to take them off, and to bring others on; as musicians use to do, with those that dance too long galliards. If you dissemble, sometimes, your knowledge of that you are thought to know, you shall be thought, another time, to know that you know not.

Speech of a man's self ought to be seldom, and well chosen. I knew one, was wont to say in scorn, He must needs be a wise man, he speaks so much of himself: and there is but one case, wherein a man may commend himself with good grace; and that is in commending virtue in another; especially if it be such a virtue, whereunto himself pretendeth. Speech of touch towards others, should be sparingly used; for discourse ought to be as a field, without coming home to any man. I knew two noblemen, of the west part of England, whereof the one was given to scoff, but kept ever royal cheer in his house; the other would ask, of those that had been at the other's table, Tell truly, was there never a flout or dry blow given? To which the guest would answer, Such and such a thing passed. The lord would say, I thought, he would mar a good dinner.

Discretion of speech, is more than eloquence; and to speak agreeably to him, with whom we deal, is more than to speak in good words, or in good order. A good continued speech, without a good speech of interlocution, shows slowness: and a good reply or second speech, without a good settled speech, showeth shallowness and weakness. As we see in beasts, that those that are weakest in the course, are yet nimblest in the turn; as it is betwixt the greyhound and the hare. To use too many circumstances, ere one come to the matter, is wearisome; to use none at all, is blunt.

Of Plantations

Plantations are amongst ancient, primitive, and heroical works. When the world was young, it begat more children; but now it is old, it begets fewer: for I may justly account new plantations, to be the children of former kingdoms. I like a plantation in a pure soil; that is, where people are not displanted, to the end, to plant in others. For else it is rather an extirpation, than a plantation. Planting of countries, is like planting of woods; for you must make account to leese almost twenty years'profit, and expect your recompense in the end.

For the principal thing, that hath been the destruction of most plantations, hath been the base and hasty drawing of profit, in the first years. It is true, speedy profit is not to be neglected, as far as may stand with the good of the plantation, but no further. It is a shameful and unblessed thing, to take the scum of people, and wicked condemned men, to be the people with whom you plant; and not only so, but it spoileth the plantation; for they will ever live like rogues, and not fall to work, but be lazy, and do mischief, and spend victuals, and be quickly weary, and then certify over to their country, to the discredit of the plantation.

The people wherewith you plant ought to be gardeners, ploughmen, laborers, smiths, carpenters, joiners, fishermen, fowlers, with some few apothecaries, surgeons, cooks, and bakers. In a country of plantation, first look about, what kind of victual the country yields of itself to hand; as chestnuts, walnuts, pineapples, olives, dates, plums, cherries, wild honey, and the like; and make use of them. Then consider what victual or esculent things there are, which grow speedily, and within the year; as parsnips, carrots, turnips, onions, radish, artichokes of Hierusalem, maize, and the like. For wheat, barley, and oats, they ask too much labour; but with pease and beans you may begin, both because they ask less labour, and because they serve for meat, as well as for bread. And of rice, likewise cometh a great increase, and it is a kind of meat. Above all, there ought to be brought store of biscuit, oat-meal, flour, meal, and the like, in the beginning, till bread may be had. For beasts, or birds, take chiefly such as are least subject to diseases, and multiply fastest; as swine, goats, cocks, hens, turkeys, geese, house-doves, and the like.

The victual in plantations, ought to be expended almost as in a besieged town; that is, with certain allowance. And let the main part of the ground, employed to gardens or corn, be to a common stock; and to be laid in, and stored up, and then delivered out in proportion; besides some spots of ground, that any particular person will manure for his own private. Consider likewise what commodities, the soil where the plantation is, doth naturally yield, that they may some way help to defray the charge of the plantation (so it be not, as was said, to the untimely prejudice of the main business), as it hath fared with tobacco in Virginia. Wood commonly aboundeth but too much; and therefore timber is fit to be one. If there be iron ore, and streams whereupon to set the mills, iron is a brave commodity where wood aboundeth.

Making of bay-salt, if the climate be proper for it, would be put in experience. Growing silk likewise, if any be, is a likely commodity. Pitch and tar, where store of firs and pines are, will not fail. So drugs and sweet woods, where they are, cannot but yield great profit. Soap-ashes likewise, and other things that may be thought of. But moil not too much under ground; for the hope of mines is very uncertain, and useth to make the planters lazy, in other things.

For government, let it be in the hands of one, assisted with some counsel; and let them have commission to exercise martial laws, with some limitation. And above all, let men make that profit, of being in the wilderness, as they have God always, and his service, before their eyes. Let not the government of the plantation, depend upon too many counsellors, and undertakers, in the country that planteth, but upon a temperate number; and let those be rather noblemen and gentlemen, than merchants; for they look ever to the present gain.

Let there be freedom from custom, till the plantation be of strength; and not only freedom from custom, but freedom to carry their commodities, where they may make their best of them, except there be some special cause of caution. Cram not in people, by sending too fast company after company; but rather harken how they waste, and send supplies proportionably; but so, as the number may live well in the plantation, and not by surcharge be in penury.

It hath been a great endangering to the health of some plantations that they have built along the sea and rivers, in marish and unwholesome grounds. Therefore, though you begin there, to avoid carriage and like discommodities, yet build still rather upwards from the streams, than along. It concerned likewise the health of the plantation, that they have good store of salt with them, that they may use it in their victuals, when it shall be necessary.

If you plant where savages are, do not only entertain them, with trifles and gingles, but use them justly and graciously, with sufficient guard nevertheless; and do not win their favor, by helping them to invade their enemies, but for their defence it is not amiss; and send oft of them, over to the country that plants, that they may see a better condition than their own, and commend it when they return. When the plantation grows to strength, then it is time to plant with women, as well as with men; that the plantation may spread into generations, and not be ever pieced from without. It is the sinfullest thing in the world, to forsake or destitute a plantation once in forwardness; for besides the dishonor, it is the guiltiness of blood of many commiserable persons.

Of Riches

I cannot call riches better than the baggage of virtue. The Roman word is better, impedimenta. For as the baggage is to an army, so is riches to virtue. It cannot be spared, nor left behind, but it hindereth the march; yea, and the care of it, sometimes loseth or disturbeth the victory. Of great riches there is no real use, except it be in the distribution; the rest is but conceit.

So saith Salomon, Where much is, there are many consume it; and what hath the owner, but the sight of it with his eyes? The personal fruition in any man, cannot reach to feel great riches: there is a custody of them; or a power of dole, and donative of them; or a fame of them; but no solid use to the owner. Do you not see what feigned prices, are set upon little stones and rarities? and what works of ostentation are undertaken, because there might seem to be some use of great riches? But then you will say, they may be of use, to buy men out of dangers or troubles. As Salomon saith, Riches are as a strong hold, in the imagination of the rich man. But this is excellently expressed, that it is in imagination, and not always in fact. For certainly great riches, have sold more men, than they have bought out. Seek not proud riches, but such as thou mayest get justly, use soberly, distribute cheerfully, and leave contentedly.

Yet have no abstract nor friarly contempt of them. But distinguish, as Cicero saith well of Rabirius Posthumus, In studio rei amplificandÃ¦ apparebat, non avaritiÃ¦ prÃ¦dam, sed instrumentum bonitati quÃ¦ri. Harken also to Salomon, and beware of hasty gathering of riches; Qui festinat ad divitias, non erit insons. The poets feign, that when Plutus (which is Riches) is sent from Jupiter, he limps and goes slowly; but when he is sent from Pluto, he runs, and is swift of foot. Meaning that riches gotten by good means, and just labour, pace slowly; but when they come by the death of others (as by the course of inheritance, testaments, and the like), they come tumbling upon a man.

But it mought be applied likewise to Pluto, taking him for the devil. For when riches come from the devil (as by fraud and oppression, and unjust means), they come upon speed. The ways to enrich are many, and most of them foul. Parsimony is one of the best, and yet is not innocent; for it withholdeth men from works of liberality and charity. The improvement of the ground, is the most natural obtaining of riches; for it is our great mother's blessing, the earth's; but it is slow. And yet where men of great wealth do stoop to husbandry, it multiplieth riches exceedingly.

I knew a nobleman in England, that had the greatest audits of any man in my time; a great grazier, a great sheep-master, a great timber man, a great collier, a great corn-master, a great lead-man, and so of iron, and a number of the like points of husbandry. So as the earth seemed a sea to him, in respect of the perpetual importation. It was truly observed by one, that himself came very hardly, to a little riches, and very easily, to great riches.

For when a man's stock is come to that, that he can expect the prime of markets, and overcome those bargains, which for their greatness are few men's money, and be partner in the industries of younger men, he cannot but increase mainly. The gains of ordinary trades and vocations are honest; and furthered by two things chiefly: by diligence, and by a good name, for good and fair dealing.

But the gains of bargains, are of a more doubtful nature; when men shall wait upon others' necessity, broke by servants and instruments to draw them on, put off others cunningly, that would be better chapmen, and the like practices, which are crafty and naught. As for the chopping of bargains, when a man buys not to hold but to sell over again, that commonly grindeth double, both upon the seller, and upon the buyer. Sharings do greatly enrich, if the hands be well chosen, that are trusted. Usury is the certainest means of gain, though one of the worst; as that whereby a man doth eat his bread, in sudore vÃ»ltus alieni; and besides, doth plough upon Sundays. But yet certain though it be, it hath flaws; for that the scriveners and brokers do value unsound men, to serve their own turn.

The fortune in being the first, in an invention or in a privilege, doth cause sometimes a wonderful overgrowth in riches; as it was with the with the first sugar man, in the Canaries. Therefore, if a man can play the true logician, to have as well judgment, as invention, he may do great matters; especially if the times be fit. He that resteth upon gains certain, shall hardly grow to great riches; and he that puts all upon adventures, doth oftentimes break and come to poverty: it is good, therefore, to guard adventures with certainties, that may uphold losses.

Monopolies, and coemption of wares for re-sale, where they are not restrained, are great means to enrich; especially if the party have intelligence, what things are like to come into request, and so store himself beforehand. Riches gotten by service, though it be of the best rise, yet when they are gotten by flattery, feeding humors, and other servile conditions, they may be placed amongst the worst. As for fishing for testaments and executorships (as Tacitus saith of Seneca, testamenta et orbos tamquam indagine capi) it is yet worse; by how much men submit themselves to meaner persons, than in service. Believe not much, them that seem to despise riches for they despise them, that despair of them; and none worse, when they come to them. Be not penny-wise; riches have wings, and sometimes they fly away of themselves, sometimes they must be set flying, to bring in more. Men leave their riches, either to their kindred, or to the public; and moderate portions, prosper best in both. A great state left to an heir, is as a lure to all the birds of prey round about, to seize on him, if he be not the better stablished in years and judgment. Likewise glorious gifts and foundations, are like sacrifices without salt; and but the painted sepulchres of alms, which soon will putrefy, and corrupt inwardly.

Therefore measure not thine advancements, by quantity, but frame them by measure: and defer not charities till death; for, certainly, if a man weigh it rightly, he that doth so, is rather liberal of another man's, than of his own.

Of Prophecies

I mean not to speak of divine prophecies; nor of heathen oracles; nor of natural predictions; but only of prophecies that have been of certain memory, and from hidden causes. Saith the Pythonissa to Saul, To-morrow thou and thy son shall be with me. Homer hath these verses: At domus Ã†neÃ¦ cunctis dominabitur oris, Et nati natorum, et qui nascentur ab illis. A prophecy, as it seems, of the Roman empire. Seneca the tragedian hath these verses: —Venient annis SÃ¦cula seris, quibus Oceanus Vincula rerum laxet, et ingens Pateat Tellus, Tiphysque novos Detegat orbes; nec sit terris Ultima Thule:

A prophecy of the discovery of America. The daughter of Polycrates dreamed that Jupiter bathed her father, and Apollo anointed him: and it came to the sun made his body run with sweat, and the rain washed it. Philip of Macedon dreamed, he sealed up his wife's belly; whereby he did expound it, that his wife should be barren; but Aristander the soothsayer, told him his wife was with child because men do not use to seal vessels, that are empty. A phantasm that appeared to M. Brutus, in his tent, said to him, Philippis iterum me videbis. Tiberius said to Galba, Tu quoque, Galba, degustabis imperium. In Vespasian's time, there went a prophecy in the East, that those that should come forth of Judea, should reign over the world: which though it may be was meant of our Savior; yet Tacitus expounds it of Vespasian. Domitian dreamed, the night before he was slain, that a golden head was growing, out of the nape of his neck: and indeed, the succession that followed him for many years, made golden times.

Henry the Sixth of England, said of Henry the Seventh, when he was a lad, and gave him water, This is the lad that shall enjoy the crown for which we strive. When I was in France, I heard from one Dr. Penal that the Queen Mother, who was given to curious arts, caused the King her husband's nativity to be calculated, under a false name; and the astrologer gave a judgment, that he should be killed in a duel; at which the Queen laughed, thinking her husband to be above challenges and duels: but he was slain upon a course at tilt, the splinters of the staff of Montgomery going in at his beaver. The trivial prophecy, which I heard when I was a child, and Queen Elizabeth was in the flower of her years, was, When Hempe is sponne, England's done.

whereby it was generally conceived, that after the princes had reigned, which had the principal letters of that word hempe (which were Henry, Edward, Mary, Philip, and Elizabeth), England should come to utter confusion; which, thanks be to God, is verified only in the change of the name; for that the King's style, is now no more of England, but of Britian. There was also another prophecy, before the year of '88, which I do not well understand.

There shall be seen upon a day,
Between the Baugh and the May,
The black fleet of Norway.
When that that come and gone,
England build houses of lime and stone,
For after wars shall you have none.

It was generally conceived to be meant, of the Spanish fleet that came in '88: for that the king of Spain's surname, as they say, is Norway. The prediction of Regiomontanus,

Octogesimus octavus mirabilis annus, was thought likewise accomplished in the sending of that great fleet, being the greatest in strength, though not in number, of all that ever swam upon the sea. As for Cleon's dream, I think it was a jest. It was, that he was devoured of a long dragon; and it was expounded of a maker of sausages, that troubled him exceedingly.

There are numbers of the like kind; especially if you include dreams, and predictions of astrology. But I have set down these few only, of certain credit, for example. My judgment is, that they ought all to be despised; and ought to serve but for winter talk by the fireside. Though when I say despised, I mean it as for belief; for otherwise, the spreading, or publishing, of them, is in no sort to be despised. For they have done much mischief; and I see many severe laws made, to suppress them. That that hath given them grace, and some credit, consisteth in three things. First, that men mark when they hit, and never mark when they miss; as they do generally also of dreams.

The second is, that probable conjectures, or obscure traditions, many times turn themselves into prophecies; while the nature of man, which coveteth divination, thinks it no peril to foretell that which indeed they do but collect. As that of Seneca's verse. For so much was then subject to demonstration, that the globe of the earth had great parts beyond the Atlantic, which mought be probably conceived not to be all sea: and adding thereto the tradition in Plato's TimÃ¦us, and his Atlanticus, it mought encourage one to turn it to a prediction. The third and last (which is the great one) is, that almost all of them, being infinite in number, have been impostures, and by idle and crafty brains merely contrived and feigned, after the event past.

Of Ambition

Ambition is like choler; which is an humour that made men active, earnest, full of alacrity, and stirring, if it be not stopped. But if it be stopped, and cannot have his way, it becometh adust, and thereby malign and venomous. So ambitious men, if they find the way open for their rising, and still get forward, they are rather busy than dangerous; but if they be checked in their desires, they become secretly discontent, and look upon men and matters with an evil eye, and are best pleased, when things go backward; which is the worst property in a servant of a prince, or state.

Therefore it is good for princes, if they use ambitious men, to handle it, so as they be still progressive and not retrograde; which, because it cannot be without inconvenience, it is good not to use such natures at all. For if they rise not with their service, they will take order, to make their service fall with them. But since we have said, it were good not to use men of ambitious natures, except it be upon necessity, it is fit we speak, in what cases they are of necessity. Good commanders in the wars must be taken, be they never so ambitious; for the use of their service, dispenseth with the rest; and to take a soldier without ambition, is to pull off his spurs.

There is also great use of ambitious men, in being screens to princes in matters of danger and envy; for no man will take that part, except he be like a seeled dove, that mounts and mounts, because he cannot see about him. There is use also of ambitious men, in pulling down the greatness of any subject that over-tops; as Tiberius used Marco, in the pulling down of Sejanus. Since, therefore, they must be used in such cases, there resteth to speak, how they are to be bridled, that they may be less dangerous. There is less danger of them, if they be of mean birth, than if they be noble; and if they be rather harsh of nature, than gracious and popular: and if they be rather new raised, than grown cunning, and fortified, in their greatness. It is counted by some, a weakness in princes, to have favorites; but it is, of all others, the best remedy against ambitious great-ones. For when the way of pleasuring, and displeasuring, lieth by the favourite, it is impossible any other should be over great. Another means to curb them, is to balance them by others, as proud as they.

But then there must be some middle counselors, to keep things steady; for without that ballast, the ship will roll too much. At the least, a prince may animate and inure some meaner persons, to be as it were scourges, to ambitions men. As for the having of them obnoxious to ruin; if they be of fearful natures, it may do well; but if they be stout and daring, it may precipitate their designs, and prove dangerous. As for the pulling of them down, if the affairs require it, and that it may not be done with safety suddenly, the only way is the interchange, continually, of favors and disgraces; whereby they may not know what to expect, and be, as it were, in a wood.

Of ambitions, it is less harmful, the ambition to prevail in great things, than that other, to appear in every thing; for that breeds confusion, and mars business. But yet it is less danger, to have an ambitious man stirring in business, than great in dependences. He that seeketh to be eminent amongst able men, hath a great task; but that is ever good for the public. But he, that plots to be the only figure amongst ciphers, is the decay of a whole age. Honor hath three things in it: the vantage ground to do good; the approach to kings and principal persons; and the raising of a man's own fortunes.

He that hath the best of these intentions, when he aspireth, is an honest man; and that prince, that can discern of these intentions in another that aspireth, is a wise prince. Generally, let princes and states choose such ministers, as are more sensible of duty than of rising; and such as love business rather upon conscience, than upon bravery, and let them discern a busy nature, from a willing mind.

Of Masques and Triumphs

These things are but toys, to come amongst such serious observations. But yet, since princes will have such things, it is better they should be graced with elegancy, than daubed with cost. Dancing to song, is a thing of great state and pleasure. I understand it, that the song be in quire, placed aloft, and accompanied with some broken music; and the ditty fitted to the device. Acting in song, especially in dialogues, hath an extreme good grace; I say acting, not dancing (for that is a mean and vulgar thing); and the voices of the dialogue would be strong and manly (a base and a tenor; no treble); and the ditty high and tragical; not nice or dainty. Several quires, placed one over against another, and taking the voice by catches, anthem-wise, give great pleasure.

Turning dances into figure, is a childish curiosity. And generally let it be noted, that those things which I here set down, are such as do naturally take the sense, and not respect petty wonderments. It is true, the alterations of scenes, so it be quietly and without noise, are things of great beauty and pleasure; for they feed and relieve the eye, before it be full of the same object.

Let the scenes abound with light, specially colored and varied; and let the masquers, or any other, that are to come down from the scene, have some motions upon the scene itself, before their coming down; for it draws the eye strangely, and makes it, with great pleasure, to desire to see, that it cannot perfectly discern. Let the gongs be loud and cheerful, and not chirpings or pulings. Let the music likewise be sharp and loud, and well placed.

The colors that show best by candle-light are white, carnation, and a kind of sea-water-green; and oes, or spangs, as they are of no great cost, so they are of most glory. As for rich embroidery, it is lost and not discerned. Let the suits of the masquers be graceful, and such as become the person, when the vizors are off; not after examples of known attires; Turke, soldiers, mariners, and the like.

Let anti-masques not be long; they have been commonly of fools, satyrs, baboons, wild-men, antics, beasts, sprites, witches, Ethiops, pigmies, turquets, nymphs, rustics, Cupids, statuas moving, and the like. As for angels, it is not comical enough, to put them in anti-masques; and anything that is hideous, as devils, giants, is on the other side as unfit. But chiefly, let the music of them be recreative, and with some strange changes. Some sweet odors suddenly coming forth, without any drops falling, are, in such a company as there is steam and heat, things of great pleasure and refreshment. Double masques, one of men, another of ladies, addeth state and variety. But all is nothing except the room be kept clear and neat. For justs, and tourneys, and barriers; the glories of them are chiefly in the chariots, wherein the challengers make their entry; especially if they be drawn with strange beasts: as lions, bears, camels, and the like; or in the devices of their entrance; or in the bravery of their liveries; or in the goodly furniture of their horses and armor. But enough of these toys.

Of Nature in Men

Nature is often hidden; sometimes overcome; seldom extinguished. Force, made nature more violent in the return; doctrine and discourse, made nature less importune; but custom only doth alter and subdue nature. He that seeketh victory over his nature, let him not set himself too great, nor too small tasks; for the first will make him dejected by often failings; and the second will make him a small proceeder, though by often prevailing. And at the first let him practice with helps, as swimmers do with bladders or rushes; but after a time let him practice with disadvantages, as dancers do with thick shoes.

For it breeds great perfection, if the practice be harder than the use. Where nature is mighty, and therefore the victory hard, the degrees had need be, first to stay and arrest nature in time; like to him that would say over the four and twenty letters when he was angry; then to go less in quantity; as if one should, in forbearing wine, come from drinking healths, to a draught at a meal; and lastly, to discontinue altogether. But if a man have the fortitude, and resolution, to enfranchise himself at once, that is the best:

Optimus ille animi vindex lÃ¦dentia pectus
Vincula qui rupit, dedoluitque semel.

Neither is the ancient rule amiss, to bend nature, as a wand, to a contrary extreme, whereby to set it right, understanding it, where the contrary extreme is no vice. Let not a man force a habit upon' himself, with a perpetual continuance, but with some intermission. For both the pause reinforceth the new onset; and if a man that is not perfect, be ever in practice, he shall as well practice his errors, as his abilities, and induce one habit of both; and there is no means to help this, but by seasonable intermissions. But let not a man trust his victory over his nature, too far; for nature will lay buried a great time, and yet revive, upon the occasion or temptation. Like as it was with Ã†sop's damosel, turned from a cat to a woman, who sat very demurely at the board's end, till a mouse ran before her. Therefore, let a man either avoid the occasion altogether; or put himself often to it, that he may be little moved with it.

A man's nature is best perceived in privateness, for there is no affectation; in passion, for that putteth a man out of his precepts; and in a new case or experiment, for there custom leaveth him. They are happy men, whose natures sort with their vocations; otherwise they may say, Multum incola fuit anima mea; when they converse in those things, they do not affect. In studies, whatsoever a man commandeth upon himself, let him set hours for it; but whatsoever is agreeable to his nature, let him take no care for any set times; for his thoughts will fly to it, of themselves; so as the spaces of other business, or studies, will suffice. A man's nature, runs either to herbs or weeds; therefore let him seasonably water the one, and destroy the other.

Of Custom and Education

Men's thoughts, are much according to their inclination; their discourse and speeches, according to their learning and infused opinions; but their deeds, are after as they have been accustomed. And therefore, as Machiavel well noteth (though in an evil-favored instance), there is no trusting to the force of nature, nor to the bravery of words, except it be corroborate by custom. His instance is, that for the achieving of a desperate conspiracy, a man should not rest upon the fierceness of any man's nature, or his resolute undertakings; but take such an one, as hath had his hands formerly in blood.

But Machiavel knew not of a Friar Clement, nor a Ravillac, nor a Jaureguy, nor a Baltazar Gerard; yet his rule holdeth still, that nature, nor the engagement of words, are not so forcible, as custom. Only superstition is now so well advanced, that men of the first blood, are as firm as butchers by occupation; and votary resolution, is made equipollent to custom, even in matter of blood.

In other things, the predominancy of custom is everywhere visible; insomuch as a man would wonder, to hear men profess, protest, engage, give great words, and then do, just as they have done before; as if they were dead images, and engines moved only by the wheels of custom. We see also the reign or tyranny of custom, what it is. The Indians (I mean the sect of their wise men) lay themselves quietly upon a stock of wood, and so sacrifice themselves by fire. Nay, the wives strive to be burned, with the corpses of their husbands. The lads of Sparta, of ancient time, were wont to be scourged upon the altar of Diana, without so much as queching.

I remember, in the beginning of Queen Elizabeth's time of England, an Irish rebel condemned, put up a petition to the deputy, that he might be hanged in a withe, and not in an halter; because it had been so used, with former rebels. There be monks in Russia, for penance, that will sit a whole night in a vessel of water, till they be engaged with hard ice. Many examples may be put of the force of custom, both upon mind and body. Therefore, since custom is the principal magistrate of man's life, let men by all means endeavor, to obtain good customs. Certainly custom is most perfect, when it beginneth in young years: this we call education; which is, in effect, but an early custom. So we see, in languages, the tongue is more pliant to all expressions and sounds, the joints are more supple, to all feats of activity and motions, in youth than afterwards. For it is true, that late learners cannot so well take the ply;

except it be in some minds that have not suffered themselves to fix, but have kept themselves open, and prepared to receive continual amendment, which is exceeding rare. But if the force of custom simple and separate, be great, the force of custom copulate and conjoined and collegiate, is far greater. For there example teacheth, company comforteth, emulation quickeneth, glory raiseth: so as in such places the force of custom is in his exaltation. Certainly the great multiplication of virtues upon human nature, resteth uponsocieties well ordained and disciplined. For commonwealths, and good governments, do nourish virtue grown, but do not much mend the deeds. But the misery is, that the most effectual means, are now applied to the ends, least to be desired.

Of Fortune

It cannot be denied, but outward accidents conduce much to fortune; favor, opportunity, death of others, occasion fitting virtue. But chiefly, the mould of a man's fortune is in his own hands. Faber quisque fortunÃ¦ suÃ¦, saith the poet. And the most frequent of external causes is, that the folly of one man, is the fortune of another. For no man prospers so suddenly, as by others' errors. Serpens nisi serpentem comederit non fit draco. Overt and apparent virtues, bring forth praise; but there be secret and hidden virtues, that bring forth fortune; certain deliveries of a man's self, which have no name. The Spanish name, desemboltura, partly expresseth them; when there be not stonds nor restiveness in a man's nature; but that the wheels of his mind, keep way with the wheels of his fortune.

For so Livy (after he had described Cato Major in these words, In illo viro tantum robur corporis et animi fuit, ut quocunque loco natus esset, fortunam sibi facturus videretur) falleth upon that, that he had versatile ingenium. Therefore if a man look sharply and attentively, he shall see Fortune: for though she be blind, yet she is not invisible. The way of fortune, is like the Milken Way in the sky; which is a meeting or knot of a number of small stars; not seen asunder, but giving light together. So are there a number of little, and scarce discerned virtues, or rather faculties and customs, that make men fortunate. The Italians note some of them, such as a man would little think. When they speak of one that cannot do amiss, they will throw in, into his other conditions, that he hath poco di matto. And certainly there be not two more fortunate properties, than to have a little of the fool, and not too much of the honest.

Therefore extreme lovers of their country or masters, were never fortunate, neither can they be. For when a man placeth his thoughts without himself, he goeth not his own way. An hasty fortune made an enterpriser and remover (the French hath it better, entreprenant, or remuant), but the exercised fortune made the able man. Fortune is to be honored and respected, and it be but for her daughters, Confidence and Reputation. For those two, Felicity breedeth; the first within a man's self, the latter in others towards him.

All wise men, to decline the envy of their own virtues, use to ascribe them to Providence and Fortune; for so they may the better assume them: and, besides, it is greatness in a man, to be the care of the higher powers. So CÃ¦sar said to the pilot in the tempest, CÃ¦sarem portas, et fortunam ejus. So Sylla chose the name of Felix, and not of Magnus. And it hath been noted, that those who ascribe openly too much to their own wisdom and policy, end infortunate. It is written that Timotheus the Athenian, after he had, in the account he gave to the state of his government, often interlaced this speech, And in this, Fortune had no part, never prospered in anything, he undertook afterwards. Certainly there be, whose fortunes are like Homer's verses, that have a slide and easiness more than the verses of other poets; as Plutarch saith of Timoleon's fortune, in respect of that of Agesilaus or Epaminondas. And that this should be, no doubt it is much, in a man's self.

Of Usury

Many have made witty invectives against usury. They say that it is a pity, the devil should have God's part, which is the tithe. That the usurer is the greatest Sabbath-breaker, because his plough goeth every Sunday. That the usurer is the drone, that Virgil speaketh of; Ignavum fucos pecus a prÃ¦sepibus arcent. That the usurer breaketh the first law, that was made for mankind after the fall, which was, in sudore vÃ»ltus tui comedes panem tuum; not, in sudore vÃ»ltus alieni. That usurers should have orange-tawny bonnets, because they do judaize. That it is against nature for money to beget money; and the like. I say this only, that usury is a concessum propter duritiem cordis; for since there must be borrowing and lending, and men are so hard of heart, as they will not lend freely, usury must be permitted. Some others, have made suspicious and cunning propositions of banks, discovery of men's estates, and other inventions.

But few have spoken of usury usefully. It is good to set before us, the incommodities and commodities of usury, that the good, may be either weighed out or called out; and warily to provide, that while we make forth to that which is better, we meet not with that which is worse.

The discommodities of usury are, First, that it makes fewer merchants. For were it not for this lazy trade of usury, money would not he still, but would in great part be employed upon merchandizing; which is the vena porta of wealth in a state. The second, that it makes poor merchants. For, as a farmer cannot husband his ground so well, if he sit at a great rent; so the merchant cannot drive his trade so well, if he sit at great usury. The third is incident to the other two; and that is the decay of customs of kings or states, which ebb or flow, with merchandizing.

The fourth, that it bringeth the treasure of a realm, or state, into a few hands. For the usurer being at certainties, and others at uncertainties, at the end of the game, most of the money will be in the box; and ever a state flourisheth, when wealth is more equally spread. The fifth, that it beats down the price of land; for the employment of money, is chiefly either merchandizing or purchasing; and usury waylays both. The sixth, that it doth dull and damp all industries, improvements, and new inventions, wherein money would be stirring, if it were not for this slug. The last, that it is the canker and ruin of many men's estates; which, in process of time, breeds a public poverty.

On the other side, the commodities of usury are, first, that howsoever usury in some respect hindereth merchandizing, yet in some other it advanceth it; for it is certain that the greatest part of trade is driven by young merchants, upon borrowing at interest; so as if the usurer either call in, or keep back, his money, there will ensue, presently, a great stand of trade. The second is, that were it not for this easy borrowing upon interest, men's necessities would draw upon them a most sudden undoing; in that they would be forced to sell their means (be it lands or goods) far under foot; and so, whereas usury doth but gnaw upon them, bad markets would swallow them quite up. As for mortgaging or pawning, it will little mend the matter: for either men will not take pawns without use; or if they do, they will look precisely for the forfeiture.

I remember a cruel moneyed man in the country, that would say, The devil take this usury, it keeps us from forfeitures, of mortgages and bonds. The third and last is, that it is a vanity to conceive, that there would be ordinary borrowing without profit; and it is impossible to conceive, the number of inconveniences that will ensue, if borrowing be cramped. Therefore to speak of the abolishing of usury is idle. All states have ever had it, in one kind or rate, or other. So as that opinion must be sent to Utopia.

To speak now of the reformation, and reiglement, of usury; how the discommodities of it may be best avoided, and the commodities retained. It appears, by the balance of commodities and discommodities of usury, two things are to be reconciled. The one, that the tooth of usury be grinded, that it bite not too much; the other, that there be left open a means, to invite moneyed men to lend to the merchants, for the continuing and quickening of trade. This cannot be done, except you introduce two several sorts of usury, a less and a greater. For if you reduce usury to one low rate, it will ease the common borrower, but the merchant will be to seek for money. And it is to be noted, that the trade of merchandize, being the most lucrative, may bear usury at a good rate; other contracts not so. To serve both intentions, the way would be briefly thus.

That there be two rates of usury: the one free, and general for all; the other under license only, to certain persons, and in certain places of merchandizing. First, therefore, let usury in general, be reduced to five in the hundred; and let that rate be proclaimed, to be free and current; and let the state shut itself out, to take any penalty for the same.

This will preserve borrowing, from any general stop or dryness. This will ease infinite borrowers in the country. This will, in good part, raise the price of land, because land purchased at sixteen years' purchase will yield six in the hundred, and somewhat more; whereas this rate of interest, yields but five. This by like reason will encourage, and edge, industrious and profitable improvements; because many will rather venture in that kind, than take five in the hundred, especially having been used to greater profit. Secondly, let there be certain persons licensed, to lend to known merchants, upon usury at a higher rate; and let it be with the cautions following. Let the rate be, even with the merchant himself, somewhat more easy than that he used formerly to pay; for by that means, all borrowers, shall have some ease by this reformation, be he merchant, or whosoever. Let it be no bank or common stock, but every man be master of his own money. Not that I altogether mislike banks, but they will hardly be brooked, in regard of certain suspicions. Let the state be answered some small matter for the license, and the rest left to the lender; for if the abatement be but small, it will no whit discourage the lender.

For he, for example, that took before ten or nine in the hundred, will sooner descend to eight in the hundred than give over his trade of usury, and go from certain gains, to gains of hazard. Let these licensed lenders be in number indefinite, but restrained to certain principal cities and towns of merchandizing; for then they will be hardly able to colour other men's moneys in the country: so as the license of nine will not suck away the current rate of five; for no man will send his moneys far off, nor put them into unknown hands.

If it be objected that this doth in a sort authorize usury, which before, was in some places but permissive; the answer is, that it is better to mitigate usury, by declaration, than to suffer it to rage, by connivance.

Of Youth and Age

A man that is young in years, may be old in hours, if he have lost no time. But that happeneth rarely. Generally, youth is like the first cogitations, not so wise as the second. For there is a youth in thoughts, as well as in ages. And yet the invention of young men, is more lively than that of old; and imaginations stream into their minds better, and, as it were, more divinely. Natures that have much heat, and great and violent desires and perturbations, are not ripe for action, till they have passed the meridian of their years; as it was with Julius CÃ¦sar and Septimius Severus.

Of the latter, of whom it is said, Juventutem egit erroribus, imo furoribus, plenam. And yet he was the ablest emperor, almost, of all the list. But reposed natures may do well in youth. As it is seen in Augustus Caesar, Cosmus Duke of Florence, Gaston de Foix, and others. On the other side, heat and vivacity in age, is an excellent composition for business. Young men are fitter to invent, than to judge; fitter for execution, than for counsel; and fitter for new projects, than for settled business. For the experience of age, in things that fall within the compass of it, directed them; but in new things, abused them.

The errors of young men, are the ruin of business; but the errors of aged men, amount but to this, that more might have been done, or sooner. Young men, in the conduct and manage of actions, embrace more than they can hold; stir more than they can quiet; fly to the end, without consideration of the means and degrees; pursue some few principles, which they have chanced upon absurdly; care not to innovate, which draws unknown inconveniences; use extreme remedies at first; and, that which doubled all errors, will not acknowledge or retract them; like an unready horse, that will neither stop nor turn. Men of age object too much, consult too long, adventure too little, repent too soon, and seldom drive business home to the full period, but content themselves with a mediocrity of success. Certainly it is good to compound employments of both; for that will be good for the present, because the virtues of either age, may correct the defects of both; and good for succession, that young men may be learners, while men in age are actors; and, lastly, good for extern accidents, because authority followeth old men, and favor and popularity, youth.

But for the moral part, perhaps youth will have the pre-eminence, as age hath for the politic. A certain rabbin, upon the text, Your young men shall see visions, and your old men shall dream dreams, inferreth that young men, are admitted nearer to God than old, because vision, is a clearer revelation, than a dream. And certainly, the more a man drinked of the world, the more it intoxicated; and age doth profit rather in the powers of understanding, than in the virtues of the will and affections. There be some, have an over-early ripeness in their years, which fadeth betimes.

These are, first, such as have brittle wits, the edge whereof is soon turned; such as was Hermogenes the rhetorician, whose books are exceeding subtle; who afterwards waxed stupid. A second sort, is of those that have some natural dispositions which have better grace in youth, than in age; such as is a fluent and luxuriant speech; which becomes youth well, but not age: so Tully saith of Hortensius, Idem manebat, neque idem decebat. The third is of such, as take too high a strain at the first, and are magnanimous, more than tract of years can uphold. As was Scipio Africanus, of whom Livy saith in effect, Ultima primis cedebant.

Of Beauty

Virtue is like a rich stone, best plain set; and surely virtue is best, in a body that is comely, though not of delicate features; and that hath rather dignity of presence, than beauty of aspect. Neither is it almost seen, that very beautiful persons are otherwise of great virtue; as if nature were rather busy, not to err, than in labour to produce excellence. Therefore they prove accomplished, but not of great spirit; and study rather behaviour, than virtue. But this holds not always: for Augustus Caesar, Titus Vespasianus, Philip le Belle of France, Edward the Fourth of England, Alcibiades of Athens, Ismael the Sophy of Persia, were all high and great spirits; and yet the most beautiful men of their times. In beauty, that of favor, is more than that of colour; and that of decent and gracious motion, more than that of favor.

That is the best part of beauty, which a picture cannot express; no, nor the first sight of the life. There is no excellent beauty, that hath not some strangeness in the proportion. A man cannot tell whether Apelles, or Albert Durer, were the more trifler; whereof the one, would make a personage by geometrical proportions; the other, by taking the best parts out of divers faces, to make one excellent. Such personages, I think, would please nobody, but the painter that made them. Not but I think a painter may make a better face than ever was; but he must do it by a kind of felicity (as a musician that made an excellent air in music), and not by rule. A man shall see faces, that if you examine them part by part, you shall find never a good; and yet altogether do well.

If it be true that the principal part of beauty is in decent motion, certainly it is no marvel, though persons in years seem many times more amiable; pulchrorum autumnus pulcher; for no youth can be comely but by pardon, and considering the youth, as to make up the comeliness. Beauty is as summer fruits, which are easy to corrupt, and cannot last; and for the most part it makes a dissolute youth, and an age a little out of countenance; but yet certainly again, if it light well, it made virtue shine, and vices blush.

Of Deformity

Deformed persons are commonly even with nature; for as nature hath done ill by them, so do they by nature; being for the most part (as the Scripture saith) void of natural affection; and so they have their revenge of nature. Certainly there is a consent, between the body and the mind; and where nature erreth in the one, she ventureth in the other. Ubi peccat in uno, periclitatur in altero. But because there is, in man, an election touching the frame of his mind, and a necessity in the frame of his body, the stars of natural inclination are sometimes obscured, by the sun of discipline and virtue. Therefore it is good to consider of deformity, not as a sign, which is more deceivable; but as a cause, which seldom faileth of the effect. Whosoever hath anything fixed in his person, that doth induce contempt, hath also a perpetual spur in himself, to rescue and deliver himself from scorn.

Therefore all deformed persons, are extreme bold. First, as in their own defence, as being exposed to scorn; but in process of time, by a general habit. Also it stirreth in them industry, and especially of this kind, to watch and observe the weakness of others, that they may have somewhat to repay. Again, in their superiors, it quencheth jealousy towards them, as persons that they think they may, at pleasure, despise: and it layeth their competitors and emulators asleep; as never believing they should be in possibility of advancement, till they see them in possession.

So that upon the matter, in a great wit, deformity is an advantage to rising. Kings in ancient times (and at this present in some countries) were wont to put great trust in eunuchs; because they that are envious towards all are more obnoxious and officious, towards one. But yet their trust towards them, hath rather been as to good spials, and good whisperers, than good magistrates and officers. And much like is the reason of deformed persons. Still the ground is, they will, if they be of spirit, seek to free themselves from scorn; which must be either by virtue or malice; and therefore let it not be marvelled, if sometimes they prove excellent persons; as was Agesilaus, Zanger the son of Solyman, Ã†sop, Gasca, President of Peru; and Socrates may go likewise amongst them; with others.

Of Building

Houses are built to live in, and not to look on; therefore let use be preferred before uniformity, except where both may be had. Leave the goodly fabrics of houses, for beauty only, to the enchanted palaces of the poets; who build them with small cost. He that builds a fair house, upon an ill seat, committed himself to prison. Neither do I reckon it an ill seat, only where the air is unwholesome; but likewise where the air is unequal;

as you shall see many fine seats set upon a knap of ground, environed with higher hills round about it; whereby the heat of the sun is pent in, and the wind gathereth as in troughs; so as you shall have, and that suddenly, as great diversity of heat and cold as if you dwelt in several places. Neither is it ill air only that made an ill seat, but ill ways, ill markets; and, if you will consult with Momus, ill neighbors.

I speak not of many more; want of water; want of wood, shade, and shelter; want of fruitfulness, and mixture of grounds of several natures; want of prospect; want of level grounds; want of places at some near distance for sports of hunting, hawking, and races; too near the sea, too remote; having the commodity of navigable rivers, or the discommodity of their overflowing; too far off from great cities, which may hinder business, or too near them, which lurcheth all provisions, and made everything dear; where a man hath a great living laid together, and where he is scanted: all which, as it is impossible perhaps to find together, so it is good to know them, and think of them, that a man may take as many as he can; and if he have several dwellings, that he sort them so, that what he wanteth in the one, he may find in the other.

Lucullus answered Pompey well; who, when he saw his stately galleries, and rooms so large and lightsome, in one of his houses, said, Surely an excellent place for summer, but how do you in winter? Lucullus answered, Why, do you not think me as wise as some fowl are, that ever change their abode towards the winter?

To pass from the seat, to the house itself; we will do as Cicero doth in the orator's art; who writes books De Oratore, and a book he entitles Orator; whereof the former, delivers the precepts of the art, and the latter, the perfection. We will therefore describe a princely palace, making a brief model thereof. For it is strange to see, now in Europe, such huge buildings as the Vatican and Escurial and some others be, and yet scarce a very fair room in them. First, therefore, I say you cannot have a perfect palace except you have two several sides; a side for the banquet, as it is spoken of in the book of Hester, and a side for the household; the one for feasts and triumphs, and the other for dwelling. I understand both these sides to be not only returns, but parts of the front; and to be uniform without, though severally partitioned within; and to be on both sides of a great and stately tower, in the midst of the front, that, as it were, joineth them together on either hand. I would have on the side of the banquet, in front, one only goodly room above stairs, of some forty foot high; and under it a room for a dressing, or preparing place, at times of triumphs.

On the other side, which is the household side, I wish it divided at the first, into a hall and a chapel (with a partition between); both of good state and bigness; and those not to go all the length, but to have at the further end, a winter and a summer parlor, both fair. And under these rooms, a fair and large cellar, sunk under ground; and likewise some privy kitchens, with butteries and pantries, and the like. As for the tower, I would have it two stories, of eighteen foot high apiece, above the two wings; and a goodly leads upon the top, railed with statuas interposed; and the same tower to be divided into rooms, as shall be thought fit.

The stairs likewise to the upper rooms, let them be upon a fair open newel, and finely railed in, with images of wood, cast into a brass colour; and a very fair landing-place at the top. But this to be, if you do not point any of the lower rooms, for a dining place of servants. For otherwise, you shall have the servants' dinner after your own: for the steam of it, will come up as in a tunnel. And so much for the front. Only I understand the height of the first stairs to be sixteen foot, which is the height of the lower room.

Beyond this front, is there to be a fair court, but three sides of it, of a far lower building than the front. And in all the four corners of that court, fair staircases, cast into turrets, on the outside, and not within the row of buildings themselves. But those towers, are not to be of the height of the front, but rather proportional to the lower building. Let the court not be paved, for that striketh up a great heat in summer, and much cold in winter. But only some side alleys, with a cross, and the quarters to graze, being kept shorn, but not too near shorn. The row of return on the banquet side, let it be all stately galleries: in which galleiies let there be three, or five, fine cupolas in the length of it, placed at equal distance; and fine colored windows of several works. On the household side, chambers of presence and ordinary entertainments, with some bed-chambers; and let all three sides be a double house, without thorough lights on the sides, that you may have rooms from the sun, both for forenoon and afternoon. Cast it also, that you may have rooms, both for summer and winter; shady for summer, and warm for winter.

You shall have sometimes fair houses so full of glass, that one cannot tell where to become, to be out of the sun or cold. For inbowed windows, I hold them of good use (in cities, indeed, upright do better, in respect of the uniformity towards the street); for they be pretty retiring places for conference; and besides, they keep both the wind and sun off; for that which would strike almost through the room, doth scarce pass the window. But let them be but few, four in the court, on the sides only. Beyond this court, let there be an inward court, of the same square and height; which is to be environed with the garden on all sides; and in the inside, cloistered on all sides, upon decent and beautiful arches, as high as the first story. On the under story, towards the garden, let it be turned to a grotto, or a place of shade, or estimation. Only have opening and windows towards the garden; and be level upon the floor, no whit sunken under ground, to avoid all dampishness. And let there be a fountain, or some fair work of statuas, in the midst of this court; and to be paved as the other court was. These buildings to be for privy lodgings on both sides; and the end for privy galleries.

Whereof you must foresee that one of them be for an infirmary, if the prince or any special person should be sick, with chambers, bed-chamber, antecamera, and recamera joining to it. This upon the second story. Upon the ground story, a fair gallery, open, upon pillars; and upon the third story likewise, an open gallery, upon pillars, to take the prospect and freshness of the garden.

At both corners of the further side, by way of return, let there be two delicate or rich cabinets, daintily paved, richly hanged, glazed with crystalline glass, and a rich cupola in the midst; and all other elegancy that may be thought upon. In the upper gallery tool I wish that there may be, if the place will yield it, some fountains running in divers places from the wall, with some fine avoidances. And thus much for the model of the palace; save that you must have, before you come to the front, three courts.

A green court plain, with a wall about it; a second court of the same, but more garnished, with little turrets, or rather embellishments, upon the wall; and a third court, to make a square with the front, but not to be built, nor yet enclosed with a naked wall, but enclosed with terraces, leaded aloft, and fairly garnished, on the three sides; and cloistered on the inside, with pillars, and not with arches below. As for offices, let them stand at distance, with some low galleries, to pass from them to the palace itself.

Of Gardens

God Almighty planted a garden. And indeed it is the purest of human pleasures. It is the greatest refreshment to the spirits of man; without which, buildings and palaces are but gross handiworks; and a man shall ever see, that when ages grow to civility and elegancy, men come to build stately sooner than to garden finely; as if gardening were the greater perfection. I do hold it, in the royal ordering of gardens, there ought to be gardens, for all the months in the year; in which severally things of beauty may be then in season.

For December, and January, and the latter part of November, you must take such things as are green all winter: holly; ivy; bays; juniper; cypress-trees; yew; pine-apple-trees; fir-trees; rosemary; lavender; periwinkle, the white, the purple, and the blue; germander; flags; orange-trees; lemon-trees; and myrtles, if they be stoved; and sweet marjoram, warm set. There followeth, for the latter part of January and February, the mezereon-tree, which then blossoms; crocus vernus, both the yellow and the grey; primroses; anemones; the early tulippa; hyacinthus orientalis; chamairis; fritellaria. For March, there come violets, specially the single blue, which are the earliest; the yellow daffodil; the daisy; the almond-tree in blossom; the peach-tree in blossom; the cornelian-tree in blossom; sweet-briar.

In April follow the double white violet; the wallflower; the stock-gilliflower; the cowslip; flower-delices, and lilies of all natures; rosemary-flowers; the tulippa; the double peony; the pale daffodil; the French honeysuckle; the cherry-tree in blossom; the damson and plum-trees in blossom; the white thorn in leaf; the lilac-tree. In May and June come pinks of all sorts, specially the blushpink; roses of all kinds, except the musk, which comes later; honeysuckles; strawberries; bugloss; columbine; the French marigold, flos Africanus; cherry-tree in fruit; ribes; figs in fruit; rasps; vineflowers; lavender in flowers; the sweet satyrian, with the white flower; herba muscaria; lilium convallium; the apple-tree in blossom.

In July come gilliflowers of all varieties; musk-roses; the lime-tree in blossom; early pears and plums in fruit; jennetings, codlins. In August come plums of all sorts in fruit; pears; apricocks; berberries; filberds; musk-melons; monks-hoods, of all colors. In September come grapes; apples; poppies of all colors; peaches; melocotones; nectarines; cornelians; wardens; quinces. In October and the beginning of November come services; medlars; bullaces; roses cut or removed to come late; hollyhocks; and such like. These particulars are for the climate of London; but my meaning is perceived, that you may have ver perpetuum, as the place affords.

And because the breath of flowers is far sweeter in the air (where it comes and goes like the warbling of music) than in the hand, therefore nothing is more fit for that delight, than to know what be the flowers and plants that do best perfume the air. Roses, damask and red, are fast flowers of their smells; so that you may walk by a whole row of them, and find nothing of their sweetness; yea though it be in a morning's dew. Bays likewise yield no smell as they grow. Rosemary little; nor sweet marjoram. That which above all others yields the sweetest smell in the air is the violet, specially the white double violet, which comes twice a year; about the middle of April, and about Bartholomew-tide. Next to that is the musk-rose. Then the strawberry-leaves dying, which [yield] a most excellent cordial smell. Then the flower of vines; it is a little dust, like the dust of a bent, which grows upon the cluster in the first coming forth. Then sweet-briar. Then wall-flowers, which are very delightful to be set under a parlor or lower chamber window. Then pinks and gilliflowers, especially the matted pink and clove gilliflower.

Then the flowers of the lime-tree. Then the honeysuckles, so they be somewhat afar off. Of beanflowers I speak not, because they are field flowers. But those which perfume the air most delightfully, not passed by as the rest, but being trodden upon and crushed, are three; that is, burnet, wild-thyme, and watermints. Therefore you are to set whole alleys of them, to have the pleasure when you walk or tread. For gardens (speaking of those which are indeed princelike, as we have done of buildings), the contents ought not well to be under thirty acres of ground; and to be divided into three parts; a green in the entrance; a heath or desert in the going forth; and the main garden in the midst; besides alleys on both sides. And I like well that four acres of ground be assigned to the green; six to the heath; four and four to either side; and twelve to the main garden.

The green hath two pleasures: the one, because nothing is more pleasant to the eye than green grass kept finely shorn; the other, because it will give you a fair alley in the midst, by which you may go in front upon a stately hedge, which is to enclose the garden. But because the alley will be long, and, in great heat of the year or day, you ought not to buy the shade in the garden, by going in the sun through the green, therefore you are, of either side the green, to plant a covert alley upon carpenter's work, about twelve foot in height, by which you may go in shade into the garden.

As for the making of knots or figures, with divers colored earths, that they may lie under the windows of the house on that side which the garden stands, they be but toys; you may see as good sights, many times, in tarts. The garden is best to be square, encompassed on all the four sides with a stately arched hedge. The arches to be upon pillars of carpenter's work, of some ten foot high, and six foot broad; and the spaces between of the same dimension with the breadth of the arch. Over the arches let there be an entire hedge of some four foot high, framed also upon carpenter's work; and upon the upper hedge, over every arch, a little turret, with a belly, enough to receive a cage of birds: and over every space between the arches some other little figure, with broad plates of round colored glass gilt, for the sun to play upon.

But this hedge I intend to be raised upon a bank, not steep, but gently slope, of some six foot, set all with flowers. Also I understand, that this square of the garden, should not be the whole breadth of the ground, but to leave on either side, ground enough for diversity of side alleys; unto which the two covert alleys of the green, may deliver you. But there must be no alleys with hedges, at either end of this great enclosure; not at the hither end, for letting your prospect upon this fair hedge from the green; nor at the further end, for letting your prospect from the hedge, through the arches upon the heath.

For the ordering of the ground, within the great hedge, I leave it to variety of device; advising nevertheless, that whatsoever form you cast it into, first, it be not too busy, or full of work. Wherein I, for my part, do not like images cut out in juniper or other garden stuff; they be for children. Little low hedges, round, like welts, with some pretty pyramids, I like well; and in some places, fair columns upon frames of carpenter's work. I would also have the alleys, spacious and fair. You may have closer alleys, upon the side grounds, but none in the main garden.

I wish also, in the very middle a fair mount, with three ascents, and alleys, enough for four to walk abreast; which I would have to be perfect circles, without any bulwarks or embossments; and the whole mount to be thirty foot high; and some fine banqueting-house, with some chimneys neatly cast, and without too much glass.

For fountains, they are a great beauty and refreshment; but pools mar all, and make the garden unwholesome, and full of flies and frogs. Fountains I intend to be of two natures: the one that sprinkleth or spouteth water; the other a fair receipt of water, of some thirty or forty foot square, but without fish, or slime, or mud. For the first, the ornaments of images gilt, or of marble, which are in use, do well: but the main matter is so to convey the water, as it never stay, either in the bowls or in the cistern; that the water be never by rest discolored, green or red or the like; or gather any mossiness or putrefaction. Besides that, it is to be cleansed every day by the hand.

Also some steps up to it, and some fine pavement about it, doth well. As for the other kind of fountain, which we may call a bathing pool, it may admit much curiosity and beauty; wherewith we will not trouble ourselves: as, that the bottom be finely paved, and with images; the sides likewise; and withal embellished with colored glass, and such things of luster; encompassed also with fine rails of low statuas. But the main point is the same which we mentioned in the former kind of fountain; which is, that the water be in perpetual motion, fed by a water higher than the pool, and delivered into it by fair spouts, and then discharged away under ground, by some equality of bores, that it stay little.

And for fine devices, of arching water without spilling, and making it rise in several forms (of feathers, drinking glasses, canopies, and the like), they be pretty things to look on, but nothing to health and sweetness. For the heath, which was the third part of our plot, I wish it to be framed, as much as may be, to a natural wildness. Trees I would have none in it, but some thickets made only of sweet-briar and honeysuckle, and some wild vine amongst; and the ground set with violets, strawberries, and primroses. For these are sweet, and prosper in the shade.

And these to be in the heath, here and there, not in any order. I like also little heaps, in the nature of mole-hills (such as are in wild heaths), to be set, some with wild thyme; some with pinks; some with germander, that gives a good flower to the eye; some with periwinkle; some with violets; some with strawberries; some with cowslips; some with daisies; some with red roses; some with lilium convallium; some with sweet-williams red; some with bear's-foot: and the like low flowers, being withal sweet and slightly. Part of which heaps, are to be with standards of little bushes pricked upon their top, and part without. The standards to be roses; juniper; hory; berberries (but here and there, because of the smell of their blossoms); red currants; gooseberries; rosemary; bays; sweetbriar; and such like. But these standards to be kept with cutting, that they grow not out of course.

For the side grounds, you are to fill them with variety of alleys, private, to give a full shade, some of them, where so ever the sun be. You are to frame some of them, likewise, for shelter, that when the wind blows sharp you may walk as in a gallery. And those alleys must be likewise hedged at both ends, to keep out the wind; and these closer alleys must be ever finely graveled, and no grass, because of going wet. In many of these alleys, likewise, you are to set fruit-trees of all sorts; as well upon the walls, as in ranges. And this would be generally observed, that the borders wherein you plant your fruit-trees, be fair and large, and low, and not steep; and set with fine flowers, but thin and sparingly, lest they deceive the trees. At the end of both the side grounds, I would have a mount of some pretty height, leaving the wall of the enclosure breast high, to look abroad into the fields.

For the main garden, I do not deny, but there should be some fair alleys ranged on both sides, with fruit-trees; and some pretty tufts of fruit-trees; and arbors with seats, set in some decent order; but these to be by no means set too thick; but to leave the main garden so as it be not close, but the air open and free. For as for shade, I would have you rest upon the alleys of the side grounds, there to walk, if you be disposed, in the heat of the year or day; but to make account, that the main garden is for the more temperate parts of the year; and in the heat of summer, for the morning and the evening, or overcast days.

For aviaries, I like them not, except they be of that largeness as they may be turfed, and have living plants and bushes set in them; that the birds may have more scope, and natural nestling, and that no foulness appear in the floor of the aviary. So I have made a platform of a princely garden, partly by precept, partly by drawing, not a model, but some general lines of it; and in this I have spared for no cost. But it is nothing for great princes, that for the most part taking advice with workmen, with no less cost set their things together; and sometimes add statuas and such things for state and magnificence, but nothing to the true pleasure of a garden.

Of Negotiating

It is generally better to deal by speech than by letter; and by the mediation of a third than by a man's self. Letters are good, when a man would draw an answer by letter back again; or when it may serve for a man's justification afterwards to produce his own letter; or where it may be danger to be interrupted, or heard by pieces. To deal in person is good, when a man's face breadth regard, as commonly with inferiors; or in tender cases, where a man's eye, upon the countenance of him with whom he speaketh, may give him a direction how far to go; and generally, where a man will reserve to himself liberty, either to disavow or to expound.

In choice of instruments, it is better to choose men of a plainer sort, that are like to do that, that is committed to·them, and to report back again faithfully the success, than those that are cunning, to contrive, out of other men's business, somewhat to grace themselves, and will help the matter in report for satisfaction's sake.

Use also such persons as affect the business, wherein they are employed; for that quickened much; and such, as are fit for the matter; as bold men for expostulation, fair-spoken men for persuasion, crafty for inquiry and observation, forward, and absurd men, for business that doth not well bear out itself. Use also such as have been lucky, and prevailed before, in things wherein you have employed them; for that breeds confidence, and they will strive to maintain their prescription. It is better to sound a person, with whom one deals afar off than to fall upon the point at first; except you mean to surprise him by some short question. It is better dealing with men in appetite, than with those that are where they would be. If a man deal with another upon conditions, the start or first performance is all; which a man cannot reasonably demand, except either the nature of the thing be such, which must go before; or else a man can persuade the other party, that he shall still need him in some other thing; or else that he be counted the honest man. All practice is to discover, or to work.

Men discover themselves in trust, in passion, at unawares, and of necessity, when they would have somewhat done, and cannot find an apt pretext. If you would work any man, you must either know his nature and fashions, and so lead him; or his ends, and so persuade him or his weakness and disadvantages, and so awe him or those that have interest in him, and so govern him. In dealing with cunning persons, we must ever consider their ends, to interpret their speeches; and it is good to say little to them, and that which they least look for. In all negotiations of difficulty, a man may not look to sow and reap at once; but must prepare business, and so ripen it by degrees.

Of Followers and Friends

Costly followers are not to be liked; lest while a man made his train longer, he make his wings shorter. I reckon to be costly, not them alone which charge the purse, but which are wearisome, and importune in suits. Ordinary followers ought to challenge no higher conditions, than countenance, recommendation, and protection from wrongs. Factious followers are worse to be liked, which follow not upon affection to him, with whom they range themselves, but upon discontentment conceived against some other; whereupon commonly ensued that ill intelligence, that we many times see between great personages.

Likewise glorious followers, who make themselves as trumpets of the commendation of those they follow, are full of inconvenience; for they taint business through want of secrecy; and they export honor from a man, and make him a return in envy. There is a kind of followers likewise, which are dangerous, being indeed espials; which inquire the secrets of the house, and bear tales of them, to others.

Yet such men, many times, are in great favor; for they are

officious, and commonly exchange tales. The following by certain estates of men, answerable to that, which a great person himself professed (as of soldiers, to him that hath been employed in the wars, and the like), hath ever been a thing civil, and well taken, even in monarchies; so it be without too much pomp or popularity.

But the most honorable kind of following, is to be followed as one, that apprehended to advance virtue, and desert, in all sorts of persons. And yet, where there is no eminent odds in sufficiency, it is better to take with the more passable, than with the more able. And besides, to speak truth, in base times, active men are of more use than virtuous. It is true that in government, it is good to use men of one rank equally: for to countenance some extraordinarily, is to make them insolent, and the rest discontent; because they may claim a due.

But contrariwise, in favor, to use men with much difference and election is good; for it made the persons preferred more thankful, and the rest more officious: because all is of favor. It is good discretion, not to make too much of any man at the first; because one cannot hold out that proportion. To be governed (as we call it) by one is not safe; for it shows softness, and gives a freedom, to scandal and disreputation; for those, that would not censure or speak in of a man immediately, will talk more boldly of those that are so great with them, and thereby wound their honor.

Yet to be distracted with many is worse; for it makes men to be of the last impression, and fun of change. To take advice of some few friends, is ever honorable; for lookers-on many times see more than gamesters; and the vale best discovered the hill. There is little friendship in the world, and least of all between equals, which was wont to be magnified. That is, is between superior and inferior, whose fortunes may comprehend the one the other.

Of Suitors

Many ill matters and projects are undertaken; and private suits do putrefy the public good. Many good matters, are undertaken with bad minds; I mean not only corrupt minds, but crafty minds, that intend not performance. Some embrace suits, which never mean to deal effectually in them; but if they see there may be life in the matter, by some other mean, they will be content to win a thank, or take a second reward, or at least to make use, in the meantime, of the suitor's hopes. Some take hold of suits, only for an occasion to cross some other; or to make an information, whereof they could not otherwise have apt pretext; without care what become of the suit, when that turn is served; or, generally, to make other men's business a kind of entertainment, to bring in their own.

Nay, some undertake suits, with a full purpose to let them fall; to the end to gratify the adverse party, or competitor. Surely there is in some sort a right in every suit; either a right of equity, if it be a suit of controversy; or a right of desert, if it be a suit of petition. If affection lead a man to favor the wrong side in justice, let him rather use his countenance to compound the matter, than to carry it. If affection lead a man to favor the less worthy in desert, let him do it, without depraving or disabling the better deserver. In suits which a man doth not well understand, it is good to refer them to some friend of trust and judgment, that may report, whether he may deal in them with honor: but let him choose well his referendaries, for else he may be led by the nose. Suitors are so distasted with delays and abuses, that plain dealing, in denying to deal in suits at first, and reporting the success barely, and in challenging no more thanks than one hath deserved, is grown not only honorable, but also gracious.

In suits of favor, the first coming ought to take little place: so far forth, consideration may be had of his trust, that if intelligence of the matter could not otherwise have been had, but by him, advantage be not taken of the note, but the party left to his other means; and in some sort recompensed, for his discovery. To be ignorant of the value of a suit, is simplicity; as well as to be ignorant of the right thereof, is want of conscience. Secrecy in suits, is a great mean of obtaining; for voicing them to be in forwardness, may discourage some kind of suitors, but doth quicken and awake others. But timing of the suit is the principal. Timing, I say, not only in respect of the person that should grant it, but in respect of those, which are like to cross it. Let a man, in the choice of his mean, rather choose the fittest mean, than the greatest mean; and rather them that deal in certain things, than those that are general. The reparation of a denial, is sometimes equal to the first grant; if a man show himself neither dejected nor discontented. Iniquum petas, ut Ã¦quum feras, is a good rule, where a man hath strength of favor: but otherwise, a man were better rise in his suit; for he, that would have ventured at first to have lost the suitor, will not in the conclusion lose both the suitor, and his own former favor. Nothing is thought so easy a request to a great person, as his letter; and yet, if it be not in a good cause, it is so much out of his reputation. There are no worse instruments, than these general contrivers of suits; for they are but a kind of poison, and infection, to public proceedings.

Of Studies

Studies serve for delight, for ornament, and for ability. Their chief use for delight, is in privateness and retiring; for ornament, is in discourse; and for ability, is in the judgment, and disposition of business. For expert men can execute, and perhaps judge of particulars, one by one; but the general counsels, and the plots and marshalling of affairs, come best, from those that are learned.

To spend too much time in studies is sloth; to use them too much for ornament, is affectation; to make judgment wholly by their rules, is the humour of a scholar. They perfect nature, and are perfected by experience: for natural abilities are like natural plants, that need proyning, by study; and studies themselves, do give forth directions too much at large, except they be bounded in by experience. Crafty men contemn studies, simple men admire them, and wise men use them; for they teach not their own use; but that is a wisdom without them, and above them, won by observation. Read not to contradict and confute; nor to believe and take for granted; nor to find talk and discourse; but to weigh and consider.

Some books are to be tasted, others to be swallowed, and some few to be chewed and digested; that is, some books are to be read only in parts; others to be read, but not curiously; and some few to be read wholly, and with diligence and attention. Some books also may be read by deputy, and extracts made of them by others; but that would be only in the less important arguments, and the meaner sort of books, else distilled books are like common distilled waters, flashy things. Reading made a full man; conference a ready man; and writing an exact man.

And therefore, if a man write little, he had need have a great memory; if he confer little, he had need have a present wit: and if he read little, he had need have much cunning, to seem to know, that he doth not. Histories make men wise; poets witty; the mathematics subtile; natural philosophy deep; moral grave; logic and rhetoric able to contend. Abeunt studia in mores. Nay, there is no stond or impediment in the wit, but may be wrought out by fit studies; like as diseases of the body, may have appropriate exercises. Bowling is good for the stone and reins; shooting for the lungs and breast; gentle walking for the stomach; riding for the head; and the like.

So if a man's wit be wandering, let him study the mathematics; for in demonstrations, if his wit be called away never so little, he must begin again. If his wit be not apt to distinguish or find differences, let him study the schoolmen; for they are cymini sectores: if he be not apt to beat over matters, and to call up one thing to prove and illustrate another, let him study the lawyers' cases. So every defect of the mind, may have a special receipt.

Of Faction

Many have an opinion not wise, that for a prince to govern his estate, or for a great person to govern his proceedings, according to the respect of factions, is a principal part of policy; whereas contrariwise, the chiefest wisdom, is either in ordering those things which are general, and wherein men of several factions do nevertheless agree; or in dealing with correspondence to particular persons, one by one. But I say not that the considerations of factions, is to be neglected. Mean men, in their rising, must adhere; but great men, that have strength in themselves, were better to maintain themselves indifferent, and neutral.

Yet even in beginners, to adhere so moderately, as he be a man of the one faction, which is most passable with the other, commonly giveth best way. The lower and weaker faction, is the firmer in conjunction; and it is often seen, that a few that are stiff, do tire out a greater number, that are more moderate. When one of the factions is extinguished, the remaining subdivideth; as the faction between Lucullus, and the rest of the nobles of the senate (which they called Optimates) held out awhile, against the faction of Pompey and Caesar; but when the senate's authority was pulled down, Caesar and Pompey soon after brake. The faction or party of Antonius and Octavianus Caesar, against Brutus and Cassius, held out likewise for a time; but when Brutus and Cassius were overthrown, then soon after, Antonius and Octavianus brake and subdivided.

These examples are of wars, but the same holded in private factions. And therefore, those that are seconds in factions, do many times, when the faction subdivided, prove principals; but many times also, they prove ciphers and cashiered; for many a man's strength is in opposition; and when that failed, he growth out of use. It is commonly seen, that men, once placed, take in with the contrary faction, to that by which they enter: thinking belike, that they have the first sure, and now are ready for a new purchase.

The traitor in faction, lightly goeth away with it; for when matters have stuck long in balancing, the winning of some one man casteth them, and he getteth all the thanks. The even carriage between two factions, proceedeth not always of moderation, but of a trueness to a man's self, with end to make use of both. Certainly in Italy, they hold it a little suspect in popes, when they have often in their mouth Padre commune; and take it to be a sign of one, that meaneth to refer all to the greatness of his own house. Kings had need beware, how they side themselves, and make themselves as of a faction or party; for leagues within the state, are ever pernicious to monarchies: for they raise an obligation, paramount to obligation of sovereignty, and make the king tanquam unus ex nobis: as was to be seen in the League of France. When factions are canied too high and too violently, it is a sign of weakness in princes; and much to the prejudice, both of their authority and business. The motions of factions under kings ought to be, like the motions (as the astronomers speak) of the inferior orbs, which may have their proper motions, but yet still are quietly carried, by the higher motion of primum mobile.

Of Ceremonies and Respect

He that is only real, had need have exceeding great parts of virtue; as the stone had need to be rich, that is set without foil. But if a man mark it well, it is, in praise and commendation of men, as it is in gettings and gains: for the proverb is true, that light gains make heavy purses; for light gains come thick, whereas great, come but now and then. So it is true, that small matters win great commendation, because they are continually in use and in note: whereas the occasion of any great virtue, cometh but on festivals. Therefore it doth much add to a man's reputation, and is (as Queen Isabella said) like perpetual letters commendatory, to have good forms.

To attain them, it almost sufficeth not to despise them; for so shall a man observe them in others; and let him trust himself with the rest. For if he labour too much to express them, he shall lose their grace; which is to be natural and unaffected. Some men's behaviour is like a verse, wherein every syllable is measured; how can a man comprehend great matters, that breaketh his mind too much, to small observations? Not to use ceremonies at all, is to teach others not to use them again; and so diminisheth respect to himself; especially they be not to be omitted, to strangers and formal natures; but the dwelling upon them, and exalting them above the moon, is not only tedious, but doth diminish the faith and credit of him that speaks.

And certainly, there is a kind of conveying, of effectual and imprinting passages amongst compliments, which is of singular use, if a man can hit upon it. Amongst a man's peers, a man shall be sure of familiarity; and therefore it is good, a little to keep state. Amongst a man's inferiors one shall be sure of reverence; and therefore it is good, a little to be familiar. He that is too much in anything, so that he giveth another occasion of satiety, made himself cheap. To apply one's self to others, is good; so it be with demonstration, that a man doth it upon regard, and not upon facility.

It is a good precept generally, in seconding another, yet to add somewhat of one's own: as if you will grant his opinion, let it be with some distinction; if you will follow his motion, let it be with condition; if you allow his counsel let it be with alleging further reason. Men had need beware, how they be too perfect in compliments; for be they never so sufficient otherwise, their enviers will be sure to give them that attribute, to the disadvantage of their greater virtues. It is loss also in business, to be too full of respects, or to be curious, in observing times and opportunities. Salomon saith, He that considereth the wind, shall not sow, and he that looketh to the clouds, shall not reap. A wise man will make more opportunities, than he finds. Men's behaviour should be, like their apparel, not too strait or point device, but free for exercise or motion.

Of Praise

Praise is the reflection of virtue; but it is as the glass or body, which giveth the reflection. If it be from the common people, it is commonly false and naught; and rather followeth vain persons, than virtuous. For the common people understand not many excellent virtues. The lowest virtues draw praise from them; the middle virtues work in them astonishment or admiration; but of the highest virtues, they have no sense of perceiving at an. But shews, and species virtutibus similes, serve best with them. Certainly fame is like a river, that beareth up things light and swoln, and drowns things weighty and solid.

But if persons of quality and judgment concur, then it is as the Scripture saith Nomen bonum instar unguenti fragrantis: it filleth all round about, and will not easily away. For the odors of ointments are more durable, than those of flowers. There be so many false points of praise, that a man may justly hold it a suspect. Some praises proceed merely of flattery; and if he be an ordinary flatterer, he will have certain common attributes, which may serve every man; if he be a cunning flatterer, he will follow the archflatterer, which is a man's self; and wherein a man thinketh best of himself, therein the flatterer will uphold him most: but if he be an impudent flatterer, look wherein a man is conscious to himself, that he is most defective, and is most out of countenance in himself, that will the flatterer entitle him to perforce, spretÃ¢ conscientiÃ¢.

Some praises come of good wishes and respects, which is a form due, in civility, to kings and great persons, laudando prÃ¦cipere, when by telling men what they are, they represent to them, what they should be. Some men are praised maliciously, to their hurt, thereby to stir envy and jealousy towards them: pessimum genus inimicorum laudantium; insomuch as it was a proverb, amongst the Grecians, that he that was praised to his hurt should have a push rise upon his nose; as we say, that a blister will rise upon one's tongue, that tells a lie. Certainly moderate praise, used with opportunity, and not vulgar, is that which doth the good. Salomon saith, He that praiseth his friend aloud, rising early, it shall be to him no better than a curse.

Too much magnifying of man or matter, doth irritate contradiction, and procure envy and scorn. To praise a man's self, cannot be decent, except it be in rare cases; but to praise a man's office or profession, he may do it with good grace, and with a kind of magnanimity.

The cardinals of Rome, which are theologues, and friars, and Schoolmen, have a phrase of notable contempt and scorn towards civil business: for they call all temporal business of wars, embassages, judicature, and other employments, sbirrerie, which is under-sheriffries, as if they were but matters, for under-sheriffs and catchpoles: though many times those under-sheriffries do more good, than their high speculations. St. Paul, when he boasts of himself, he doth oft interlace, I speak like a fool; but speaking of his calling, he saith, magnificabo apostolatum meum.

Of Vain-glory

It was prettily devised of sop; The fly sat upon the axle-tree of the chariot wheel, and said, What a dust do I raise! So are there some vain persons, that whatsoever goeth alone, or moveth upon greater means, if they have never so little hand in it, they think it is they that carry it. They that are glorious, must needs be factious; for an bravery stands upon comparisons.

They must needs be violent, to make good their own vaunts. Neither can they be secret, and therefore not effectual; but according to the French proverb, beaucoup de bruit, peu de fruit; much bruit, little fruit. Yet certainly, there is use of this quality in civil affairs. Where there is an opinion and fame to be created, either of virtue or greatness, these men are good trumpeters. Again, as Titus Livius noteth, in the case of Antiochus and the Ã†tolians, There are sometimes great effects of cross lies; as, if a man that negotiates between two princes, to draw them to join in a war against the third, doth extol the forces of either of them, above measure, the one to the other: and sometimes he that deals between man and man, raiseth his own credit with both, by pretending greater interest than he hath in either.

And in these and the like kinds, it often falls out, that somewhat is produced of nothing; for lies are sufficient to breed opinion, and opinion brings on substance. In militar commanders and soldiers, vain-glory is an essential point; for as iron sharpens iron, so by glory, one courage sharpeneth another. In cases of great enterprise upon charge and adventure, a composition of glorious natures, doth put life into business; and those that are of solid and sobre natures, have more of the ballast, than of the sail. In fame of leaming, the flight will be slow without some feathers of ostentation. Qui de contemnendÃ¢ gloriÃ¢ libros scribunt, nomen, suuminscribunt. Socrates, Aristotle, Galen, were men full of ostentation.

Certainly vain-glory helpeth to perpetuate a man's memory; and virtue was never so beholding to human nature, as it received his due at the second hand. Neither had the fame of Cicero, Seneca, Plinius Secundus, borne her age so well, if it had not been joined with some vanity in themselves; like unto varnish, that makes ceilings not only shine but last. But all this while, when I speak of vain-glory, I mean not of that property, that Tacitus doth attribute to Mucianus; Omnium, quÃ¦ dixerat feceratque, arte quÃ¢dam ostentator: for that proceeds not of vanity, but of natural magnanimity and discretion; and in some persons, is not only comely, but gracious.

For accusations, cessions, modesty itself well governed, are but arts of ostentation. And amongst those arts, there is none better than that which Plinius Secundus speaketh of, which is to be liberal of praise and commendation to others, in that, wherein a man's self hath any perfection. For saith Pliny, very wittily, In commending another, you do yourself right; for he that you commend, is either superior to you in that you commend, or inferior. If he be inferior, if he be to be commended, you much more; if he be superior, if he be not to be commended, you much less. Glorious men are the scorn of wise men, the admiration of fools, the idols of parasites, and the slaves of their own vaunts.

Of Honor and Reputation

The winning of honor, is but the revealing of a man's virtue and worth, without disadvantage. For some in their actions, do woo and effect honor and reputation, which sort of men, are commonly much talked of, but inwardly little admired. And some, contrariwise, darken their virtue in the show of it; so as they be undervalued in opinion. If a man perform that, which hath not been attempted before; or attempted and given over; or hath been achieved, but not with so good circumstance; he shall purchase more honor, than by effecting a matter of greater difficulty or virtue, wherein he is but a follower.

If a man so temper his actions, as in some one of them he doth content every faction, or combination of people, the music will be the fuller. A man is an ill husband of his honor, that entered into any action, the failing wherein may disgrace him, more than the carrying of it through, can honor him. Honor that is gained and broken upon another, hath the quickest reflection, like diamonds cut with facets. And therefore, let a man contend to excel any competitors of his in honor, in out shooting them, if he can, in their own bow. Discreet followers and servants, help much to reputation: Omnis fama a domesticis emanat. Envy, which is the canker of honor, is best extinguished by declaring a man's self in his ends, rather to seek merit than fame; and by attributing a man's successes, rather to divine Providence and felicity, than to his own virtue or policy.

The true marshalling of the degrees of sovereign honor, are these: In the first place are conditores imperiorum, founders of states and commonwealths; such as were Romulus, Cyrus, CÃ¦sar, Ottoman, Ismael. In the second place are legislatores, lawgivers; which are also called second founders, or perpetui principes, because they govern by their ordinances after they are gone; such were Lycurgus, Solon, Justinian, Eadgar, Alphonsus of Castile, the Wise, that made the Siete Partidas. In the third place are liberatores, or salvatores, such as compound the long miseries of civil wars, or deliver their countries from servitude of strangers or tyrants; as Augustus CÃ¦sar, Vespasianus, Aurelianus, Theodoricus, King Henry the Seventh of England, King Henry the Fourth of France. In the fourth place are propagatores or propugnatores imperii; such as in honorable wars enlarge their territories, or make noble defence against invaders. And in the last place are patres patriÃ¦; which reign justly, and make the times good wherein they live. Both which last kinds need no examples, they are in such number. Degrees of honor, in subjects, are, first participes curarum; those upon whom, princes do discharge the greatest weight of their affairs; their right hands, as we call them.

The next are duces belli, great leaders in war; such as are princes' lieutenants, and do them notable services in the wars. The third are gratiosi, favorites; such as exceed not this scantling, to be solace to the sovereign, and harmless to the people. And the fourth, negotiis pares; such as have great places under princes, and execute their places, with sufficiency.

There is an honor, likewise, which may be ranked amongst the greatest, which happeneth rarely; that is, of such as sacrifice themselves to death or danger for the good of their country; as was M. Regulus, and the two Decii.

Of Judicature

Judges ought to remember, that their office is jus dicere, and not jus dare; to interpret law, and not to make law, or give law. Else will it be like the authority, claimed by the Church of Rome, which under pretext of exposition of Scripture, doth not stick to add and alter; and to pronounce that which they do not find; and by show of antiquity, to introduce novelty. Judges ought to be more learned, than witty, more reverend, than plausible, and more advised, than confident. Above all things, integrity is their portion and proper virtue. Cursed (saith the law) is he that removeth the land-mark. The mislayer of a mere-stone is to blame. But it is the unjust judge, that is the capital remover of landmarks, when he defineth amiss, of lands and property. One foul sentence doth more hurt, than many foul examples.

For these do but corrupt the stream, the other corrupteth the fountain. So with Salomon, Fons turbatus, et vena corrupta, est justus cadens in causÃ¢ suÃ¢ coram adversario. The office of judges may have reference unto the parties that use, unto the advocates that plead, unto the clerks and ministers of justice underneath them, and to the sovereign or state above them. First, for the causes or parties that sue. There be (saith the Scripture) that turn judgement into wormwood; and surely there be also, that turn it into vinegar; for injustice made it bitter, and delays make it sour.

The principal duty of a judge, is to suppress force and fraud; whereof force is the more pernicious, when it is open, and fraud, when it is close and disguised. Add thereto contentious suits, which ought to be spewed out, as the surfeit of courts. A judge ought to prepare his way to a just sentence, as God useth to prepare his way, by raising valleys and taking down hills: so when there appeareth on either side an high hand, violent prosecution, cunning advantages taken, combination, power, great counsel, then is the virtue of a judge seen, to make inequality equal; that he may plant his judgment as upon an even ground.

Qui fortiter emungit, elicit sanguinem; and where the wine-press is hard wrought, it yields a harsh wine, that tastes of the grape-stone. Judges must beware of hard constructions, and strained inferences; for there is no worse torture, than the torture of laws. Specially in case of laws penal, they ought to have care, that that was meant for terror, be not turned into rigor; and that they bring not upon the people, that shower whereof the Scripture speaketh, Pluet super eos laqueos: for penal laws pressed, are a shower of snares upon the people. Therefore let penal laws, if they have been sleepers of long, or if they be grown unfit for the present time, be by wise judges confined in the execution: Judicis officium est, ut res, ita tempora rerum, c.

In causes of life and death, judges ought (as far as the law permitteth) in justice to remember mercy; and to cast a severe eye upon the example, but a merciful eye upon the person. Secondly, for the advocates and counsel that plead. Patience and gravity of hearing, is an essential part of justice; and an overspeaking judge is no well-tuned cymbal. It is no grace to a judge, first to find that, which he might have heard in due time from the bar; or to show quickness of conceit, in cutting off evidence or counsel too short; or to prevent information by questions, -though pertinent.

The parts of a judge in hearing, are four: to direct the evidence; to moderate length, repetition, or impertinency of speech; to recapitulate, select, and collate the material points, of that which hath been said; and to give the rule or sentence. Whatsoever is above these is too much; and proceedeth either of glory, and willingness to speak, or of impatience to hear, or of shortness of memory, or of want of a staid and equal attention. It is a strange thing to see, that the boldness of advocates should prevail with judges; whereas they should imitate God, in whose seat they sit; who represseth the presumptuous, and giveth grace to the modest.

But it is more strange, that judges should have noted

favorites; which cannot but cause multiplication of fees, and suspicion of by-ways. There is due from the judge to the advocate, some commendation and gracing, where causes are well handled and fair pleaded; especially towards the side which obtaineth not; for that upholds in the client, the reputation of his counsel, and beats down in him the conceit of his cause.

There is likewise due to the public, a civil reprehension of advocates, where there appeareth cunning counsel, gross neglect, slight information, indiscreet pressing, or an overbold defence. And let not the counsel at the bar, chop with the judge, nor wind himself into the handling of the cause anew, after the judge hath declared his sentence; but, on the other side, let not the judge meet the cause half way, nor give occasion to the party, to say, his counsel or proofs were not heard.

Thirdly, for that that clerks and ministers. The place of justice is an hallowed place; and therefore not only the bench, but the foot-place; and precincts and purprise thereof, ought to be preserved without scandal and corruption. For certainly, Grapes (as the Scripture saith) will not be gathered of thorns or thistles; either can justice yield her fruit with sweetness, amongst the briars and brambles of catching and polling clerks, and ministers. The attendance of courts, is subject to four bad instruments. First, certain persons that are sowers of suits; which make the court swell, and the country pine.

The second sort is of those, that engage courts in quarrels of jurisdiction, and are not truly amici curiÃ¦, but parasiti curiÃ¦, in puffing a court up beyond her bounds, for their own scraps and advantage. The third sort, is of those that may be accounted the left hands of courts; persons that are full of nimble and sinister tricks and shifts, whereby they pervert the plain and direct courses of courts, and bring justice into oblique lines and labyrinths.

And the fourth, is the poller and exacter of fees; which justifies the common resemblance of the courts of justice, to the bush whereunto, while the sheep flies for defence in weather, he is sure to lose part of his fleece. On the other side, an ancient clerk, skilful in precedents, wary in proceeding, and understanding in the business of the court, is an excellent finger of a court; and doth many times point the way to the judge himself.

Fourthly, for that which may concern the sovereign and estate. Judges ought above all to remember the conclusion of the Roman Twelve Tables Salus populi suprema lex; and to know that laws, except they be in order to that end, are but things captious, and oracles not well inspired. Therefore it is an happy thing in a state, when kings and states do often consult with judges; and again, when judges do often consult with the king and state: the one, when there is matter of law, intervenient in business of state; the other, when there is some consideration of state, intervenient in matter of law.

For many times the things deduced to judgment may be meum and tuum, when the reason and consequence thereof may trench to point of estate: I call matter of estate, not only the parts of sovereignty, but whatsoever introduceth any great alteration, or dangerous precedent; or concerneth manifestly any great portion of people. And let no man weakly conceive, that just laws and true policy have any antipathy; for they are like the spirits and sinews, that one moves with the other.

Let judges also remember, that Salomon's throne was supported by lions on both sides: let them be lions, but yet lions under the throne; being circumspect that they do not check or oppose any points of sovereignty. Let not judges also be ignorant of their own right, as to think there is not left to them, as a principal part of their office, a wise use and application of laws. For they may remember, what the apostle saith of a greater law than theirs: Nos scimus quia lex bona est, modo quis ea utatur legitime.

Of Anger

To seek to extinguish anger utterly, is but a bravery of the Stoics. We have better oracles: Be angry, but sin not. Let not the sun go down upon your anger. Anger must be limited and confined, both in race and in time. We will first speak how the natural inclination and habit to be angry may be attempted and calmed. Secondly, how the particular motions of anger may be repressed, or at least refrained from doing mischief. Thirdly, how to raise anger, or appease anger in another.

For the first; there is no other way but to meditate, and ruminate well upon the effects of anger, how it troubles man's life. And the best time to do this, is to look back upon anger, when the fit is thoroughly over. Seneca saith well, that anger is like ruin, which breaks itself upon that it falls. The Scripture exhorteth us to possess our souls in patience. Whosoever is out of patience, is out of possession of his soul. Men must not turn bees; —animasque in vulnere ponunt.

Anger is certainly a kind of baseness; as it appears well in the weakness of those subjects in whom it reigns; children, women, old folks, sick folks. Only men must beware, that they carry their anger rather with scorn, than with fear; so that they may seem rather to be above the injury, than below it; which is a thing easily done, if a man will give law to himself in it.

For the second point; the causes and motives of anger, are chiefly three. First, to be too sensible of hurt; for no man is angry, that feels not himself hurt; and therefore tender and delicate persons must needs be oft angry; they have so many things to trouble them, which more robust natures have little sense of. The next is, the apprehension and construction of the injury offered, to be, in the circumstances thereof, full of contempt: for contempt is that, which putteth an edge upon anger, as much or more than the hurt itself. And therefore, when men are ingenious in picking out circumstances of contempt, they do kindle their anger much.

Lastly, opinion of the touch of a man's reputation, doth multiply and sharpen anger. Wherein the remedy is, that a man should have, as Consalvo was wont to say, telam honoris crassiorem. But in all refrainings of anger, it is the best remedy to win time; and to make a man's self believe, that the opportunity of his revenge is not yet come, but that he foresees a time for it; and so to still himself in the meantime, and reserve it. To contain anger from mischief, though it take hold of a man, there be two things, whereof you must have special caution. The one, of extreme bitterness of words, especially if they be aculeate and proper; for cummunia maledicta are nothing so much; and again, that in anger a man reveal no secrets; for that, makes him not fit for society. The other, that you do not peremptorily break off, in any business, in a fit of anger; but howsoever you show bitterness, do not act anything, that is not revocable.

For raising and appeasing anger in another; it is done chiefly by choosing of times, when men are frowardest and worst disposed, to incense them. Again, by gathering (as was touched before) all that you can find out, to aggravate the contempt. And the two remedies are by the contraries. The former to take good times, when first to relate to a man an angry business; for the first impression is much; and the other is, to sever, as much as may be, the construction of the injury from the point of contempt; imputing it to misunderstanding, fear, passion, or what you will.

Of Vicissitude of Things

Salomon saith, There is no new thing upon the earth. So that as Plato had an imagination, that all knowledge was but remembrance; so Salomon giveth his sentence, that all novelty is but oblivion. Whereby you may see, that the river of Lethe runneth as well above ground as below. There is an abstruse astrologeı that saith, if it were not for two things that are constant (the one is, that the fixed stars ever stand a like distance one from another, and never come nearer together, nor go further asunder; the other, that the diurnal motion perpetually keepeth time), no individual would last one moment. Certain it is, that the matter is in a perpetual flux, and never at a stay.

The great winding-sheets, that bury all things in oblivion, are two; deluges and earthquakes. As for conflagrations and great droughts, they do not merely dispeople and destroy. Phaeton's car went but a day. And the three years' drought in the time of Elias was but particular, and left people alive. As for the great burnings by lightnings, which are often in the West Indies, they are but narrow. But in the other two destructions, by deluge and earthquake, it is further to be noted, that the remnant of people which hap to be reserved, are commonly ignorant and mountainous people, that can give no account of the time past; so that the oblivion is all one, as if none had been left.

If you consider well of the people of the West Indies, it is very probable that they are a newer or a younger people, than the people of the Old World. And it is much more likely, that the destruction that hath heretofore been there, was not by earthquakes (as the Egyptian priest told Solon concerning the island of Atlantis, that it was swallowed by an earthquake), but rather that it was desolated by a particular deluge. For earthquakes are seldom in those parts. But on the other side, they have such pouring rivers, as the rivers of Asia and Africk and Europe, are but brooks to them.

Their Andes, likewise, or mountains, are far higher than those with us; whereby it seems, that the remnants of generation of men, were in such a particular deluge saved. As for the observation that Machiavel hath, that the jealousy of sects, doth much extinguish the memory of things; traducing Gregory the Great, that he did what in him lay, to extinguish all heathen antiquities; I do not find that those zeals do any great effects, nor last long; as it appeared in the succession of Sabinian, who did revive the former antiquities.

The vicissitude of mutations in the superior globe, are no fit matter for this present argument. It may be, Plato's Great Year, if the world should last so long, would have some effect; not in renewing the state of like individuals (for that is the fume of those, that conceive the celestial bodies have more accurate influences upon these things below, than indeed they have), but in gross. Comets, out of question, have likewise power and effect, over the gross and mass of things; but they are rather gazed upon, and waited upon in their journey, than wisely observed in their effects; specially in their respective effects; that is, what kind of comet, for magnitude, colour, version of the beams, placing in the reign of heaven, or lasting, produceth what kind of effects.

There is a toy which I have heard, and I would not have it given over, but waited upon a little. They say it is observed in the Low Countries (I know not in what part) that every five and thirty years, the same kind and suit of years and weathers come about again; as great frosts, great wet, great droughts, warm winters, summers with little heat, and the like; and they call it the Prime. It is a thing I do the rather mention, because, computing backwards, I have found some concurrence.

But to leave these points of nature, and to come to men. greatest vicissitude of things amongst men, is the vicissitude of sects and religions. For those orbs rule in men's minds most. The true religion is built upon the rock; the rest are tossed, upon the waves of time. To speak, therefore, of the causes of new sects; and to give some counsel concerning them, as far as the weakness of human judgment can give stay, to so great revolutions.

When the religion formerly received, is rent by discords; and when the holiness of the professors of religion, is decayed and full of scandal; and withal the times be stupid, ignorant, and barbarous; you may doubt the springing up of a new sect; if then also, there should arise any extravagant and strange spirit, to make himself author thereof. All which points held, when Mahomet published his law. If a new sect have not two properties, fear it not; for it will not spread. The one is the supplanting, or the opposing, of authority established; for nothing is more popular than that. The other is the giving license to pleasures, and a voluptuous life. For as for speculative heresies (such as were in ancient times the Arians, and now the Arminians), though they work mightily upon men's wits, yet they do not produce any great alterations in states; except it be by the help of civil occasions. There be three manner of plantations of new sects. By the power of signs and miracles; by the eloquence, and wisdom, of speech and persuasion; and by the sword.

For martyrdoms, I reckon them amongst miracles; because they seem to exceed the strength of human nature: and I may do the like, of superlative and admirable holiness of life. Surely there is no better way, to stop the rising of new sects and schisms, than to reform abuses; to compound the smaller differences; to proceed mildly, and not with sanguinary persecutions; and rather to take off the principal authors by winning and advancing them, than to enrage them by violence and bitterness.

The changes and vicissitude in wars are many; but chiefly in three things; in the seats or stages of the war; in the weapons; and in the manner of the conduct. Wars in ancient time, seemed more to move from east to west; for the Persians, Assyrians, Arabians, Tartars (which were the invaders) were all eastern people. It is true, the Gauls were western; but we read but of two incursions of theirs: the one to Gallo-GrÃ¦cia, the other to Rome.

But east and west have no certain points of heaven; and no more have the wars either from the east or west, any certainty of observation. But north and south are fixed; and it hath seldom or never been seen that the far southern people have invaded the northern, but contrariwise. Whereby it is manifest that the northern tract of the world, is in nature the more martial region: be it in respect of the stars of that hemisphere; or of the great continents that are upon the north, whereas the south part, for aught that is known, is almost all sea; or (which is most apparent) of the cold of the northern parts, which is that which, without aid of discipline, doth make the bodies hardest, and the courages warmest.

Upon the breaking and shivering of a great state and empire, you may be sure to have wars. For great empires, while they stand, do enervate and destroy the forces of the natives which they have subdued, resting upon their own protecting forces; and then when they fail also, all goes to ruin, and they become a prey. So was it in the decay of the Roman empire; and likewise in the empire of Almaigne, after Charles the Great, every bird taking a feather; and were not unlike to befall to Spain, if it should break. The great accessions and unions of kingdoms, do likewise stir up wars; for when a state grows to an over-power, it is like a great flood, that will be sure to overflow. As it hath been seen in the states of Rome, Turkey, Spain, and others.

Look when the world hath fewest barbarous peoples, but such as commonly will not marry or generate, except they know means to live (as it is almost everywhere at this day, except Tartary), there is no danger of inundations of people; but when there be great shoals of people, which go on to populate, without foreseeing means of life and sustentation, it is of necessity that once in an age or two, they discharge a portion of their people upon other nations; which the ancient northern people were wont to do by lot; casting lots what part should stay at home, and what should seek their fortunes. When a warlike state grows soft and effeminate, they may be sure of a war. For commonly such states are grown rich in the time of their degenerating; and so the prey invited, and their decay in valor, encouraged a war.

As for the weapons, it hardly felled under rule and observation: yet we see even they, have returns and vicissitudes. For certain it is, that ordnance was known in the city of the Oxidrakes in India; and was that, which the Macedonians called thunder and lightning, and magic. And it is well known that the use of ordnance, hath been in China above two thousand years. The conditions of weapons, and their improvement, are; First, the fetching afar off; for that outruns the danger; as it is seen in ordnance and muskets. Secondly, the strength of the percussion; wherein likewise ordnance do exceed all arietations and ancient inventions. The third is, the commodious use of them; as that they may serve in all weathers; that the carriage may be light and manageable; and the like.

For the conduct of the war: at the first, men rested extremely upon number: they did put the wars likewise upon main force and valor; pointing days for pitched fields, and so trying it out upon an even match and they were more ignorant in ranging and arraying their battles. After, they grew to rest upon number rather competent, than vast; they grew to advantages of place, cunning diversions, and the like: and they grew more skilful in the ordering of their battles. In the youth of a state, arms do flourish; in the middle age of a state, learning; and then both of them together for a time; in the declining age of a state, mechanical arts and merchandize. Learning hath his infancy, when it is but beginning and almost childish; then his youth, when it is luxuriant and juvenile; then his strength of years, when it is solid and reduced; and lastly, his old age, when it waxeth dry and exhaust. But it is not good to look too long upon these turning wheels of vicissitude, lest we become giddy. As for the philology of them, that is but a circle of tales, and therefore not fit for this writing.

Of Fame

The poets make Fame a monster. They describe her in part finely and elegantly, and in part gravely and sententiously. They say, look how many feathers she hath, so many eyes she hath underneath; so many tongues; so many voices; she pricks up so many ears.

This is a flourish. There follow excellent parables; as that, she gathered strength in going; that she go upon the ground, and yet hided her head in the clouds; that in the daytime she sited in a watch tower, and filet most by night; that she mingled things done, with things not done; and that she is a terror to great cities. But that which passed all the rest is: They do recount that the Earth, mother of the giants that made war against Jupiter, and were by him destroyed, thereupon in an anger brought forth Fame. For certain it is, that rebels, figured by the giants, and seditious fames and libels, are but brothers and sisters, masculine and feminine. But now, if a man can tame this monster, and bring her to feed at the hand, and govern her, and with her fly other ravening fowl and kill them, it is somewhat worth. But we are infected with the style of the poets. To speak now in a sad and serious manner:

There is not, in all the politics, a place less handled and more worthy to be handled, than this of fame. We will therefore speak of these points: What are false fames; and what are true fames; and how they may be best discerned; how fames may be sown, and raised; how they may be spread, and multiplied; and how they may be checked, and laid dead. And other things concerning the nature of fame. Fame is of that force, as there is scarcely any great action, wherein it hath not a great part; especially in the war.

Mucianus undid Vitellius, by a fame that he scattered, that Vitellius had in purpose to remove the legions of Syria into

Germany, and the legions of Germany into Syria; whereupon the legions of Syria were infinitely inflamed. Julius Caesar took Pompey unprovided, and laid asleep his industry and preparations, by a fame that he cunningly gave out: Caesar's own soldiers loved him not, and being wearied with the wars, and laden with the spoils of Gaul, would forsake him, as soon as he came into Italy. Livia settled all things for the succession of her son Tiberius, by continual giving out, that her husband Augustus was upon recovery and amendment, and it is an usual thing with the pashas, to conceal the death of the Great Turk from the janizaries and men of war, to save the sacking of Constantinople and other towns, as their manner is. Themistocles made Xerxes, king of Persia, post apace out of Grecia, by giving out, that the Grecians had a purpose to break his bridge of ships, which he had made athwart Hellespont.

There be a thousand such like examples; and the more they are, the less they need to be repeated; because a man met with them everywhere. Therefore, let all wise governors have as great a watch and care over fames, as they have of the actions and designs themselves....

Chapter 5

Pruning by Study: Self-Cultivation in Bacon's Essays

The question of the relationship of Bacon's Essays to his scientific project is a recurring commonplace of Bacon criticism. Generally, critics have argued over the degree to which the Essays conform to Bacon's inductive method, as described and demonstrated in The Novum Organon and The Advancement of Learning. Jacob Zeitlin's influential essay of 1928 was one of the first to argue that the Essays represent the application of induction to "civil knowledge, which of all others is most immersed in matter, and hardliest reduced to axiom", resulting in a "science of pure selfishness".

Some more recent studies suggest a different approach to the question; these stress the coherence of the writings by arguing not so much that the Essays are (or are not) informed by the principles and methods of the scientific writings, as that both are the products of common anxieties, concerns, or socio-political conditions. Robert Faulkner, for instance, discovers underlying the Essays "foundational" definition of the Baconian subject as "a needy self that must make its own provision to the point of making its own world". From such a self, Faulkner argues, springs both the Essays' concern with personal security and power, and the will to power over nature which is the end of the scientific project.

The following essay will begin, likewise, by exploring the nature of the self—and its "selfishness"—on which the Essays are predicated. The self portrayed in the Essays, and for which they are written, is motivated by a powerful anxiety about its ability to control and distribute its creative energies. This anxiety, in turn, highlights a significant difference between the two projects—The Advancement of Learning and the advancement of the self—and thus illuminates an important methodological distinction between the two. While the scientific writings concern the present and future work of many minds, the Essays address the needs of a single concrete self, bounded by time and space, and ambitious to achieve concrete results within those bounds. Knowledge, the goal of The Advancement of Learning, is long; but life, the subject of the Essays, is short.

While the Novum Organon argues that induction, properly practiced, will proceed more efficiently than science had hitherto, it warns especially against the dangers of haste in method, particularly such haste as is encouraged by the desire to see results, whether in the form of abstract axioms or concrete, practical "fruits." For the individual contingent self, however, results do count. For that self, therefore, efficiency becomes paramount concern. The contingent self, as both subject and audience of the Essays, thus determines their difference from Bacon's progressive writings.

This difference explains and can be illustrated by a consistent difference in the uses to which a common set of figures are put in the Essays and in the scientific writings. Brian Vickers has described Bacon's use of horticultural metaphors such as seeds, fruit, gardens, and irrigation to represent the potential for the growth of knowledge from the well cultivated "seeds" which the scientific writings are supposed to plant. Such figures figure prominently in the Essays as well. There, however, they are most often used as images of unrestrained growth to an opposite effect: to represent the inefficient expenditure of the self limited creative resources. Figures of fecundity in The Advancement of Learning become, in the Essays, metaphors for profligacy.

This concern with protecting the resources of the contingent self is most evident in those essays which describe the borders of public life. These include the essays on the relationship between public and domestic life, a relationship which is necessarily competitive within the economy of the selfs limited energies. Among other things, these essays discover a greater security in the public realm, in part because the expression of creative energies is more easily controlled through the fashioning of an artificial public self—a reputation—than through the making of separate and individual selves through physical procreation.

The essays on education—the process of transition from private to public life—also endorse a jealous strategy of careful investments in future returns; it is in these essays that the contrast is clearest between the processes of advancing one's own learning and those for the advancement of general knowledge. The following argument will first discuss how the essays on public and private life and on education represent the economy of the self, and will conclude by examining similar representations in two essays which prescribe the matured public relationships which are the fruits of such jealous cultivation.

Three essays first published in the 1612 edition of the Essays—"Of Parents and Children," "Of Marriage and Single Life," and "Of Love"—address more directly than any others the domestic side of men's (and occasionally and indirectly women's) life. If, as has often been suggested, the Essays attempt to fill a gap in The Advancement of Learning's discussion of the "three wisdoms" of "civil knowledge," then these three essays may have been introduced in the 1612 edition to address concerns not attended to in the first edition. Indeed, these essays are primarily concerned not so much with domestic issues as with the relationship between domestic and public life. Each of these essays represent this relationship as a competition between the two spheres for the individual's limited creative energies; the 1625 revisions of these essays only tend to emphasize this theme. The management of that competitive relationship thus involves economic decisions about the allocation of those resources.

The first paragraph of "Of Parents and Children" represents this competition by invoking a commonplace metaphor for public works.

The perpetuity by generation is common to beasts; but memory, merit, and noble works, are proper to men. And surely a man shall see the noblest works and foundations have proceeded from childless men; which have sought to express the images of their minds, where those of their bodies have failed. So the care of posterity is most in them that have no posterity.

Bacon, however, does not mean the analogy between works and children metaphorically but literally: the two forms of self-reproduction conflict with one another, forcing a choice. The passage clearly suggests that works, which are "proper to men," ought to be valued by the essay's audience above the getting and raising of children, which is "common to beasts" (and women).

That generation which is "proper to men" is defined by public perception: its products are "memory, merit, and noble works," objects "a man can see." This public approbation seems as integral to the value of such works as their usefulness; even the "care of posterity" suggests not only the future benefits of one's work but one's historical reputation as well. By contrast, according to the essay's opening sentence, " the joys of parents are secret, and so are their griefs and fears." Thus, the first paragraph of "Of Parents and Children" implies that its titular topic is a less valuable and less valued form of creativity, while the creation of works which serve the public is both "proper to men" and validated by the less ambiguous reward of public recognition.

Though reputation may seem a less substantial commodity than flesh and blood offspring, it is the coin which buys preferment and other benefits in the public sphere. Despite its subsequent attention to the practical matters of getting and raising children, this essay begins by declaring its topic to be a distraction from the business of "civil life," which is the business of the Essays.

The discussion of these practical matters also involves a concern with conserving resources. The second, longer paragraph of the essay describes how family size and "nature" itself can work to limit parents' control over the development of their offspring. In addition to implying that smaller families are easier to manage, the paragraph describes parenting as primarily concerned with the curbing the child's "affection." One way to do this is to avoid driving the child to "harmful error" through parental "illiberality." In the 1625 version of the essay, however, the paragraph concludes by urging the control and timely amputation of the individual inclinations of one's children:

> Let parents choose betimes the vocations and courses they mean their children should take; for then they are most flexible; and let them not too much apply themselves to the disposition of their children, as thinking they will take best to that which they have most mind to. It is true that if the affection or aptness of the children be extraordinary, then it is good not to cross it; but generally the precept is good, optimum elige, suave et facile illud faciet consuetudo.

This advice may partially explain why parental Joys remain secret, for the engineering of a child's options from an early age involves a kind of deception on the parent's part. Custom (consuetudo), the essay promises, will make the child's imposed career tolerable to him; it may also help to inculcate the retentive habits of adulthood which the essay prescribes for both the getting and raising of children. Throughout the process of self-reproduction, whether through works or through human offspring, the chief danger seems to be a loss of control over these versions of oneself. Thus both the getting and raising of children require strategies to conserve the resources which fuel such "generation" and to control its products.

In another domestic essay that first appears in 1612, "Of Marriage and Single Life," a similar economics or husbandry of the self is the basis for weighing the merits of marriage. The essay' s opening sentence formulates a model of the relationship of private and public work used consistently in the essay to compare the suitability of married and single life to a catalog of various occupations and ambitions.

> He that hath wife and children hath given hostages to fortune; for they are impediments to great enterprises, either

of virtue or mischief. Certainly the best works, and of greatest merit for the public, have proceeded from the unmarried or childless men; which both in affection and means have married and endowed the public.

The rhetorical progression of these two sentences seems to promise a third in which the second sentence's discussion of "great enterprises of virtue" will be balanced with one making the same point about those of "mischief." Instead of this second affirmation of the opening maxim, however, we get a series of equivocations on its plausibility which then digresses subtly into a consideration of the causes of bachelorhood before returning to consequences:

Yet it were great reason that those that have children should have greatest care of future times; unto which they know they must transmit their dearest pledges. Some there are who, though they lead a single life, yet their thoughts do end with themselves, and account future times impertinences. Nay, there are some other that account wife and children but as bills of charges. Nay more, there are some foolish rich covetous men, that take a pride in having no children, because they may be thought so much the richer....But the most ordinary cause of a single life is liberty, especially in certain self-pleasing and humorous minds, which are so sensible of every restraint, as they will go near to think that girdles and garters to be bonds and shackles. Unmarried men are best friends, best masters, best servants; but not always best subjects; for they are light to run away; and almost all fugitives are of that condition.

Rather than turning to the costs that bachelors inflict on others, as the opening sentence seem to promise it will do, the essay shifts its attention to the selfish motives of such men. The common denominator in each instance is greed and covetousness of resources, not "great enterprises...of mischief." Such greed results in the same wasteful draining of potentially productive resources as living dependents inflict on the family man: in each case these resources are taken out of public circulation, in the one case to support an enterprise "common to beasts," in the other simply to be hoarded to appease a familiar form of human folly. After several sentences of delay, we finally arrive at "the most ordinary cause of a single life," a rhetorical, if not logical, completion of the Partitio promised in the essay's first sentence. The delayed fulfillment of this expectation adds to the reader's uncertainty about the paragraph's direction and conclusion and particularly about the costs, if any, of not marrying.

Throughout this passage the language of economics merges with the language of political restraint, duty, and liberty, contributing to the passage's ambiguities. The connotations of the term "liberty," for instance, shift over the course of the passage. The context initially associates liberty with "self-pleasing and humorous minds," of the kind perhaps produced by the "illiberality" faulted in parents in "Of Parents and Children." As it turns out, however, the "humorous" conceits of such minds are true: "girdles and garters" are in fact the "bonds and shackles" from which the many "fugitives...of that condition" flee.

Thus political liberty becomes a figure not for "illiberality" but for liberation from constraining obligations. Marriage seems to enforce social bonds through a kind of hostage-holding similar to that noted in the essay's opening clause; what keeps a man in subjection, whether to society or to family, is what keeps him from the great enterprises through which he might advance society's interests. The man of business must thus be free of such conventional but baser obligations in order to fulfill the greater ones to which he aspires.

The ambiguities arising from the debate between "liberty" and "restraint" lead to the essay's most succinct and resonant description of the dynamics of the conservation of self: "A single life doth well with churchmen; for charity will hardly water the ground where it must first fill a pool" (VI: 392). In context of the Essays, the metaphor is supremely sly. The vehicle of the metaphor strongly suggests the very mechanism of the generation "common to beasts," thus linking charity to the act of fertilization, at the same time that its sense is in fact the opposite. The consequent implication is that the "churchman" who does not marry is in fact more of a father than he who does, for his energies are put to the most efficient creative use. The "pool"—static, enclosed, useless (perhaps a decorative garden pool is the precise referent)—figures the "secret" work of the home; placed beside the fruitfully watered ground it seems almost onanistic.

The same equation of domesticity and wasted resources reappears at the end of the essay "Of Love": There is in man's nature a secret inclination and motion towards love of others, which if it be not spent upon some one or a few, doth naturally spread itself towards many, and maketh men become humane and charitable; as it is seen sometimes in friars. Nuptial love maketh mankind; friendly love perfecteth it; but wanton love corrupteth and embaseth it.

The language of this passage relates "Of Love" to the two other "domestic" essays previously discussed, by invoking the "secret" nature of this "inclination." "Of Parents and Children" recommends that this secrecy be used to regulate family life more efficiently, by suppressing both the parents' expressions of joy or grief and the children's expressions of their private inclinations. However, domestic life also seems to bottle up other public forms of self-expression within the "secret" economy of the home. Thus are one's "love," "water," "wealth," or generation" "spent" rather than "spread," wasted in secret on one or a few" rather than invested in work validated by public and historical recognition.

As in the early lines of "Of Marriage and Single Life," an initially even-handed presentation of two opposing alternatives is ultimately resolved in favor of alternative about which Bacon has the least to say. Echoing the same opposition between domestic and public life developed in the two earlier essays, the remainder of the sentence equates the "humane and charitable" man, he whose generative power is greatest, with celibacy and rejection of domesticity. The "friendly love" of the last sentence, though never defined or discussed elsewhere in the essay, is presumably that which "spreads" one's resources like water across a field, rather than merely filling the domestic pool. Unlike the act of "making mankind," which, as we have seen in "Of Parents and Children," is "common to beasts," this "friendly love perfecteth" mankind. It is, in other words, what is "proper" to mankind. As the reader has seen in "Of Parents and Children," what is "proper" to man is the channeling of the creative impulse towards works which receive public validation. "Friendly love" and charity thus involve the careful husbandry of the self required of the public man. Nuptial love, however, as the essay states earlier, "maketh men that they can no ways be true to their own ends".

In the context of the Essays' general concern with "the wisdom of business," these three essays on domestic or personal topics attend to issues which do not fall within the realm of public affairs but rather influence it from outside. All share certain themes and concerns.

Most striking is the model of the self which informs each essay, according to which the self represents a font of limited resources whose expenditure requires economic decisions. Though each essay makes gestures which seem to reserve judgment on the relative value of using these resources in one sphere or the other, in fact each essay clearly argues for the greater value of public over private work.

This conclusion seems to arise from an anxiety over loss of control of the self and its reproductions which is high lighted by the model of a self motivated by a kind of economic jealousy. This anxiety explains in part the recurring emphasis in these essays on appearances and reputation as measures of public success; such abstract reproductions of the self are easier to manipulate and control than those corporeal offspring which grow inevitably into independent personalities.

Beginning with the 1612 edition, these three essays help determine the audience of the remainder of the Essays as those who have chosen public life over private (or have had it chosen for them by their parents) and are aware of the effects of that choice on their other social and personal relationships. The next step in one's fashioning for "civil life" is education. Though "Of Studies" is the first essay in the 1597 group of ten, in subsequent editions it appeared towards the end of the Essays, following the essays on domestic relations. Nevertheless, "Of Studies" still appears as a kind of preface to the rest of the

Essays, offering instructions on how to read, warnings against the misuses of reading, and particular recommendations regarding the therapeutic values of reading for various readers.

The method of critical reading advocated in "Of Studies" in 159'7 is seconded eight years later in The Advancement of Learning, where a cautious, "Probative" approach to textual authority is prescribed: Read not to contradict and confute; nor to believe and take for granted; nor to find talk and discourse; but to weigh and consider. Disciples do owe unto masters only a temporary belief and a suspension of their own judgment until they be fully instructed, and not an absolute resignation or perpetual captivity.

As Croll and others have argued, the aphoristic style of the Essays appears consistent with Bacon's description of the style appropriate to scientific investigation:...Aphorisms, except they should be ridiculous, cannot but be made of the pith and heart of sciences for discourse of illustration is cut off; recitals of example are cut off; discourse of connexion and order is cut off; descriptions of practice are cut off; so there remaineth nothing to fill the Aphorisms but some good quantity of observation...Aphorisms, representing a knowledge broken, do invite men to enquire farther...Thus, the pursuit of knowledge, whether through the study of texts or through direct observation of phenomena, is presented in both "Of Studies" and the Advancement as requiring a cautious skepticism of hasty generalization and precedent authorities.

Both texts also place importance on the distinction between the discovery of knowledge and the application of that knowledge. Their use of this distinction, however, reveals the fundamental difference between the situation of the scientist and the predicament of the self. While the ultimate goal of Bacon's properly to be made before taking the preparatory steps of such a career. It may be that the importance of such issues occurred to Bacon, who himself married late in life and had no children, only as an afterthought. scientific method is useful knowledge, consideration of the practical "fruits" of knowledge threatens to warp the process of scientific inquiry by polluting the inductive process with predetermined ends. Thus the application of the scientist's discoveries is left to the "arts mechanical," i.e., to technology. In education, however, studies and experience must be combined in a single enterprise in order to achieve the proper end common to both: the formation of the self. In describing how these two elements combine in the education of the individual, Bacon uses language familiar from our examination of the conflict between the public and the private self:

Studies perfect nature, and are perfected by experience: for natural abilities are like natural plants, that need pruning by study; and studies themselves do give forth directions too much at large, except they be bounded in by experience.

Insofar as "perfection" here implies the unique and proper telos of a thing, study would appear to be the proper activity of man, actualizing his "natural abilities." The simile which expands on the aphorism emphasizes the idea of a growth directed towards a predetermined end. Pruning a "natural plant" directs the plant's growth by blocking the wasteful or inefficient use of its resources in order that they may be expended, and the plant expanded, in a narrower yet more fruitful direction. The educational process thus resembles the secret prunings of illiberality in children prescribed in "Of Parents and Children." Studies and experience direct the individual's energies by a careful, cooperative modulation of control and release.

The subordinate clause in which the "pruning" simile appears in this sentence, was added in the final 1625 edition. The other 1625 additions to this essay are likewise interesting for what they suggest about Bacon's developing conception not only of the essay's form but of the Essays' audience and purpose as well. As many critics have noted, Bacon's revisions of earlier essays, as well as those essays which appear for the first time in 1612 and 1625 editions, evince a greater emphasis on formal Partitio. If this tendency seems less evident in the revisions of "Of Studies," it is because the initial version of 1612 already divides its topic quite artfully into a series of roughly parallel triplicates, starting with the opening sentence: "Studies serve for delight, for ornament, and for ability." Many of the 1625 additions to this essay—among them the "pruning" simile—tend to expand on the third element of a triplicate. These elaborations tend to mark more clearly the boundaries of the various topics; they also confirm that each triplicate represents an ascending order of importance: thus "delight" is a less valuable application of studies than "ornament," which is in turn less valuable than "ability." At the same time, however, many such elaborations in the later editions of the Essays tend to render an initial aphorism ambiguous by illustrating it with observations which qualify rather than confirm it.

The revisions of "Of Studies" reveal both of these tendencies in the structural development of the Essays. In addition, however, they seem to reflect a parallel development in the student towards a kind of self-organization. In the following passage from "Of Studies," the 1625 additions have been underlined to illustrate this new emphasis: Studies' chief use...for ability is in the judgment and disposition of business. For expert men can execute, and perhaps judge of particulars one by one; but the general counsels and the plots and marshaling of affairs come best from those that are learned. In the 1597 and 1612 versions the last clause reads: "but learned men are fittest to judge or censure."

The revision of this passage clarifies the distinction between execution and judgment by elaborating on each one. Moreover, though, the revision is itself an act of the "disposition" and "marshalling" which are the results of study. The concern with such organization is not, in this essay at least, simply a rhetorical revision; rather it seems to incorporate the "wisdom" of business which the later version of the essay emphasizes both here and in the earlier "pruning" simile. The martial connotations of the words "disposition" and "marshalling" suggest the potential dangers contained and controlled by learning; the "expert," on the other hand, deals with such "affairs" only case-by-case. A consequence of learning is thus an increased sense of security, maintained by strategies of containment and control. Another major revision to "Of Studies," added in 1612 and expanded in 1625, likewise describes study as a process of channeling and controlling creative energies.

> Nay, there is no stond or impediment in the wit, but may be wrought out by fit studies;...So if a man's wit be wandring, let him study the mathematics; for in demonstrations. if his wit be called away never so little. he must begin again. This wit be called away never so little, he must begin again. If wit be not apt to distinguish or find differences, let him study the schoolmen; for they are cymini sectores. If he be not apt to beat over matters, and to call up one thing to prove and illustrate another in 1612 edition: "find out resemblances", let him study the lawyer's cases.

Those essays which deal with domestic ties tended to recommend a redirecting of energy which would otherwise be bottled up in less profitable pursuits; this passage argues that studies can both unclog and fortify the channels through which those energies will be translated into action. In addressing questions of conduct in the world of action more directly, the majority of the remaining essays develop this notion of husbandry into a more jealous view of the self which places a much greater premium on conservation than on useful or creative production.

One other essay focuses primarily on the process of education. Unlike "Of Studies," "Of Travel," which appears only in 1625, and thus well after the formulation of the scientific method, describes education as a project clearly distinct in both method and intent from scientific investigation. The inductive method of investigation is an inherently inefficient process: it resists the efficiencies offered by the "Idols" of received opinion which prematurely exclude, preclude, or edit new observations and information. It defers as long as possible the formation of coherent axioms and keeps those it does form provisional and insecure. Education, on the other hand, because it is concerned with forming a discrete self which has to exist in the real world, cannot afford such inefficiencies. Unlike induction, the aim of education is not just discovery but use. The aim in "Of Travel" is efficiency. Though recommending exposure to a variety of objects of study, it encourages a specific, narrow focus on points of practical, contemporary interest, especially commercial and governmental institutions. Thus the "havens and harbors" of the Continent are as worthy of study as its "antiquities and ruins." The structure of the essay itself, centered on a lengthy list of such "things to be seen and observed," suggests an almost comical haste.

The whirlwind pace of this catalog justifies the recommendation which precedes it, that a diary "be brought in use." The aim of the tour is to "have a young man to put his travel into a little room, and in short time to gather much," to "abridge his travel with much profit." Important above all, therefore, is to keep moving:

Let him keep also a diary. Let him not stay long in one city or town; more or less as the place deserveth, but not long; nay, when he stayeth in one city or town, let him change his lodging from one end and part of the town to another. In his rush, Bacon seems to forget that he has already packed his diary several sentences earlier. In seeking out guides—like the diary, another efficient mediation between the student and the objects of his studies—Bacon recommends employing ambassadorial staff:

As for the acquaintance which is to be sought in travel; that which is most of all profitable is acquaintance with the secretaries and employed men of ambassadors: for so in travelling in one country he shall suck the experience of many.

Such vampirism (deriving from the conventional figure of the student as a bee who sups at many flowers) complements the premium placed on efficiency in "Of Studies." The influx of information is susceptible to and ought to be controlled by the same mechanisms of conservation which are elsewhere recommended to regulate the student's future output. The xenophobic impulse which seems to want to hurry the student through this necessary step in his education arises in part from a related fear of allowing the self to be absorbed into the massive selflessness represented by the detailed variety of the world outside both one's country and oneself. The essays examined so far represent supporting arches buttressing the central structure of (he project of the Essays, a structure which, not unlike the scientific project, is composed of discrete units of knowledge. The primary difference between the two projects is that science is allowed the luxury of reaching its Fulfillment in properly developed axioms, unhurried by any pressure to produce useful results on a schedule. Science can wait for its results.

The project of the essays, however, aims at the production of a man who can participate in the world. While some of the essays, including those already discussed, are primarily concerned with guiding such a man to the world, the majority aim at guiding him through it. The same model of the self, expressed in similar metaphors, informs the majority of these essays on the "science of negotiation." "Of Counsel" and "Of Friendship" are a useful pair by which to illustrate the persistence and use of this underlying model of the self, because both concern the relationship of the self to other selves.

"Of Counsel" focuses on the self in what would seem to be its most secure and efficiently potent state: kingship. However, the paranoia which in fact characterizes the selfs position at the top of the hierarchy of its fellow selves is not unique to that position. Rather, kingship represents the paradigm of the matured self in the world: now able to exercise its power, yet all the more susceptible to and jealous of losing control of how that power is deployed. "Of Counsel" is consequently concerned with almost nothing but the maintenance of control over one's power, as epitomized in the problems of kingship. The myth of Athena's birth figures the desire of the matured self jealously to guard its own powers so as neither to depend on the infusions of others nor to disperse wastefully one's own vital energies.

> The ancient times do set forth in figure both the incorporation and inseparable conjunction of counsel with kings, and the wise and politic use of counsel by kings: the one, in that they say Jupiter did marry Metis, which signifieth counsel; whereby they intend that Sovereignty is married to

Counsel: the other in that which followeth, which was thus: They say, after Jupiter was married to Metis, she conceived by him and was with child, but Jupiter suffered her not to stay till she brought forth, but eat her up; whereby he became himself with child, and was delivered of Pallas armed, out of his head. Which monstrous fable containeth a secret of empire; how kings are to make use of their counsel of state.

That first they ought to refer matters unto them, which is the first begetting or impregnation; but when they are elaborate, moulded, and shaped in the womb of their Counsel, and grow ripe and ready to be brought forth, that then they suffer not their Counsel to go through with the resolution and direction, as if it depended on them; but take the matter back into their own hands, and make it appear to the world that the decrees and final directions (which, because they come forth with prudence and power, are resembled to Pallas Armed) proceeded from themselves; and not only from their authority, but (the more to add reputation to themselves) from their head and device.

The force of this "monstrous Fable"—a rare device in the Essays—is not so much in its illumination of the political stratagem described, but rather in its almost literal embodiment of the problem of personal power. The figure is an assertion—similar to others noted above—of the dependence of physical body on the control of creative power. The jealousy it represents is not simply a jealousy of one's "Authority" but of one's personal security. For the close reader of the essays, the politics of the counsel room recalls the economics of the self detailed in the essays on domestic relations and education.

The fable also illustrates, however, that with proper handling this threat of loss or dismemberment can in fact be turned to profit, for the marriage to Metis can be redeemed as marriage to one's wife cannot. As the domestic essays have shown, a wife cannot increase the efficiency of the economy of self-hood, but is rather a drain on the self. Metis, on the other hand, can be swallowed by the clever king; in fact, it is his ability to do so which constitutes and preserves his power over others. Authority is maintained by maintaining the appearance that ideas gleaned from others in fact emanate from oneself. As in several of the domestic essays, the efficient use of personal power is validated by public recognition, though "Of Counsel" suggests that, like domestic exertions, public work may also involve a certain secrecy. To maintain this fiction of self-sufficiency, and thus personal power, counselors must be made dependent for their own safety on the safety of the king.

Most of the rest of this essay is devoted to enumerating "the inconveniencies of counsel, and...the remedies". These "inconveniencies" are three: the difficulty of maintaining secrecy, the threat to authority described in the "Fable," and the more specific threat posed by "unfaithful" or self-interested counsellors. In each case counsel represents a threat to the process of maintaining power; absent is any mention of the benefits of counsel.

This, it turns out, is the subject addressed in the 1625 revision of "Of Friendship. In 1612, this topic generated only a brief, highly aphoristic essay, one of the shortest in the collection. The revised version retains the favor of the earlier essay only in its opening paragraph. The rest details the three "fruits" of friendship. This metaphor echoes figural language used in both the essays on domestic life and those on education. As in those, the concern is exclusively with the fruits which grow on the boughs of the self. The first and most completely discussed o: these "fruits" sets the tone for all the rest: A principal fruit of friendship is the ease and discharge of the fulness and swellings of the heart, which passions of all kinds do cause and induce. We know diseases of stoppings and suffocations are the most dangerous in the body; and it is not much otherwise in the mind; you may take sarza to open the liver, steel to open the spleen, flower of sulphur for the lungs, castoreum for the brain; but no receipt openeth the heart, but a true friend; to whom you may impart griefs, joys, fears, hopes, suspicions, counsels, and whatsoever lieth upon the heart to oppress it, in a kind of civil shrift or confession. (VI: 437-38)

Thus the "principal fruit of friendship" is based on the model of the self sketched out so far, on both the necessity of giving its energies proper outlets and the attendant jealousy with which those energies ought to be husbanded. The ideal friend is a confessor: an anonymous receptacle of potentially dangerous passions, into which the over flowings of the self are vented and in which they are contained in secrecy.

Like the ends of education, the function of a "true friend" is not understood to exist in any benefits beyond those to the self, but only in terms of his ability to help safely direct and secure the creative—and thus potentially disruptive—forces of the self. The second and third fruits of friendship are no less selfish. The second fruit arises from conversation, the benefit of which proceeds not from the combination of two perspectives or opinions but from hearing one's own ideas aired: certain it is that whosoever hath his mind fraught with many thoughts, hi wits and understanding do clarify and bread up, in the communicating and discoursing with another; he tosseth his thoughts more easily; he marshalleth them more orderly; he seeth how they look when they are turned into words: finally, he waxeth wiser than himself; and that more by an hour's discourse than by a day's meditation.

The military figure for the disposition of energies is familiar, as is the ultimately selfish nature of this sort of improvement. One might almost as well be talking to oneself; it is the regulation of an internal pressure—here apparently intellectual though elsewhere less clearly specified—that is important, not the regulator itself:

Neither is this second fruit of friendship, in opening the understanding, restrained only to such friends as are able to give a man counsel; (they indeed are best;) but even without that, a man learneth of himself, and bringeth his own thoughts to light, and whetteth his wits as against a stone, which itself cuts not. In a word, a man were better relate himself to a statua or a picture, than to suffer his thoughts to pass in smother. The final fruit of friendship—the ability of friends to do things one cannot do oneself—is likewise couched entirely in terms of a profitable economy the self. Friends become one's "deputies," lesser yet functional extensions of the self. Though by this point in the essay the more specific initial focus on the friends of kings has been dropped, interpersonal relations at all levels continue to be represented hierarchically: the self is sovereign and as such embodies its own state and its own bounded economy striving for self-sufficiency. This economy represents the mature stage of the self first developed in the essays on domestic relations and education. Those introductory essays represent the self as an entity possessed of limited resources which must be profitably employed within a limited span of time and opportunity.

The essays on domestic life are concerned with harnessing those energies so as to maximize their productivity; metaphors of agriculture and husbandry help these essays to argue that domesticity exploits these energies inefficiently and even dangerously. The essays on education offer ways to develop the self and its energies as quickly and efficiently as possible. Finally, in at least two essays addressing the apparently matured self, the economic model of the self culminates in the view of the self as a jealous sovereign anxious about maintaining and securing its power and dominion in the public sphere. A consistent corollary of this model is that the selfs security is a function of public perception.

Thus Bacon's Essays return consistently to the importance of fashioning a specifically public self which is constituted in the responses of others. These responses are the final, delicate fruit of the self-cultivation the Essays recommend to the public man. Compared to the fruits which are the goals and justification posited for Bacon's scientific methods, reputation might seem an ephemeral good and one even opposed to truth. Within the tangible spatial and temporal compass of an individual life, however, reputation produces concrete benefits. The scientist, on the other hand, working his way carefully and warily towards truths, must acknowledge, as Bacon did of his own unfinished scientific project, that the work may not bear fruits in his lifetime.

The individual self is the object of the Essays. Though their model of induction may inform the style of the Essays, the scientific writings differ in both object and, consequently, purpose. The scientific works set forth a programme which encourages patience in the interests of a cautious expansion of knowledge in the public interest. The Essays, however, reveal—and in fact arise from—an anxiety over the concerns of personal and professional security to which the individual, political flesh is heir. The Essays therefore value efficiency over methodological rigor, conservation over progress, personal over public good, the self over truth. The Essays demonstrate a recognition of the limits of the scientific programme as a guide of practical conduct, for the methods of Baconian science do not apply within the micro-economics of the bounded self.

Chapter 6

Francis Bacon and the True Ends of Skepticism

Long ago, Bacon asserted that science must begin with doubts in order to end in certainties, a paradox that stills leads to misunderstandings about Bacon and about science.

Detractors of modern science sometimes refer to themselves as skeptics, because they dare to question long-accepted doctrine. But skepticism as a method is not just a resolve to disagree. It is the presumption of error and fallibility on which our science is based. This paradox was first put forth by Francis Bacon in The New Organon (1620), building on his previous Advancement of Learning (1605). He announced that great things were possible in science, provided that nearly all the old methods and beliefs were cast away. What struck him was the mixture of unproductive dogma and unresolved controversy over basic theory in science despite long centuries of data-collecting and thought. He had ideas about a remedy, yet he believed no remedy could be complete because the human mind itself had faults and limitations that made it almost incapable of seeing truly. Today, when people claim as a novel discovery that scientists are not godlike beings, that thought may be limited by emotions and culture, and that languag e is not the same as natural fact, they are merely reiterating Bacon's starting assumptions.

We think of the seventeenth century as a golden age of science. Yet when Bacon considered the matter, inquiry was busy but not very fruitful. Cosmology was up for grabs, the old Scholastic system of four elements offered no definite path to new discoveries, alchemists were at odds about basic laws of chemistry, and when an innovator such as William Gilbert1 (1540—1603) did achieve knowledge about magnetism, he then went overboard with mystical extensions of his discoveries. Whether stressing reason and logic, symbolic connections and intuition, or hands-on experiment, the active disciplines had yielded few outcomes solid enough to be built upon.

But there was practical progress in navigation, engineering, and astronomy. Empiricism was not lacking, but it did not underlie broad scientific theories. These tended to soar aloft, in obedience to what Bacon called "Idols of the mind" because they diverted men from examining divinely created nature. What was needed was "a closer and purer league between... the experimental and the rational (such as has never yet been made)" (Bacon 1960, 95).

Bacon's Paradox

Bacon saw that good thinking is a sort of paradox. The mind is all too effective, not only in feeling and imagining, but even in reasoning. Fastening on one idea, it traces implications, follows up parallels, leaps to conclusions, and creates a tight and persuasive system of beliefs. This power can be useful, if properly disciplined, but it tends to shrug aside direct observation of nature. Man, according to Bacon, does nor have a privileged intuition into the construction of the cosmos—a direct link to the Creator's intentions—as many then believed.

He must let the actions of nature in the uncontrollable future be the arbiters of his theory's soundness. Initial speculations must issue in a well-formulated experiment, and that, in turn, must yield to a sensory judgment of the experiment's result. Though Bacon didn't think of double-blind testing, he saw that these stages must be made as distinct from each other as possible (1960; 2, 50).

Bacon called endemic human limitations "Idols of the Tribe." Even the cleverest minds leap to generalizations, notice striking events more than typical ones, and seek out supportive data more than counterexamples. They fasten on apparent patterns too quickly and don't let go. "Idols of the Cave" were the individual's limitations and enthusiasms. He may apply favourite ideas or remedies to every-thing, like a wonder drug. "Idols of the Marketplace" were the limitations of common language, suitable for everyday life, but not to describe nature accurately. "Substance," "heavy," "moist," and "dense" were all vague terms. New words must refer to measurable physical phenomena (1960, 41—60).

In developing these ideas, Bacon outlined a devastating critique that might well doom any science. When the human mind has once despaired of finding truth, its interest in all things grows fainter, and the result is that men turn aside to pleasant disputatious and discourses and roam as it were from object to object... a wandering kind of inquiry that leads to nothing. But he rejected the immobile skepticism, common at that time, which doubted whether any human theory about nature would ever be a clear advance. Some raise doubts, he said, as lawyers do, without any aim of settling a question. They may embrace a "deliberate and factitious despair" of learning anything new, for the sake of thinking their own thought perfect.

Here Bacon aptly depicts that spongy indecisiveness of mind that can masquerade as "being critical." Today many academics, having grown uneasy about the concept of seeking truth, deal mainly in ingenious detractions, aimed at proving that various forms of supposed excellence are really (but not "in truth") invidious shams. If public debate is mere entertainment and debunking is an automatic reflex with no drive to find central, usable insights, we are imitating the learned men whom Bacon criticized, whose scholarship sought just to get by according to some group's limited conventions. But Bacon wanted people to address great issues and strive to be adequate to their demands.

Just as analyzing government mismanagement should actually give hope (Bacon wistfully reflected) because it shows the failure was not inevitable, so he will offer "arguments of hope," by analyzing the bad habits of mind and futile methods so far used in science (1960, 94). Both mind and senses are unreliable, yet the right method of using mind to correct mind, as we look from a different angle to correct sight, might repair our faults just enough to achieve reliable theories. And this, in essence, has proven true.

Bacon's Checks and Balances

Unlike most revolutionaries (but like the American founders), Bacon offers not a cure, but "helps": checks and balances (1960, 37). First is the thinker's deliberate attention to each pitfall. Second, his limits will be bypassed by involving diverse inquirers. And finally, the theory-making urge itself must be challenged by experimental tests of each assumption and conclusion. The inquirer's thinking will also be affected. What counts as a theory or a scientific term will be guided by his awareness that an eventual empirical test is in the offing. (And, conversely, dubious scientific thought is influenced by the knowledge that no rigorous test will be applied.)

Bacon's paradoxical message—the mind is faulty, the mind can achieve wonders—is usually misunderstood, ignored, or quoted misleadingly. Yet it is at the heart of the mission of SKEPTICAL INQUIRER. For Bacon grasped that scientific method must be intimately linked with a critique of pseudo-science, and that such a critique was not to be just a start-up routine for modern science, but would be of continuing, even increasing, importance. The more that inquiry prospered, the more its intellectual, semantic, and institutional offshoots would be vulnerable to the Idols of the mind.

Bacon saw that the three Idols might generate whole systems of belief, tightly inwoven, fiercely defended, securely institutionalized, and thus hard to dislodge. His fourth category, "Idols of the Theatre," referring to the "vain show" of such a system, incorporates all the others. Though familiar mainly with the Scholastic system, he expected that as freer thought was permitted, many new, specious systems would arise (1960, 61-66, 44). The fame of his initiating role for modern science has obscured his concern with the perennial.

Even Stephen J. Gould, in a recent article, mentions only "outmoded," or "older, traditional" systems as Bacon's target, rather than the system-making propensity of the human mind. Bacon did not envisage the mathematical physics to come; indeed, he could hardly know what a powerful theory would look like. Thus he thought more generally about the search for meaningful patterns in the confusion of phenomena, making his ideas particularly relevant to fledgling and would-be sciences. He hoped that ethics and politics would also yield to his ideas: But the notion of creating a science of society tends to make people aim for universal laws, exact measurements (of something), and the prestige of a system. Soon after Bacon's death, Thomas Hobbes attempted such a science, with simple mechanical principles in the style of physics.

But such efforts ought to be "scientific" first in heeding Bacon's warnings about straying from the facts and clinging to assumptions or terminology that cannot lead to new, testable insight. Bacon would have us spend more time with tentative "middle principles." Pioneers such as Freud, eager to make their ideas science, are in danger of taking any plausible mechanism to be a universal principle. Bacons reluctance to assume uniformity, though misplaced in physics, is more pertinent in studying human nature.

Bacon's list of features in Scholasticism that held back inquiry is surprisingly up-to-date. For example, he includes worship of antiquity; worship of the new; picking on points for argument rather than new discovery; didactic presentation of what is not yet understood; premature formalizing of dubious beliefs; reverence toward an oft-quoted founder; and eloquent elaboration of trivial ideas.

We still rush to call things knowledge and teach formally what we cannot yet be sure of. In alternative medicine the ancient and the brand-new are equally valued for that trait alone. Excessive quoting of a founder (whether Lenin or Freud) whom experience has superseded suggests that one is not trying to move on. Bacon thought Aristotle and others should he treated as "counselors" to give advice, not "dictators" to enforce belief. Thus he himself offered not an opinion to be held, but a work to be done".

What Bacon called "contentious" learning originated in

the twelfth century as a laudable attempt to consider more than one view. But the formal debate had become a mere contest in which flooring an opponent took precedence over gaining new insight. Similarly, modern talk shows, debates, and documentaries may virtuously state contrasting views without working them over to reach new insight.

Bacon's value is in pressing us to question the systems or rhetorical habits of many modern gurus, from Hegel, Marx, and Freud to Derrida, Foucault, and Lacan. Posing questions of pertinent concreteness is, to be sure, a central intellectual skill. Mastering it may require a long struggle with one or more slippery systems finally abandoned. Alexander Herzen, in nineteenth-century Russia, discovered in Bacon's New Organon a radicalism more exact than the left-wing Hegelianism of his time. This quintessential liberal critic of right and left extremes felt surprising affinity with Bacon's thought, as we may also.

Dilution and Misunderstanding of Bacon's Method

Bacon's ideas were both heeded and ignored in the centuries following. His insistence that theory be in continual interchange with experiment is fundamental to science and was assumed by Galileo, Kepler, and Newton. Yet the rise of mathematical physics, which seemed to contain its own safeguards against error, encouraged renewed trust in reason alone. Descartes's influence also gave authority to the mathematical mind and reasserted the old hunger for intuitive certainty, in contrast with Bacon's portrayal of a tricky, self-doubting, circuitous quest.

In the 1660s, promoters of experimental methods in England hoped that direct study of nature would offer a refuge from the theological wrangling and ensuing violence of the Civil War. Bacon's talk of enchanted mirrors and idolatries of mind had an almost Calvinist ring to those eager to link religion with the clear light of reason. Even Robert Boyle, who was closest to Bacon in his methods, intentions, and interests, wanted science and religion mutually to vindicate one another in "natural theology." But Bacon regarded scientific assumptions derived from religion as "anticipations of nature" which had always prevented sound discoveries. Specifically, he rejected attempts to use the book of Genesis as an authority for science (1960, 65).

But in the heyday of natural theology (the eighteenth century), this was forgotten, and it was possible for a geologist to think he was heeding Bacon just because he looked at physical evidence, though his purpose was to vindicate the account in Genesis. The historian of science Charles Gillispie points out the discrepancy while offering another distortion. He derides Bacon for his "popular" notion that science required "not difficult abstract thought but only patience and the right method." He makes the common mistake of assuming that some mechanical ascent from experiment to theory is all that Bacon proposed (Gillispie 1951, 62-63; 1960, 81-82). Actually, Bacon's wished-for method of constantly questioning and retesting one's thought, going from works to axioms and back, as he put it, could hardly be more difficult (1960, 117).

In fact, Bacon feared that people would judge his ideas wholly by his tentative suggestions for moving from data to low-level hypotheses. And that is exactly what has happened. These proposals (which have some limited value) are usually cited as the Baconian method, then dismissed as inadequate. Often, as Henry Bauer does in Scientific Literacy and the Myth of Scientific Method, critics proceed to their own view of what is important, ending up with reflections similar to Bacon's about pitfalls in the mind. Bacon himself said that his positive proposals should be thrown out if they didn't serve. What mattered was the empirical testing of each theory's assumptions and conclusions, neither accepting old dogmas nor hurriedly forming new ones. For "the art of discovery" would also improve as science advanced.

The point is that Bacon's "method" is really a meta-method, a set of principles underlying method. He assumed that native wit would generate theories and that the real problem was to discipline them (1960, 130).

But the false "Baconianism" is not the only shadow blotting out Bacon's meaning. A common misconception is that he wanted science to aim at power instead of truth. He is associated with the modern slogan, "knowledge is power," which he did not say. Usually, people mean by it that knowledge will bring us worldly triumph. Or, at best, that knowledge brings power to humanity in the form of useful technology. Bacon did want to achieve the latter eventually. But he was referring to the proof of scientific theories in saying:

Knowledge and power meet in one; for where the cause is not known, the effect cannot be produced. Nature to be commanded must be obeyed; and that which in contemplation is as the cause is in operation as the rule. (1960, 3) That is, only by making nature act a certain way (exercising "power") can you be sure that you understand how it does act, and only by knowing that can you control it.

This simple idea, like Dewey's "learning by doing," is far-reaching in implication. It reflects an appreciation of how people usually do behave: they talk highfalutin nonsense that is far from any facts. In Bacon's famous triad, they produce "fantastical," "contentious," or "delicate" learning; statements that are false, rhetorically persuasive only, or merely aesthetic wordplay. Bacon's hope of eventual technology is regularly confused with his methodological concern with experiment (power) to verify knowledge.

He didn't want people to stop at quick practical gains. To shrink from intellectual challenge was as cowardly as to fear testing one's suppositions against reality. "Works themselves are of greater value as pledges of truth than as contributing to the comforts of life." Yet he did believe that to ease human misery was a noble purpose. Most people, he said, seek knowledge for professional advancement, profit, or to triumph over rivals; sometimes for idle curiosity. The benefit of one's country was a higher end, and better than all these, the good of mankind. In The Advancement of Learning, Bacon explained that by "use" he didn't mean achieving wealth or success, but what would be "solid and fruitful" as opposed to "vain and fantastical." If it is real knowledge, it has implications; it leads on, and makes one want to try it out. The hypothetical path to concrete reality should be intelligible, however complex. Sometimes people embrace dense ideologies of politics or psychoanalysis while avoiding the question, "But how exactly will any of this help?" even though their stated purpose is social reform or healing.

Grand philosophic systems are the fruit of struggle with some human problem. If their adherents retreat to obscurantism, often they have failed and refuse to admit it. When Khrushchev (a Baconian at times) asserted that there is "no Communism without sausages," the Marxist-Leninst experts in Moscow saw him as a buffoon. But his down-to-earth concern about hunger was part of a drive to truth that also made him speak out about Stalin and recognize the madness of nuclear war.

What is called "utility" or "pragmatism" can be given different slants. William James tended to accept the practical value of ideas (loosely applied) that might not strictly be true. George Orwell, in 1984, showed the dire everyday consequences of living by lies. For Bacon, practice proved the worth of ideas, but also (as for Orwell) showed the failure of false ones.

Bacon saw clearly the dichotomy between the shifty language of men and nature's power, which could not be bought off by flattery or incantation. "To overcome not an adversary in argument, but nature in action" was his aim and the most important distinction he made. He knew he was surrounded, as we are now, by adroit rhetoricians who refused to accept that words sometimes succeed and sometimes fall to get close to the things they purport to describe, and that it matters. The idea that thought can never be anything but rhetoric or "conversation" will only satisfy those who never feel obliged to act, and therefore to get reality right.

Iron and Love, Science and Art

Our literary-aesthetic traditions place great value on the metaphorical use of words that reached its height in the poetry of Bacon's day. This drew on the very habits of symbolism that Bacon saw must be eliminated from strict science, which uses language differently. The query, "Is this really love?" will never fully parallel, "Is this really iron?" We have agreed-upon tests to determine that a thing is iron. Love is an open concept, and iron, since modern chemistry, a closed one.

Science adds knowledge by showing what can't be. Mystical thinking sets no such bounds. Its glory is to give meaning to every perceived pattern, and its method permits any number of meanings apply. Sensitivity in pursuing metaphors is essential to art; it is needed only sparingly in science. Today, the revivers of pre-scientific medicine often use language evocatively, as advertisers do, piling on terms without indicating and proving what thing does what. Attempting to heal by suggestion or placebo is not alternative, but "aesthetic" medicine.

In setting himself against such habits, Bacon was indeed saying that the aesthetic way of thought could not be the scientific one, and people have been saying "ouch!" ever since. But should they? Must we have one big thing, the unified art-science that has become so fashionable a craving, rather than two different, equally valuable things? Must the universe melt down into a beautiful dream of our own—can it not be seen as a separate thing that we must specially equip our minds to decipher?

Science seeks ways to give a definite "no" to a plausible idea; in literature, plausibility is all. If a Shakespeare play has many interpretations, we say it is rich and complex. If a natural phenomenon does, we say the science is incomplete. Art frees us by creating a refuge against the time flux, but science frees us by enabling us to "command" nature by "obeying" her. It uses necessity to create freedom, as art uses freedom to create its own formal necessity.

Art may spur us to a scientific inkling; science, to an aesthetic one but that is all. The distinction should be cherished, not broken down. It permits us to value our mental motions for their own sake, or to adapt them for use in action, without confusion or self-deception.

The mingled promise and disarray of natural philosophy in his time led Bacon to appreciate two great freedoms of the mind. We can question whole systems that seem to violate evidence or logic. It does not matter how many people swear by such beliefs, or for how many centuries they have done so, or with what coercive power. But we can do better than reject the affirmations of the madding crowd. We can thread our own path through the forests of unsorted experience, trusting our minds not to guess right, but to devise tests for detecting falseness. Bacon did no science that today would have won him a Nobel prize. He founded no schools of philosophy. He was not, like Aristotle, "the master of them that know." But he was the friend of those who think, and for that reason, his writings should not be laid aside.

Chapter 7

Bacon and the Rose Cross

Much has been said of Bacon's connection with that influential Society which flourished in England in the reigns of Elizabeth and James, known as "Rosicrucian," whose very existence was so carefully concealed that few outside of it's fellowship knew of its existence. At what date in the world's history it originated we will hardly venture to inquire; it is sufficient to our purpose that the public announcement of its existence occurred in 1614, when was published in Cassel the " Allegemeine and General-Reformation der ganzen weiten Welt." This work declares that it was first formed by four persons only, and by them was made the magical language and writing, with a large dictionary, which we yet daily use God's praise and glory.

Says Mackey:—

Many writers have sought to discover a close connection between the Rosicrucians and the Freemasons, and some, indeed, have advanced the theory that the latter are only the successes of the former. Whether this opinion be correct or not, there are sufficient coincidences of character between the two to render the history of Rosicrucianism highly interesting to the Masonic student.(Albert G. Mackey, *An Encyclopedia of Freemasonry*, vol.II p.639. 1912

In England, there still exists a society of Rosicrucians which was "founded upon the remains of the old German association." We are told that:

Modern times have eagerly accepted, in the full light of science, the precious inheritance of knowledge bequeathed by the Rosicrucians.... It is not desirable, in a work of this kind, to make disclosures of an indiscreet nature. The Brethren of the Rosy Cross will never and should not, at peril and under alarm, give up their secrets. This ancient body has apparently disappeared from the field of human activity, but it's labors are being carried on with alacrity, and with a sure delight in an ultimate success. (*Beyond Masonic Cyclopadia.* London, 1877)

Among the members of the ancient Society appear these initials, " Fra. F.B.; M.P.A.; " which, plainly stated, stand for Francis Bacon, Magister, Pictor, Architectus. Waite, perhaps the best historian of the Rosicrucian Order, introduces it to us in these words:-

Beneath the broad tide of human history there flow the stealthy undercurrents of the secret societies which frequently determine in the depths the changes that take place upon the surface. The facts and documents concerning the Fraternity of the Rose Cross are absolutely unknown to English readers. Even well-informed people will learn with astonishment the extent and variety of the Rosicrucian literature, which hitherto has lain buried in rare pamphlets, written in the old German tongue, and in Latin commentaries of the later alchemists. Says Heckthorne:—

A halo of poetic splendor surrounds the order of the Rosicrucians; the magic lights of fancy play round their graceful day dreams, while the mystery in which they shrouded themselves lends additional attraction to their history. But their brilliancy was that of a meteor. The literature of every European country contains hundreds of pleasing fictions, whose machinery has been borrowed from their system of philosophy, though that itself has passed away. (C.W.Heckthorne, *Secret Societies in All Ages and Countries. London, 1897*

The writer has long been a member of the Masonic order of the Red Cross, which is popularly supposed to have inherited the title from the Rosicrucian Brotherhood, a supposition which, having a knowledge of the history of this and other societies akin to Masonry, he believes to of doubtful validity.

The title of the Brotherhood is derived from Rosa-Crux, a red rose affixed to a cross, presumably of gold. So many intellectual subtleties have been employed by fanciful theorists in attempts to explain the precise signification of these ancient symbols, believed to be older than the Christian era, that their more obvious and truer significance has been unnecessarily obscured. To the Rosicrucians of the age of Elizabeth, it hardly seems questionable that the rose was the symbol of silence, as among the ancients it was originally derived from the pagan tradition that the God of Love made the first rose, which he presented to the God of Silence.

From this tradition originated the custom of carving a rose on the ceilings of banquet halls, or rooms where people met for gayety and diversion, to intimate that under it, whatever was spoken or done was not to be divulged; hence our term *sub rosa* used to indicate secrecy.The Cross,of course, signified salvation, to which the Society of the Rose-Cross devoted itself by teaching mankind the love of God and the beauty of brotherhood, with all that they implied.

The following has been recognized as having been written by Bacon, and will not be doubted by any acquainted intimately with his style:- I was twenty when this book was finished; but methinks I have outlived myself; I begin to be weary of the sun. I have shaken hands with delight, and know all is vanity, and I think no man can live well once but he that could live twice. For my part I would not live over my hours past, or begin again the minutes of my days; not because I have not lived well, but for fear that I should live them worse. At my death I mean to make a total adieu of the world, not caring for the burthen of a tombstone and epitaph, but in the universal Register of God I fix my contemplations on Heaven. I writ the Rosicrucian Infallible Axiomata in four books, and study, not for my own sake only, but for them that study not for themselves. In the law I began to be a perfect clerk; I writ the idea of the Law, et., for the benefit of my friends, and practice in King's Bench.(the reader is referred to Bacon's Historia Vitae et Mortis, and legal writings including the Attorney's Academy.) I envy no man that knows more than myself, but pity them that knows less..... Now, intake midst of all my endeavours there is but one thought that dejects me, that my acquired parts must perish with myself, nor can be legacied amongst my dearly beloved and honoured friends.

The striking phrase, "I begin to be weary of the sun," is duplicated in "Macbeth," v, 5: "I 'gin to be a weary of the sun." We would gladly indulge in a more comprehensive exposition of this interesting fraternity were it not necessary to limit ourselves to a single member of it, Francis Bacon, its putative head in England, though Robert Fludd, whom Waite describes as "the great English mystical philosopher of the seventeenth century, a man of immense erudition, of exalted mind, and, to judge by his writings, of extreme personal sanctity,"(A. S. Waite, *The Real History of the Rosicrucians,* p.283 London 1887.) was its chief exponent.

Of course he was a friend of Bacon, if the latter belonged to the English fraternity, and so must have been Maier, the chief among German writers of the order, who was also in England the year of the actor's death(Shakespere) and Bringern, another associate with him in upholding the honor of Rosicrucianism on the continent. It is to this association that we desire to call especial attention. In 1617 a year after the death of the Stratford actor, Fludd was in Frankfort engaged in seeing his "Defence of Rosicrucianism" through the press. At the same time Bringern was printing the *"Fama Fraternitatis."* In this work appears, on pages 52 and 53, the following:—

We must earnestly admonish you that you cast away, if not all, yet most of the worthless books of pseudo chymists (the term "chymist" used figuratively signified poets or romanticists.) to whom it is a jest to apply the Most Holy Trinity to vain things, or to deceive men with monstrous symbols and enigmas, or to profit by the curiosity of the credulous; our age doth produce many such, one of the greatest being a stage player, a man with sufficient ingenuity for imposition; such doth the enemy of human welfare mingle among the good seed, thereby to make the truth more difficult to be believed, which in herself is simple and naked, while falsehood is proud, haughty, and colored with a lustre of seemingly godly and humane wisdom. Ye that are wise eschew such books and have recourse to us, who seek not your moneys, but to offer unto you our great treasures.

The allusion is evidently to the Stratford actor, for the plays, as well as Bacon's other works, are saturated with Rosicrucian thought. Dr. Ingleby should include it in a new edition of his "Allusions." Certainly it is much clearer than many he has published. But further to identify the actor with the titles "false poet" and "stage player" we will call attention to a method which these literary Bo-Peeps had of revealing their meaning to the initiated. If they wished to inform their reader who a person alluded to was, they placed the allusion on a page the number of which corresponded so the number which he was known,or to the date of some well-known event connected with him. This allusion was placed on pages 52 and 53; the first to indicate the age of "false poet and stage player," which was 52, and the second to show the relation between him and Bacon, whose number as we shall see later was 53.

It may be asked, why did a member of the Brotherhood and friend of Bacon speak of the plays in this manner if he knew they were the work of a good Rosicrucian? It should be understood that in the Brotherhood the largest liberty of expression was allowed, and that many, especially those who were of Puritan extraction, looked upon the stage with abhorrence. Bringern was among these, and took this way of expressing his disapproval of mingling things sacred and profane. He was occupied, as so many are even in our day, with methods of reform, while Bacon was looking to results.

The Rose-Cross order is greatly misunderstood. Writers upon the subject have permitted themselves to be led astray form the motive which vitalized it, and have been hoodwinked by its mysteries, as though it exalted mystery above faith, the shadow above the substance, paying scant heed to the patent fact, that secrecy, was its only safeguard against rack and thumbscrew. It was not a searcher for gold, but a Christian organization composed of studious and thoughtful men, impressed by the mysteries amidst which the Creator had placed them, and which Science and Philosophy have ever been striving to solve. They were mystical, —how could they be otherwise?—and were regarded as heretics, or free-thinkers, then synonymous terms, though now they would be called conservative, for history teaches that the error of one age may be the truth of a later one.

There were many in Elizabeth's reign who chafed at the restrictions, and abhorred the obsequious attitude which placed and power imposed them; but though the Advancement of Learning was the cornerstone of their temple, they naturally differed as to methods of advancement. Some among them, like Bacon, found in Poetry and Romance he most convenient vehicles for delivering to the world, either by means of the printed page or the living drama, the truths they so ardently desired it to possess. The influence of these upon the literature of the Elizabethan age is evident, and if it is true that the caged bird sings sweeter than the free, the saying may furnish a reason for its matchless charm. To the mind of the writer, Swedenborg's ethically religious system, which makes the dual precepts,love to God and love to man, its science, quite faithfully expresses that of the Rosicrucians. To love God and man sufficiently to serve both to the best of their ability was their religion, and realizing the wickedness about them, they undertook a crusade of education to lead men to a recognition of their duty to God and their fellows, the "Universal Reformation of the Whole Wide World."

These mysteries were simply cloaks to protect them from danger,not it is true, of modern style, though fantastic garb is still all too much in evidence in the world; for then, Religion and even Science sported strange attire, and they naturally reflect the fashion of their time. It was an age of isms in which men flung loose the jesses of Fancy, and soared aimlessly amid the drifting clouds of fiction, or were ensnared in the toils of superstition; an age in which men mad with the lust of power crushed with mailed heel those with helplessness should have been their protection. But in no age has God been without faithful witnesses, who, braving the terrors of torture and death, were ready to give their lives to the emancipation of their fellowmen, and it was among such that Rosicrucianism found a proper field for it activities.

Unless we pay less attention to the peculiarities of their outward habiliments, and more to them as men, living the common life, and sharing the common aspirations of thinking and well-meaning mortals, we shall fail to understand them.

It is interesting to note that the Rosicrucian Brotherhood especially flourished in England during Bacon's life, and that its existence was not made known to the world, and then on the Continent, until the year of the actor's death. We have already spoken of Maier, the Rosicrucian Protagonist, and of his sojourn in England. Returning to Frankfort, he published in September, 1616, five months after the actor's death, three works, one being his "Lusus Serius," which he dedicated to a triumvirate of Rosicrucians, at whose head appeared *Don Francisco Antonio, Londin, Anglo, Seniori.* This combination of the names of Francis and Anthony, the latter of whom had been dead fifteen years, was of course, understood by the Brotherhood, among whom such books only found readers. To have dedicated it openly to Francis Bacon might have attracted unpleasant attention, if, by chance, it fell under the eye of any but a friend, though at this time, while it might have been injurious, it might not have been dangerous if it had been known that he was a member of the Brotherhood. It is suggestive to note that in his book Maier gives us a paraphrase of the story of Christopher Sly in the "Taming of the Shrew," which he uses to point a moral. Maier concludes the story by restoring the poor sot to his former condition, while in the play he is left unrestored.

This story of Sly, Wigston interprets as showing the relation between the actor and Bacon, the former representing "a man of low extraction, set up like a nobleman by Bacon in his own place with regard to plays or players." (Maier's paraphrase, under the title of the *Waking Man's Dream,* may be found in the Shakespeare Library of Hazlitt. Cf. *Francis Bacon, etc. versus Phantom Captain Shakespeare,* et.,p.xxxii et seq.London, 1891)

It is certainly suggestive that Sly, in the "Taming of the Shrew", remains unrestored to his former condition, as if to suggest that the joke of the actor's false role on the stage of literature was to go on while it continued to amuse the world. The story of Sly is in the Quarto of 1594. It is worth noticing that parts of the play are duplicated in Tamburlaine and Faustus, whose assumed author died in 1593.

When we come to the consideration of Symbolism, we shall learn more of the secret methods employed by Rosicrucians for conveying information, though many of them may never be fully disclosed. It should be noted that the stronghold of the Brotherhood was in England, and that its period of greatest influence was during Bacon's life.

Of the fact that Bacon was a Rosicrucian, Spedding, in his preface to "The New Atlantis," shows himself to have been entirely oblivious. Had he known this, John Heydon's Voyage to the Land of the Rosicrucians" would have opened to him a line of thought which would have greatly enlightened him, for Heydon's "Voyage," largely word for word the same, would have enabled him to understand many passages in his author's works ever which he puzzled in vain. "The New Atlantis" was published in 1627, after Bacon's death, by Rawley, his executor, in connection with the "Sylva Sylvarum," as Bacon "designed," says Spedding, and "Solomon's House," or "The Temple of Wisdom"—as Heydon has it—"is nothing more than a vision of the practical results which he anticipated from the study of natural history diligently and systematically carried on through successive generations,"and that "of it has told us all that he was yet qualified to tell."

Talbot, Heydon's biographer, gives the date of his birth as 1630, four years after Bacon's death. He represents him as a great traveller, and a man of high character. How it came for him to use almost the same description of his penetration into the riddle of Rosicrucianism that Bacon used in his "fable" which Rawley says " he devised to the end that he might exhibit therein a model or description of a college instituted for the interpreting of nature, and the production of great and marvelous works for the benefit of men, under the name of Solomon's House, or the College of the Six Days' Works?" A fair answer seems to be that Bacon used a sketch for his "Atlantis" familiar to the Hermetic Brotherhood, which was limned by him as its head, to exhibit what might be accomplished by wise means for the regeneration of society, making some minor changes to adapt it to a new purpose, and that Heydon, who was a Rosicrucian, unaware of the existence of Bacon's "Atlantis," preserved for the world the original or an accurate copy of it. It is, however, as reasonable to suppose that Heydon becoming acquainted with the "Atlantis," in his admiration of a work in which he discerned the embodiment of the Rosicrucian spirit, adopted it as an exposition of the beauty and strength of the Holy House. In commenting upon Bacon's "Atlantis," Spedding justly says:—

Perhaps there is no single work of his which has so much of himself in it. The description of Solomon's House is the description of the vision in which he lived— the vision not of an ideal world released from the natural conditions to which ours is subject, but of our own as it might be made if we did our duty by it, of a state of things which he believed would one day be actually seen upon this earth, such as it is, by men such as we are, and the coming of which he believed that his own labors were sensibly hastening.

Before dismissing this phase of our subject, let us compare extracts from the "Atlantis" and Heydon's " Voyage."

A study of the two books from which these few and brief extracts are made, in connection with the works of Waite, Wigston, and Hargrave Jennings on the Rosicrucians, opens to us a realm of thought to which so many of us in our less trammeled age are oblivious, and helps in blazing a way to a conception of what has seemed to us a fantastic and futile method for one of the greatest intellects which the world has known, to employ in playing his role on the human stage.

This conception is reached when we clearly understand that Rosicrucianism meant in the seventeenth century the universal brotherhood of humanity; that it was a society closely allied to Freemasonry; derived its cult through the same channels from the event— the building of Solomon's House; employed the same symbols, and that the Invisibles, as the Rosicrucians entitled themselves, worked by hidden ways to bring about their proposed reformation of society, and found that the field of literature afforded sure and safe highways to human minds—the highways of Philosophy, Science, and

History; Poetry, Romance, and Drama; reached in the one instance by different paths of abstract thought, experiment, analysis, and comparison; in the other by the more alluring byways of imagination and fancy. Reaching this conception, a comprehension of Bacon's literary methods, and even of the cipher mystery, becomes less difficult; in fact, difficulties quite vanish when one reflects that the reformer of our day works in the same way, and uses the same means that the Invisibles did, but with this difference, that he labours in the sunshine of hope, while they wrought in the shadow of fear.

From the "New Atlantis"

The father of the Family, whom they call the Tirsan, two days before the feast, taketh to him three of such friends as he liketh to choose; and is assisted also by the governor of the city or place where the feast is celebrated; and all the persons of the family, of both sexes, are summoned to attend him. These two days the Tirsan sitteth in consultation concerning the good estate of the family. Then, if there be any discord or suits between any of the family, they are compounded and appeased.

From Heydon's "Voyage to the Land of the Roscicrucians"

The Father of the fraternity, whom they call the R.C., two days before the feast taketh to him three of such friends as he liketh to chase, and is assisted also by the governor of the city where the feast is celebrated, and all the persons of the family, of both sexes, are summoned to attend upon him. Then, if there be any discords or suits, they are compounded and appeased.

From the "New Atlantis"

And as we were thus in conference, there came one that seemed to be a messenger, in a rich hue, that spake with the Jew; whereupon he turned to me and said: "You will pardon me, for I am commanded away in haste." The next morning he came to me again, joyful as it seemed, and said, "There is word come to the governor of the city, that one of the Fathers of Salomon's House will be here this day seven-night: we have seen none of them this dozen years. His coming is in state;

but the cause of his coming is secret. I will provide you and your fellows of a good standing to see his entry." I thanked, and told him, I was most glad of the news.

From Heydon's "Voyage to the Land of the Roscicrucians"

As we were thus in conference, there came one that seemed to be a messenger, in a rich hue, that spake with the Jew, whereupon he turned to me and said, " You will pardon me, for I am commanded away in haste." The next morning he came to me joyful, and said—"There is word come to the Governor of the city that one of the Fathers of the Temple of the Rosie Cross, or Holy House, will be here this day seven-night. We have seen none of them this dozen years. His coming is in state, but the cause is secret. I will provide you and your fellows of a good standing to see his entry." I thanked him and said I was most glad of the news.

From the "New Atlantis"

God bless thee, my son; I will give thee the greatest jewel I have. For I will impart unto thee, for the love of God and men, a relation of the true state of Salomon's House. Son, to make you know the true state of Salomon's House, I will keep this order. First, I will set forth unto you the end of our foundation. Secondly, the preparations and instruments we have for our works. Thirdly, the several employments and functions whereto our fellows are assigned. And fourthly, the ordinances and rites which we observe. The End of our Foundation is the knowledge of Causes, and secret motions of things; and the enlarging of the bounds of Human Empire, to the effecting of all things possible.

From Heydon's "Voyage to the Land of the Roscicrucians"

God bless thee, my son; I will give thee the greatest jewel I have; I will impart unto thee, for the love of God and men, a relation of the true state of the Rosie Crosse. First, I will set forth the end of our foundation; secondly the preparations and instruments we have for our workes; thirdly, the several functions whereto our fellows are assigned; and fourthly, the ordinances and rights which we observe. The end of our foundation is the knowledge of causes and secret motions of things, and the enlarging of the bounds of Kingdoms to the effecting of all things possible.

That the order of the Rose-Cross was a Christian organization these extracts from the Rosicrucian prayer alone prove:—

Jesus Mihi Omnia

Oh Thou everywhere and good of all, whatsoever I do remember, I beseech Thee, that I am but dust, but as a vapour sprung from earth, which even Thy smallest breath can scatter. Thou hast given me a soul and laws to govern it; let that fraternal rule which Thou didst first appoint to sway man order me; make me careful to point at Thy glory in all my wayes, and where I cannot rightly know Thee, that not only my understanding but my ignorance may honour Thee— I cast myself as an honourer of Thee at Thy feet, and because I cannot be defended by Thee unless I believe after Thy laws, keep me, O my soul's Sovereign, in the obedience of Thy Will, and that I wound not conscience with vice and hiding Thy gifts and graces bestowed upon me, for this, I know, will destroy me within, and make Thy illumination Spirit leave me.

I am afraid I have already infinitely swerved from the revelations of that Divine Guide which Thou hast commanded to direct me to the truth, and for this I am a sad prostrate and penitent at the foot of Thy throne. I appeal only to the abundance of Thy remissions, O God, my God. For outward things I thank thee, and such as I have I give unto others, in the name of the Trinity, freely and faithfully..... In what Thou hast given me I am content— I beg no more than Thou hast given, and that to continue me uncontemnedly and upittiedly honest. Take me from myself and fill me but with Thee. Sum up Thy blessings in these two, that I may be rightly good and wise, and these, for Thy eternal truth's sake, grant and make grateful.(Waite, *The Real History*, et., pp. 444-61)

If the reader will compare this prayer with the acknowledged and unquestioned prayers of Francis Bacon, we are confident that he will not doubt that this is the coinage of the same brain and the expression of the same heart.

Francis Bacon's God

In 1968 Howard B. White published *Peace among the Willows*, the first book-length analysis of Bacon's "New Atlantis." White, a political theorist who regards Bacon as a principal shaper of modern political ideas, maintains that it is this utopian work and not one of Bacon's philosophical treatises that provides the fullest statement of Bacon's political theory. White is especially interested in what he regards as Bacon's secularization of politics and glorification of the power of science to serve the interests of the secular state.

In developing his argument, White maintains that "New Atlantis" must be read with meticulous care in order to understand Bacon's complex interweaving and transformation of political iconography, ancient history and fables, religious symbols, scientific methodologies, and pseudo-scientific concepts. White devotes considerable attention to Bacon's use of religious themes and argues that he manipulates them in order to subvert Christian ideas and transform them into a culturally acceptable justification for a preoccupation with luxury and materialism.

According to White, Bacon's purpose is to transform the human quest from the search for the "heavenly city" to the creation of the well-governed country, and to change the philosophical quest from an effort to understand God, God's Creation, and humanity's place in it to a pursuit to understand what humans can make of themselves.

White's work has been highly influential and augmented more recently by another political philosopher, Jerry Weinberger. Weinberger also argues that Bacon's utopia provides a primary source for understanding the transitional phase from early modern political ideas to those of the modern age, and he maintains that Bacon manipulates religious language and concepts to conceal his secular agenda. Recently, considerable attention to Bacon's "New Atlantis" has also come from the new historical criticism. Studies by Charles

Whitney, Amy Boesky, and others have analyzed utopian literature as a primary source for understanding the "founding fictions" and political ideologies underpinning nationalism, imperialism, colonialism, and overseas expansion. Like White and Weinberger, many cultural historians treat Bacon's manipulation of religious ideas as a way of providing cultural authority for his political agenda.

Marina Leslie, for example, asserts that Bacon inverts the spiritual and material worlds, and claims that Bacon transforms spiritual salvation into material well-being accomplished by humans and not by God.

David Innes, a theologian influenced by White, contends that Bacon is responsible for transmuting Christian hope for spiritual salvation into a secular dream of material comfort and argues that the Christianity of Bensalem is actually a "fundamental assault upon, transformation of and ultimate displacement of Christianity."

Denise Albanese asserts that Bensalemite Christianity "first serves as yet another instance of reverse colonialism, with the natives' conversion already an accomplished fact" and as the "code for an intellectual imperialism." This essay contends that it is a misunderstanding and distortion to view Bacon's use of religious language and concepts as disingenuous and manipulative. It demonstrates that Bacon's programme of utopian reform, as presented in "New Atlantis," is grounded in genuinely and deeply felt religious convictions, which serve as the foundation for his programme of political and social prosperity through the advancement of learning.

Developing the evidence to support a position that stands in marked contrast to prevailing interpretations requires careful attention to the details of Bacon's utopian narrative. We need to examine each episode of the story, from the storm that brings European sailors to Bensalem, through the Europeans' interviews with the Governor of the Strangers' House and with Joabin, to the climactic audience with a Father of Solomon's House. We need to pay careful attention to the accounts of Bensalem's conversion to Christianity and to the early history of Bensalem, Atlantis, and other great sea-going civilizations. While only one of these, the conversion to Christianity, is explicitly religious, examination of the other episodes demonstrates Bacon's pervasive use of two key religious themes: *providential deliverance* and *special election*. In discussing the primordial history of Bensalem and Atlantis, we need to compare Bacon's version of the myth of Atlantis to the one found in Plato's *Critias* and *Timaeus*. Bacon uses this primordial history to portray a golden age that has been virtually lost from memory; as a result, humanity has been left with a truncated account of its past achievements. Bacon refers to an ancient wisdom that has been lost and replaced by impotent, inferior philosophies. Yet the purpose of the Platonic myth in "New Atlantis" is to instill hope that this knowledge can be recovered and the state of civilizational excellence restored.

We then need to turn to the complex themes surrounding the activities of Solomon's House. This episode typically receives the most extended discussion, but the focus is usually on Bacon's description of collaborative efforts of specialized sciences to advance empirical knowledge and bring relief to the human condition. The analysis offered here will place Bacon's references to Solomon and Solomon's House in the context of the iconography of the court of the British King James I, particularly portrayals of James I as the new Solomon, who would restore Solomon's Temple and usher in a providential age of peace, harmony, and prosperity.

Bacon conceives of Solomon's House (i.e., the recovery of natural philosophy) as the complement to the rebuilding of Solomon's Temple (i.e., the restoration of true religion). This is the heart of Bacon's programme of instauration: first, a thoroughgoing reform of religion that restores humanity's relation to God, and second, a thoroughgoing recovery of the principles of natural philosophy that restores humanity's dominion over nature.

In the end, Bacon's "great instauration" is not a secular, scientific advance through which humanity gains dominion over nature and mastery of its own destiny. Bacon's instauration is a programme for rehabilitating humanity and its relation to nature, guided by divine Providence and achieved through pious human effort. To make this contrarian case, let us follow Bacon's story as it unfolds.

The Discovery of Bensalem

The story begins with a European expedition sailing from Peru en route to China and Japan being blown off course and becoming lost "in the greatest wilderness of the waters in the world." Helpless and disoriented, the sailors pray to God, begging for mercy and deliverance. Night closes in leaving them to wonder at their fate. When dawn comes, they discover that their prayers have been answered and they have been brought within sight of land. As they approach the uncharted island, people on shore warn the Europeans not to disembark. The Europeans beg for assistance explaining that they have several sick sailors on board, who might die without medical attention. In response to this urgent need, an official of the country sails out to their ship and offers provisions, medication, and repairs that will enable the Europeans to get underway. This offer is presented on a scroll written in four languages (Hebrew, Latin, Greek, and Spanish), and marked by a cross and a pair of cherubim's wings.

(The cross is an obvious Christian symbol, and cherubim's wings are a key symbol from the Old Testament, representing God's presence among His chosen people.) The apprehension of the Europeans is relieved by the obvious charity and learning of the inhabitants of this country, but most of all by the familiar sign of the cross. Similarly, the Bensalemites relax their guarded reception of the foreigners when they declare themselves to be from a Christian land, and the Europeans are invited to the island to recuperate.

This opening segment is noteworthy for its introduction of the leitmotif of divine intervention and salvation. In describing the event, the Europeans compare their experience to that of Jonah and acknowledge that it was divine grace that brought them to Bensalem. Were these the only references to deliverance or salvation, their significance could be discounted or attributed to the language conventions of Bacon's day. This is not the case, however. The theme of salvation and deliverance is developed further as the Europeans experience the charity of the Bensalemites. The sailors are so struck by the people and by the society that they declare that it "seemed to us that we have before us a picture of our salvation in heaven; for we that were awhile since in the jaws of death." On another occasion, they say that they had "come into a land of angels."

The Conversion of Bensalem

When given an opportunity to learn about this remarkable island, the first question that the Europeans hope to have answered is how the island had been converted to Christianity. The Governor of the Strangers' House explains that the conversion occurred as the result of a miraculous event which happened about twenty years after the Resurrection and Ascension. One night a great column of light topped by a cross appeared about a mile out on the ocean. A few brave souls from Renfusa, the nearest city, boarded boats and sailed out toward the hierophany.

When they had come within about 60 yards, they were mysteriously restrained from drawing closer. One of the boats, however, had a member of Solomon's House on board, who offered this prayer: "Lord God of Heaven and Earth, Thou hast vouchsafed of Thy grace to those of our order, to know Thy works of Creation, and the secrets of them; and to discern... between divine miracles, works of Nature, works of art, and impostures and illusions of all sorts." He then declared the column to be a genuine miracle and begged God to reveal its true meaning. The wise man was allowed to move closer, and, as he did, the Pillar of Cloud was transformed, leaving an ark (small chest) floating in the water.

As the wise man moved toward it, the chest opened to reveal a book and a letter. The book found in the ark contained canonical books familiar to the Europeans and "some other books of the New Testament which were not at that time written." The letter was from the apostle Bartholomew, who stated that he had received a vision in which God instructed him "to commit the ark to the floods of the sea." When the ark reached its appointed destination, the people of that land would receive "salvation and peace and goodwill from the Father and from the Lord Jesus."

Several aspects of this account deserve comment and development: Bensalem's conversion does not occur through ordinary missionary activity. It results from direct intervention by God, Who has chosen the island for a special benediction. In addition, Bensalem's conversion occurred shortly after Christ's Ascension—a period when Christ's teachings and deeds were vivid in the minds of the apostles.

The Christianity of Bensalem, therefore, is pure and unadulterated by the human error and misinterpretation that occur with the passage of time. This is a primary difference between Europe and Bensalem. The sacred texts available to the Bensalemites are more extensive than those available to European Christianity.

So, another contrast between Bensalem and Europe is that Bensalem not only has a pure form of gospel Christianity, it also has a fuller scriptural base to guide it. Moreover, the Bensalemites have evidently been able to preserve the purity of the Christian kerygma and have founded a true Christian kingdom: one that the Europeans likened to Heaven and its inhabitants to angels. Again, the purity of religion in Bensalem stands in contrast to the degenerated Christianity of Europe, where doctrinal disputes and ecclesiastical corruption have contaminated the lifeblood of the faith.

The ark that brings salvation to Bensalem calls to mind the ark that saved Noah and his family from the devastating flood that destroyed all other peoples. An ark is also an integral part of the history of God's selection of the Hebrews as His chosen people. The culminating event of the Exodus-Sinai experience is Moses' placement of the God-given law in the Ark of the Covenant, which served as the throne of God's presence among His chosen people. This ark is, therefore, the most sacred object in Hebrew history, playing a ritual role in the crossing of the Jordan River into the Promised Land, the establishment of the Davidic-Solomonic kingship, and in the consecration of Jerusalem as the seat of religious and political order. The ark functions similarly in the account of Bensalem's conversion, where it is a prime symbol of the special election of the Bensalemites as God's new chosen people. Perhaps this is why the country is named Bensalem (heir of peace or inheritor of Jerusalem's renown). The name also establishes a parallel with England as the New Jerusalem, a common apocalyptic motif during the reign of James I, who was portrayed as the new Solomon who would install the new Jerusalem. The choice of Bartholomew as the apostle who receives the vision and sends the ark on its way is also noteworthy in three ways.

First, according to tradition, Bartholomew was the great missionary to the remote parts of the world: India, Persia, and Mesopotamia. Second, Bartholomew is the apostle who had a special ability to receive and interpret dreams and revelations. Finally, tradition holds that Bartholomew was the author of two non-canonical works: "The Gospel of Bartholomew" and "The Book of the Resurrection of Christ," both of which contain accounts of Christ's Resurrection, harrowing of Hell, and rescue of Adam. Bartholomew is thus another important symbol of a pure religion capable of healing the ruptured union with God and recovering humanity's condition prior to the Fall. These symbols and episodes of providential rescue refer to an entire people or nation, not a few select individuals. The Pillar of Cloud and the Ark are symbols of the selection of the Hebrews as God's chosen people. Adam, as his name indicates, represents humanity. Even Jonah's rescue is a prelude to the conversion of the people of Nineveh. Within the "New Atlantis," salvation also comes to the entire nation. And the European sailors, in the context of this utopia, are representative of European society as the whole.

The function of the member of Solomon's House is important to note and to understand properly. Though this appearance is brief, it establishes Solomon's House as the interpreter of both natural and supernatural or divine events. So from the first, Solomon's House is presented in a religious context, not as a secular, scientific think tank. The description of the activities of Solomon's House, provided in a later interview, makes it clear that the Brethren study the Creation in order to better understand God. Theirs is a pious search for the benefits in nature provided by the divine.

Howard White is wrong, therefore, when he says that the ability to interpret the miracle only serves to grant "power over miracles to the wise men of Solomon's House" and means "control of natural philosophy over theology." The wise man is not a secular scientist able to command the supernatural to obey; he is devoted to the search for truth in its natural and its supernatural forms. The demeanor of the member of Solomon's House is reverent: He prays to God to reveal the meaning of a supernatural event that he is able to recognize as a miracle, but which he cannot interpret without divine revelation.The role of the wise man in the episode is also important in coming to understand why Bensalem was chosen for this special benediction. Christian revelation comes to the land because the Bensalemites already believed in an all-knowing, all-powerful God; they devoted efforts to studying both the natural and the divine and were able to distinguish the two. That the ark comes to Bensalem is, therefore, not a result of accident or caprice. God selects Bensalem because it is capable of receiving and perpetuating a pure form of gospel Christianity.

The account of the island's conversion establishes parallels between the experience of the Bensalemites and those who first received the good news of Christ's birth. The community that first sees the hierophany is called "Renfusa," or sheep people. The person on the ship who is able to interpret the miracle is a wise man. This parallels the miraculous announcement of the birth of the Messiah to the shepherds and to the Magi. White chooses to associate the name of the community with gullibility, and Laurence Lampert claims that Renfusa is evidence that "Christianity was introduced by a wise scientist as an instrument to lead the sheep." But these interpretations are difficult to maintain or support when the reference to Renfusa is read in relation to the other symbols and motifs associated with the conversion of Bensalem.

Why Bensalem Remains Hidden

During the second interview with the Governor of the Strangers' House, the Europeans ask why such a great civilization has chosen to remain hidden from the rest of humanity, while it obviously knows about all other existing civilizations, including Europe. The Governor begins his answer with an account of ancient history virtually unknown to the Europeans. In the distant past, worldwide navigation and commerce were commonplace, until disrupted by natural catastrophe. The only vestige of the golden age known to the Europeans is in Plato's account of the glorious civilization of Atlantis, which was destroyed by earthquake and flood as punishment for its avarice and will to power.

According to the Governor's account, the early history of navigation was far more advanced than even the impressive recent accomplishments of the Europeans. In the ancient past, many great civilizations sailed to the farthest regions of the world and carried on trade with Bensalem and its neighbor Atlantis. This period was brought to an end by earthquakes and floods that "Divine Revenge" used to punish Atlantis for its proud enterprises. These calamities devastated the country, the people, and the great civilization that they had created. Human civilization was never fully able to recover following these catastrophes; the civilization of Atlantis left only the primitive culture of America and the New World.

"So you see," the Governor explains, "by this main accident of time, we lost our traffic with the Americans.... As for the other parts of the world, it is most manifest that in the ages following (whether it were in respect of wars, or by a natural revolution of time) navigation did every where greatly decay; and specially far voyages."

This account explains how other civilizations had been cut off from Bensalem and how knowledge of its greatness had been lost to the rest of the world. It does not explain, however, why Bensalem chose to keep its existence secret even though it was in contact with other nations. To give an adequate explanation requires the Governor to discuss the policies of the great king Solamona and his creation of Solomon's House.

The Governor explains that about 1,900 years earlier the Bensalemite king Solamona decided that his nation was far superior to all others in every way and could not benefit from direct intercourse with them. His country was wholly self-sufficient, morally upright, and could be "a thousand ways altered to the worse, but scarce any one way to the better" from traffic with other civilizations.

For this reason, he took steps to prevent the influx of customs and ideas from inferior nations. One of his steps was to offer to allow all foreign travelers to take up residence in Bensalem rather than return to their own countries. The Governor reports that this policy had been followed ever since and only thirteen individuals ever chose to leave during the 1,900-year span. As a result, almost nothing has been reported back to other nations in two millennia; and the few reports that were made were dismissed as fantasy because the quality of life in Bensalem seemed to be an improbable delusion.

King Solamona also prohibited his subjects from leaving to prevent them from revealing too much or from becoming corrupted by what they encountered abroad. Only members of Solomon's House are sent on secret reconnaissance missions. The purpose of these trips is to gather information about other nations, especially the "sciences, arts, manufacturers, and inventions of all the world; and withal to bring unto us books, instruments, and patterns in every kind."

The Governor makes it clear that the purpose of these efforts is not to acquire "gold, silver, or jewels; nor for silks; nor for spices; nor any other commodity of matter; but only for God's first creature, which was Light." The Governor explains that King Solamona created Solomon's House to "find out the true nature of all things; (whereby God might have the more glory in the workmanship of them, and men the more fruit in the use of them)."

This parenthetic statement links the pious study of the Creation and devotion to the Creator with the discovery of the benefits God placed in nature for humanity's use. As we will see, Bacon repeatedly warns that humanity cannot gain the benefits in nature without proper piety.

The Governor next explains that the name Solomon's House is inspired by the biblical Solomon's reputation for wisdom; but the Governor adds that Bensalem possessed Solomon's *Natural History,* a text which was lost to the Europeans. This text held special knowledge of the workings of nature, which Solomon's House used as the foundation of its remarkable work.

Following his description of the founding of the House of Solomon, and of the reconnaissance missions of its members, the Governor offers to help the Europeans return to their country or to allow them to stay in Bensalem. The Europeans enthusiastically accept the offer to stay. This account introduces or reinforces several critical themes:

Atlantis is destroyed by the gods because of its drive to expand its empire through conquest and world domination. This *libido dominandi* stands in stark contrast to Bensalem, which is characterized as an embodiment of the cardinal Christian virtues of faith, charity, peace, and justice. Even after the series of natural disasters, which weakened or destroyed other civilizations, Bensalem does not seize the opportunity to invade lands and enslave their inhabitants. Instead, it chooses to withdraw in order to live in peace. While Atlantis used navigation and exploration for material gain, Bensalem seeks knowledge that it can use for the welfare of its people.

The activities of Solomon's House have theological as well as scientific dimensions. The study of nature, which brings practical benefits, is also a study of the Creation in order to know the Creator. In addition, the account of the conversion of Bensalem to Christianity makes it clear that the members of Solomon's House are able to discern the miraculous from the natural. This episode contains another reference to sacred texts unknown or lost to Europe, and these texts play an essential role in the well-being of the nation and its people.

It is important to recognize that the age of Solamona and the founding of Solomon's House occur before the conversion to Christianity. The island, therefore, is already devoted to the spiritual and material well-being of its inhabitants. Perhaps this is why it is chosen by God for a "special benediction."

In the discussion of the conversion to Christianity, reference was made to Bartholomew and the two writings attributed to him, which described Christ's harrowing of Hell and rescue of Adam. Before the Fall, humanity had dominion over nature and was able to draw from Creation all of the benefits that God had placed in it. The work of Solomon's House reflects this prelapsarian condition in which humanity has mastery over nature and is able to create paradisiacal conditions.

Finally, it is important to note that Bensalem is the only civilization that has been spared devastation. Neither natural catastrophes nor the ravages of war have interrupted its history. It is able to preserve ancient truth and build upon it rather than being reduced to an primitive state of subsistence living and intellectual poverty.

These themes need further investigation in order to understand how they contribute to Bacon's concept of instauration. But three other episodes need to be examined first: the "Feast of the Family" ceremony, the meeting with Joabin, and the audience with a Father from Solomon's House.

The Feast of the Family

As already noted, the Europeans readily accept the Governor's invitation to become citizens. They move about the country in an attempt to learn more about its customs and practices, and soon they have the opportunity to observe the Feast of the Family ceremony. The account of the Feast of the Family serves primarily as a model to juxtapose to the pervasive disorder in European society, a theme which is taken up again during the Europeans' meeting with Joabin. Briefly, the stated purpose of the ceremony is to honor the patriarch of a family, who has supplied the king with many subjects. The celebration is thus a ritual affirmation of the abundance and prosperity of the country.

More than fecundity is being celebrated, however. The ceremony stresses the patriarch's role as the source of order, justice, and moral instruction within the family and by extension within the nation as a whole. The patriarch's first ceremonial duty, for example, is to resolve any conflict within the family before the actual celebration can begin. Moreover, the honor accorded the patriarch is proportional to the success of his children as productive, responsible citizens of the state. That the moral dimension of family life is central to the ceremony and to the well-being of the country is made clear in the discussion with Joabin.

This discussion begins when the European narrator asks Joabin if polygamy is practiced in Bensalem (since it is obvious that the country honors large families). "I desired to know of him what laws and customs they had concerning marriage; and whether they kept marriage well; and whether they were tied to one wife? For that where population is so much affected [desired] and such as with them it seemed to be, there is commonly permission of plurality of wives."

Joabin replies that the marital bond is the nucleus of familial and social order in Bensalem and that the people are not given to passion or sexual excess: "there are no stews [brothels], no dissolute houses, no courtesans, nor any thing of that kind." He adds, however, that his familiarity with the deplorable condition of European society allows him to understand how such a question might be the paramount interest and logical assumption of the Europeans.

"They [the Bensalemites] say ye have put marriage out of office: for marriage is ordained the remedy for unlawful concupiscence; and natural concupiscence seemeth as a spur to marriage. But when men have at hand a remedy more agreeable to their corrupt will, marriage is almost expulsed." This passage is followed by a scathing criticism of libidinal immorality in Europe that has destroyed the family, the desire for children, and the orderly social life that emerges from a stable family. The disorder resulting from libidinal corruption in individuals is compounded by misguided social customs and laws. In order to prevent the greater evils of adultery, the deflowering of virgins, and unnatural lust, society permits "change and the delight in meretricious embracements."

Such compromises and accommodations, however, are destined to fail. According to Joabin, lust is like a furnace: If you stop the flames altogether, it will go out, "but if you give it any vent, it will rage." He then asserts that vice and corrupt appetites reflect a profound disorder of the soul that obstructs religious and moral instruction, and without a firm moral and religious base, no society can endure. The analysis here is restricted to the most literal meaning of the text. We shall see later that Bacon repeatedly uses the "marriage" image in reference to the productive union of the mind with nature. This image is contrasted to the sterile state when men become obsessed with their intellectual creations.

Joabin the Jew

The exchange between Joabin and the Europeans is interrupted by a messenger who has come to tell Joabin that a Father of Solomon's House is going to visit the city and Joabin is needed to help make suitable arrangements. Although Joabin appears only briefly, his role in Bacon's parable is crucial. The references to Solomon's House and Joabin's name provide the principal clue to his role in Bacon's parable. The stem of Joabin's name is Joab. The biblical Joab was one of King David's generals, whose most important role was in retrieving the Ark of the Covenant from the Philistines.

As we have already noted, the Ark of the Covenant is the prime symbol of the Hebrews election as God's special people. The Ark's recovery and subsequent placement in the Temple were essential elements of the establishment of Jerusalem as a religious and political centre for the Jewish people. So there is a direct connection between the biblical Joab, Jerusalem, and Solomon's Temple. Joabin also has a key function in Bensalem and an important tie to the activities of Solomon's House. These equivalences of symbolization augment the earlier discussion of King Solamona and reinforce other symbols that associate Bensalem with God's chosen people and the New Jerusalem.

Joabin's connection with other key themes in "New Atlantis" is found in his account of the ancestry of the Bensalemites. According to Joabin, the people of Bensalem are descended from Abraham and their laws were given by Moses.

The descent from Abraham is supposed to come from his son Nachoran. Joabin's statement, therefore, provides a further link of the Bensalemites to a biblical benediction (Abraham is described elsewhere in "New Atlantis" as "Father of the faithful"). The reference to Moses includes the statement that he "by a secret cabala ordained the laws of Bensalem which they now use." The political order of Bensalem, therefore, is founded on God's law.

But the law available to Bensalem extends beyond the Old Testament. It includes the secret teachings revealed to Moses during the 40 days on Mount Sinai. While Joabin speaks specifically of the Cabala in relation to political law, mention of the Cabala reinforces the discussion of Solomon's *Natural History*: From the Middle Ages into the Renaissance there was a widespread tradition that the secret teachings given to Moses were preserved in the Ark of the Covenant and transmitted to Solomon. This complex of symbolic linkages between Bensalem and Jerusalem, Solomon's Temple, and Solomon's House is further augmented by the initial description of Joabin as a Jew unlike those in Europe. The chief difference between the Jews of Bensalem and the Jews of Europe is that the Bensalemite Jews expect that the coming of the Messiah will usher in a New Jerusalem or a Kingdom of God on earth, and they expect that the king of Bensalem, as a representative of a people who have received a special benediction, will sit on the right hand of the enthroned messiah.

Joabin's function, therefore, is to set the stage for the discussion of Solomon's House by introducing symbolic linkages between Solomon's House and Solomon's Temple. Joabin also serves as a representative of a pure form of Judaism, which complements Bensalem's pure form of Christianity. Joabin's pure form of Judaism follows the traditions of Abraham and Moses, respects Christianity, and waits for the Messiah, who will deliver His chosen people from spiritual and temporal disorder. Joabin's identification of Bensalem as a chosen people, whose king will sit on the right hand of God, reinforces the emphasis on piety, charity, faith, and good works as the traits of God's chosen people. God's "chosen" do not belong to a specific ethnic group. They are those who attempt to live under the Old and New Covenants.

The Father of Solomon's House

Shortly after Joabin is called away to assist with the arrival of the Father from Solomon's House, the narrator gives a detailed description of the pomp and ceremony surrounding the Father's entry into the city. The people crowd the streets to catch a glimpse of this high-level state official, who is surrounded by religious paraphernalia. His attendants, for example, carry a crosier, a symbol of ecclesiastical authority, and a staff, a symbol of pastoral function. Moreover, his demeanor is clearly ecclesiastical—he "held up his bare hand as he went, as blessing the people." Because the Europeans have heard about and seen how highly the Brethren are valued, they are anxious for an opportunity to gain an audience, and Joabin is able to make the arrangements. This interview is the climactic episode of "New Atlantis."

When the Europeans enter, the Father greets them with a gesture of blessing, and they kneel to kiss the hem of his robe (as they have been instructed). The Father then provides an extended account of the purpose, the activities, and the contributions of Solomon's House. The purpose is first succinctly stated: "The End of our Foundation is the knowledge of Causes and secret motions of things; and the enlarging of the bounds of Human Empire, to the effecting of all things possible." A detailed description of the investigation of the natural world then follows: from caves to mountain observatories to marine investigations.

These investigations produce a breadth and depth of knowledge beyond anything imagined in Europe. But these investigations are only the preliminary stage. The intent is to use them to improve the human condition through the improvement of existing orders and to create new phenomena. Experiments in the Lower Region, for example, produce new artificial metals, which are used for curing diseases. There is also a "great variety of composts, and of soils, for the making of the earth fruitful." There are also a number of artificial wells and fountains, including one called Water of Paradise, which was created by the brethren "for health and the prolongation of life." The Father further indicates that "we have also large and various orchards and gardens... [and] make them also by art greater much than their nature; and their fruit greater and sweeter.... And many of them we so order as they become of medicinal use." The Father also explains that Solomon's House has apothecaries, centers for the mechanical arts, furnaces, laboratories for light, acoustics, as well as houses for the study and exposure of deceit, impostures, and illusions.

The Father next explains the duties or offices of the various members, which include advancing the practical aspects of research, developing new theoretical insights, and producing new products and inventions that benefit the nation. The Europeans are told that Solomon's House guards its work carefully and takes pains to prevent the government or the citizenry from obtaining information that might be misunderstood or misused.

This last statement—along with the earlier statement that foreign travel is restricted to members of Solomon's House—has prompted extensive comment by White, Weinberger, Boesky, and others, who see these practices as further evidence of totalitarian state control or evidence of the creation of scientists as a new political-intellectual elite, who are able to provide creature comforts to the citizens and produce political order and stability for political rulers. Such interpretations fail to take into account Bacon's concept of human nature, which is based upon the concept of Original Sin.

Since the Fall, humans are prone to being self-centered and inclined to become preoccupied with material concerns. Only the members of Solomon's House have attained the level of spiritual discipline to overcome this materialistic preoccupation and use the rich benefits to be derived from God's Creation for charitable purposes.

The Father ends by describing daily religious observances intended, evidently, to remind the brethren of their religious and moral obligations to use their God-given wisdom prudently: "We have certain hymns and services, which we say daily, of laud, and thanks to God for his marvellous works: and forms of prayers, imploring his aid and blessing for the illumination of our labours, and the turning of them into good and holy uses." Here is another instance where Bacon associates knowledge of nature with piety and charity, which Bacon contrasts to the sins of pride and selfishness. Shortly after the statement that "we do also declare natural divinations of diseases, plagues, swarms of harmful creatures, scarcity, tempests, earthquakes, great inundations, comets and (etc.)," the text breaks off.

This account of the collective efforts to advance the theoretical and practical applications of the study of nature is the reason some scholars describe Solomon's House as a model for the Royal Society. But the analysis offered here demonstrates that Bacon presents Solomon's House after establishing a context of religious imagery of salvation, deliverance, and rehabilitation. We need, therefore, to consider the function of Solomon's House in relation to these motifs in more detail, especially the motifs of rescue and renewal. More specifically, we need to examine the linkages Bacon establishes between Bensalem's Solamona and the biblical Solomon and between Solomon's House and Solomon's Temple. For it is here that we might discover the true character of Bacon's concept of instauration.

Solamona and Solomon's House

We should begin by recalling the Governor's account of King Solamona and his founding of Solomon's House:

There reigned in this island, about nineteen hundred years ago, a King whose memory of all others we most adore; not superstitiously, but as a divine instrument, though a mortal man; his name was Solamona: and we esteem him as the lawgiver of our nation. This king had a *large heart*, inscrutable for good; and was wholly bent to make his kingdom and people happy.... [A]mongst the excellent acts of that king, one above all hath the preeminence. It was the erection and institution of an Order or Society which we call *Salomon's House*; the noblest foundation (as we think) that ever was upon the earth; and the lanthorn of this kingdom. It is dedicated to the study of the Works and Creatures of God. Some think it beareth the founder's name a little corrupted, as if it should be Solamona's House. But the records write it as it is spoken. So as I take it to be denominate of the King of the Hebrews, which is famous with you, and no stranger to us. For we have some parts of his works which with you are lost; namely, that Natural History which he wrote, of all plants, from the *cedar of Libanus* to the *moss that groweth out of the wall*, and of all *things that have life and motion*. (emphasis added)

The first notable feature of this account is the connection between Solamona's "large heart," that is, his piety and charity, and the establishment of Solomon's House. Bacon's reference to Solamona's "large heart" evokes the use of the phrase in I Kings 4:29 to describe Solomon. According to the text, Solomon found favor with God and God offered to grant him any wish. Solomon asked for wisdom in order to be able to rule his kingdom with intelligence and compassion. The request pleased God and it was granted. God also gave Solomon great material wealth as well. The biblical reference to a "large heart" is augmented in the Governor's account of Solamona's reign, describing the king's devotion to making his kingdom and his people happy and to perpetuating peace and prosperity.

This emphasis on the benevolence of the king also defines his kingship in terms of the primary Christian virtue: charity. "New Atlantis" makes it clear that benevolence and charity are the motives for Solamona's establishing Solomon's House. It is referred to several times as "the lanthorn of the kingdom," providing enlightenment and prosperity; enlightenment encompasses religious knowledge as well as philosophical knowledge of the workings of nature that can be applied for the benefit of humanity. Scholars who are determined to portray Bacon as an advocate of imperialism and colonization continue to overlook the Solomonic model of political order that is so obvious here and in Bacon's other writings.

Solomon's House and Bacon's Instauration

While Bacon uses biblical descriptions of Solomon's piety

and charity to link Solamona's kingship with the Hebrew King, he significantly modifies the conventional notions of Solomonic wisdom. The famous biblical account of the judgment of Solomon accents the psychological insight that allowed him to understand his subjects and to rule them justly. In "New Atlantis," Bacon associates Solomonic wisdom with his understanding of the workings of nature, and the Governor claims that Bensalem possesses a copy of Solomon's *Natural History;* and its ongoing work advances the knowledge it contains. There is, of course, no mention of this *Natural History* in the biblical accounts. Bacon makes the biblical connection by quoting fragments from the biblical description of Solomon's knowledge of the natural order: "of all plants, from the *cedar of Libanus* to *the moss that groweth out of the wall,* and of *all things that have life and motion.*" Bacon connects Solomonic knowledge to charity and piety; the work of Solomon's House brings relief to "man's estate" and demonstrates the love and mercy of the Creator.

The transformation of the attributes of Solomonic wisdom is complemented by transformation of the Solomonic Temple into Solomon's House. Charles Whitney has provided the most penetrating study of this transformation, and has shown how the references to the biblical Solomon and to the appropriation of the Solomonic Temple are tied to Bacon's concept of instauration. As Whitney explains, the Vulgate edition of the Bible created a typology that centered on the apocalyptic motif of the rebuilding of the Temple of Jerusalem. Because the Temple held the Ark of the Covenant, it stood as a symbol of God's presence among the Hebrews and associated the kingdom with religious piety and justice. It also identified the kingdom as the agency for both God's justice and His mercy. The kingdom reached its zenith during the reign of Solomon, when the Hebrews enjoyed unprecedented prosperity and freedom from religious or political interference by neighboring powers. After Solomon, however, the Hebrew nation was overrun and lost its political autonomy and religious freedom. In 624 B.C., pressure from neighboring powers waned, and the young king Josiah was able to institute political and religious reforms, including rebuilding of the Temple. During reconstruction, the Temple's Mosaic Law (the Deuteronomic Code) was rediscovered, and this crucial recovery was interpreted as the beginning of a renewed covenant with God. The biblical account makes it clear that the project of rebuilding was understood as providentially guided and signaled the restoration of God's relation to the people. The term used in the Vulgate for the rebuilding is *instauro,* which has the dual meaning of building up (construction) and rebuilding.

Whitney demonstrates that Bacon uses the notion of instauration as no previous author had, making it the root symbol for his programme. Moreover, according to Whitney, Bacon employs the connotation of building or rebuilding as edification or re-edification. The word *edifice* and its derivatives can denote a physical structure or can refer to the building up or construction of knowledge (*edification*). Bacon chooses to emphasize the latter. For him, instauration depends upon a recovery of knowledge that clears away accumulated epistemological errors and re-establishes a proper foundation. This notion of instauration is developed in "New Atlantis" by utilizing the dual meaning of edifice and edification. King Solamona builds an edifice—Solomon's House—that is responsible for rebuilding and advancing knowledge (edification).

According to Whitney, Bacon's emphasis on the revitalization of natural philosophy, that is, the rebuilding of Solomon's House, displaces the biblical notion of a spiritual recovery and advance represented by the apocalyptic motif of the rebuilding of Solomon's Temple. But this is incorrect: "New Atlantis" does not depict Solomon's House as a displacement of Solomon's Temple; it presents it as its complement. In "New Atlantis" Bacon several times demonstrates the importance of purified religion as a spiritual basis for the well-being of the people and associates it with providential action on behalf of the people.

Bacon does not dismiss or displace the idea of spiritual renewal; indeed, regulation of gospel Christianity was one of his principal concerns. He chooses, however, to emphasize what for him is an equally important part of recovery or rebuilding: to rebuild natural philosophy so that human beings can recover the benefits God instilled in Creation. The description of Solomon's House makes it clear that its first pursuit is light. Light as enlightenment is a basic religious motif, and Bacon never changes its religious connotation.

At the same time, natural philosophy leads not only to reverence for God and God's Creation but also provides practical insights into how to relieve human suffering and improve the human condition. While others stress the need for spiritual regeneration, Bacon emphasizes the need for the complementary instauration of knowledge. While the symbolic ties between Solomon's Temple and Solomon's House are the key to understanding Bacon's concept of instauration, they do not explain how Bacon's instauration of knowledge involves recovery and rebuilding in the way that the apocalyptic dream of rebuilding Solomon's Temple does. To adequately develop this concept requires an examination of the Governor's account of the prehistory of Bensalem and Atlantis, an episode that has been largely ignored by most scholars.

The Prehistory of Civilization

According to the Governor, Bensalem, Atlantis, and civilizations from the far-flung corners of the world carried out a mutual exchange of learning and material goods, while living in peace. A series of cataclysms destroyed the other great civilizations and left most nations in an infantile state, having lost all records of their previous greatness and all ability to restore themselves to their former condition. Not only were the civilizations reduced to infancy and the memory of their own past greatness eclipsed, they also forgot about the other great civilizations as well.

Consequently, Bensalem, the only civilization to be spared, chooses to remain obscure; the country has nothing to gain and much to lose by making itself known to the rest of the world. As previously noted, the island does continue to monitor developments in other countries throughout the world and brings back any information that can be used by Bensalem.

The most learned and incorruptible inhabitants of Bensalem, the members of Solomon's House, carry out these expeditions in secret, however. In recounting these remarkable events, the Bensalemite official notes that the only records of the great primeval age available to the Europeans are the brief references in the work of "one of your philosophers."

The allusion is to Plato's discussion of the golden age of Athens and to the demise of the great sea-going empire, Atlantis, found in the *Timaeus* and the *Critias*. As Plato retells in recounting the fate of Athens and other countries, "your people and the others are but newly equipped, every time, with letters and all such arts as civilized States require; and when, after the usual interval of years, like a plague, the flood from heaven comes sweeping down afresh upon your people, it leaves none but you the unlettered and uncultured so that you become young as ever, with no knowledge of all that happened in old times in this land or in your own."

The purpose of the Platonic accounts of the fate of Atlantis and of a golden age virtually lost from memory is made clear in the opening dialogue of the *Timaeus*. The participants in the dialogue are discussing the best form of society. Their intent is to limit the discussion to actually existing societies, not unattainable ideal states. But the dialogue makes it clear that the historical horizon has to be expanded beyond the immediate past. The present age is not one in which humanity has realized its full potential. It is a period of iron, not gold.

In the Platonic dialogues, it is evident that the primary difference between the primordial golden age and the current state of degeneration lies in the eclipse of knowledge of the divine and in the loss of the skills of divination, medicine, engineering, agriculture, and navigation.

In the Platonic context, then, it is clear that an essential requirement for recovering the capacity for human excellence lies in re-attaining the original, pure forms of knowledge. The two Platonic myths, taken together, give an account of the creation of the cosmos and the primordial age before man's hubris led to corruption and degeneration. After the cosmos is created, the gods amicably divide the territories. Athena, for example, becomes the patroness of Athens, and Poseidon becomes the patron of Atlantis. The human race that the gods create is a combination of divine spirit and matter. The gods' gifts to the human race include an idyllic world, and human beings have dominion over all terrestrial things.

Using their god-given abilities, they are able to accomplish great feats of engineering and navigation. The Atlantans, as the children of Poseidon, were especially accomplished navigators. But the idyllic age is destroyed when the material aspect of human nature gained prominence. The predominance of the material leads to avarice and to the will to dominate and control, and Atlantis uses its navigational skills to subjugate other civilizations. According to the *Critias*, the hubris of Atlantis is brought to an end by the gods. Zeus, the god of justice, calls a council of the gods to decide on a proper punishment.

This punishment must be severe enough to end Atlantis's marauding, but it is not to be so severe as to annihilate Atlantis. The text states that Atlantis can be brought back again at some future date. White has incorrectly characterized this ending speech by Zeus as being about destruction. In fact, Zeus is the minister of justice and is responsible for the restoration of order. The Atlantans have violated their place in the order of things and that order has to be restored by the gods. The emphasis is not on destruction; it is on the restoration of order. And the punishment is not to be a total destruction. While order must be restored in the present, Atlantis will have an opportunity to rise again in the future. This promise of restoration perhaps explains why Bacon chooses to call his text "New Atlantis."

Perhaps Bacon uses the myth of Atlantis and the promise or restoration (instauration) to complement the prevalent apocalyptic theme in England of the re-establishing of Jerusalem. While James I exploited the political elements of the idea of a renewal of the Solomonic kingdom, the primary association was with religious renewal. And, as we have noted, Bacon regarded the renewal of natural philosophy as the necessary complement to the religious renewal that was underway. Bacon apparently wishes to augment the apocalyptic religious images associated with the New Jerusalem with the prospects of the renewal of Atlantis. Atlantis was known for its engineering and navigation, and its great accomplishments in these areas reflected its wise use of the gifts the gods had provided.

Atlantis only declined after it fell away from divine intent and became dominated by material concerns. Its renewal would be allowed by the gods, once Atlantis had come to recognize the errors of its ways and had returned to a spiritual state. Perhaps Bacon intends to suggest that England's spiritual renewal coupled with his reform of knowledge will permit it to emulate the engineering and navigational feats of Atlantis; therefore, England can become the new Atlantis.

And, of course, a chastened Atlantis would also greatly resemble Bensalem. If this is Bacon's intent, then it might also explain why Bacon leaves his story incomplete. Bacon is proposing that England continue its emphasis on religious recovery and begin the recovery of natural philosophy. Whether this will be done or not is out of Bacon's hands. It will depend on whether or not James I is like Solomon and Solamona and will choose to implement the pious study of nature in order to draw from Creation the benefits that God has provided. There are, of course, significant differences in Bacon's uses of the myth of a primordial age of human excellence and those of Plato. The focus of the Platonic dialogue is on the development of right political order.

Bacon's interest in political order and disorder is secondary. His utopia makes it clear that political order derives from right religion and the proper study of nature. One of the biggest obstructions to the recovery of right knowledge—in Bacon's view—is the misplaced reverence for Platonic and Aristotelian philosophy. Through the Platonic dialogues and Bacon's own account of the prehistory of the world, we are shown that the period of Greek civilization valued by the Europeans is not an age of wisdom and high civilizational attainment. It is a period of infancy or childhood following on natural calamities. Most efforts were necessarily devoted to subsistence living; and once a civilization was stable enough to devote itself to considerations of political order and justice or to the study of the natural order, it would have little or no frame of reference, because the records of the great achievements of the past had been lost. Bacon makes this point in "New Atlantis" by having the Governor of the House of Strangers tell them first that there are Scriptures and ecclesiastical traditions that are not available in Europe, and then he tells them that Bensalem possesses Solomon's natural history which is unknown in Europe.

Moreover, his description of the activities of Solomon's House clearly do not follow Platonic or Aristotelian methods of investigation and deduction. They are based upon more ancient and purer forms of philosophy. The significance of the ancient wisdom for the (re)building of knowledge is presented in Bacon's *Wisdom of the Ancients* of 1609, which augments the primordial history of Atlantis and Bensalem. By examining the key themes in this work, we can more fully understand Bacon's description of the work of Solomon's House and how the recovery of ancient wisdom relates to Bacon's instauration of natural philosophy.

Ancient Wisdom and the Instauration of Knowledge

In the preface to *Wisdom of the Ancients,* Bacon explains that the fables of Homer and Hesiod "must be regarded as neither being the inventions nor belonging to the age of the poets themselves, but as sacred relics and light airs breathing out of better times, that were caught from the traditions of more ancient nations and so received into the flutes and trumpets of the Greeks." The problem is that their true meaning has been lost, obscured, or distorted over time; and previous generations have been unqualified to interpret them. Bacon's purpose, therefore, is to re-present the fables and give them their proper interpretation.

For the present purpose, our discussion can be confined to the fable of Orpheus, which is for Bacon the story of the decline of philosophy as it descends from the natural philosophy of the ancient wisemen to moral and civil philosophy and finally to a state of almost total disintegration. In its pristine state, according to Bacon, "natural philosophy proposes to itself as its noblest work of all, nothing less than the restitution and renovation [*instauratio*] of things corruptible, and (what is indeed the same thing in a lower degree) the conservation of bodies in the state in which they are, and the retardation of dissolution and putrefaction." he effort at retardation, however, means arduous labour, and failure leads to frustration and to the adoption of the easier task—the management of human affairs through moral and civil philosophy.

This stage of philosophy remains stable for a while, but it too declines with the passage of time, and moral and civil laws are put to silence. And if such troubles last, Bacon warns, "it is not for long before letters also and philosophy are so torn in pieces that no traces of them can be found but a few fragments, scattered here and there." When philosophy and civilization reach this low point, barbarism sets in and disorder prevails "until, according to the appointed vicissitude of things, they break out and issue forth again, perhaps among other nations, and not in the places where they were before."

Three elements of this Baconian fable are worthy of emphasis. The pure, original philosophy takes as its task the restitution and renovation of things corruptible. This god-given ability is lost through the lack of human effort and will. The decline, however, is not permanent. According to "the appointed vicissitude of things"—which is to say, providential intervention—true philosophy will return, and humanity will be restored to its primordial condition, but not necessarily in the place it originated.

With this brief discussion of Bacon's fable of the degeneration of the original, pure form of philosophy in mind, we can now better understand the activities of Solomon's House as the preservation and perpetuation of natural philosophy in its original, pure form. The investigations of Solomon's House are aimed at finding "the knowledge of Causes, and secret motions of things"; they produce new artificial metals, which are used for curing diseases, and blended mineral waters created by the brethren "for health and prolongation of life." The activities of Solomon's House are reminiscent of Bacon's accounts in *Wisdom of the Ancients* of the original, pure philosophy used to retard age, prolong life, and restore corruptible things to their original, pure state.

This emphasis on the restitution of health and the prolongation of life runs throughout "New Atlantis," and no function of Solomon's House appears to be more important. The European sailors who are sick are given a fruit with remarkable restorative properties; it causes the sick to think that they had been "cast into some Divine Pool of healing." White and others see this emphasis on "prolonging life" and drawing other benefits from nature as evidence of Bacon's materialism and secularism. It is more accurate to see these results as evidence that the reverent study of nature by Solomon's House allows them to overcome the alienation from God and nature that is the consequence of Original Sin. The Brethren understand nature and are able to enjoy the benefits God intended humanity to possess. This return to Eden is a result of the spiritual quest that has purged the members of Solomon's House of pride (the cause of the Fall) and the pious devotion to God that has prompted them to "love the neighbor as the self." In addition, the reference to Solomon's *Natural History* seems to allude to a Jewish esoteric tradition in which Solomon was not only wise in the way described in the Biblical accounts, he also possessed a deep understanding of the mysteries of the Creation. Several variations of this tradition were fairly widely known in the early modern period. In one version, the original esoteric knowledge is given to Adam but lost through the Fall. Another version has the knowledge given to Moses on Mount Sinai and placed in the Ark of the Tabernacle, where it was accessible only to the High Priest. The Ark and then later Solomon's Temple became a centre for communing with the powers and principalities governing the world. The work of Solomon's House, then, is clearly in accord with both the "pagan" tradition of a pure ancient wisdom and with the Jewish esoteric traditions associating Solomon and Solomon's Temple with cabalistic knowledge.

The Dimensions of Instauration

Taken as a whole, "New Atlantis" presents a two-fold view or description of instauration. One is represented by Bensalem and involves a spiritual rejuvenation. The other is a recovery of natural philosophy represented by the work of Solomon's House and by Atlantis before it became corrupted. Bacon chooses to stress the latter in his utopia because he was concerned that the recovery or instauration of natural philosophy was being overlooked. For Bacon, the instauration of knowledge or the building of Solomon's House was as important to creating a Solomonic kingdom as was the religious recovery.

It is important to recognize the predominance of these religious motifs in order to understand the full scope of Bacon's programme for a great instauration through the advancement of learning. This programme is not a secular or humanistic departure from traditional religion and Solomon's House is not the prototype for a modern scientific think tank. Careful reading of the full text demonstrates that the activities of Solomon's House cannot be separated from the underlying themes of providential salvation and deliverance. The aim is to rebuild man's relation to God and recover the benefits God placed in nature for human beings to enjoy. The work of Solomon's House is thus tied to the spiritual as well as the material well-being of the people. Reverence toward nature as God's Creation is essential to derive the benefits from the Creation. The pious study of nature also guards against humanity's pride and its effort to create its own fantasy world. The Solomonic wisdom alluded to in Solomon's House is the wisdom of the workings of nature and the ability to use that knowledge for the benefit of humankind.

Yet Bacon's emphasis on Solomon's House rather than on Solomon's Temple reveals the way in which Bacon's vision of renewal or instauration is unique. The work of Solomon's House is not a substitute for the work of the Temple; it is the complement to it. Bacon indicates in several other writings that he believes religious reform is underway. What is crucial but lagging is the reform of natural philosophy. This is where

Bacon directs his foremost attention. The biblical themes of instauration are reinforced by references to the prehistory of the world before human ignorance and error resulted in divine punishment. This primeval golden age offers another vision of what a well-ordered empire can be, with Atlantis serving as a proper symbol of Bacon's intent and as a complement to Bensalem. Atlantis also provides an object lesson regarding the need for right religion to guide the efforts of natural philosophy. If pride replaces piety, science and technology will become sterile or self-destructive.

That Bacon sees the two aspects of instauration as complementary is evident in his other writings. In *The New Organon*, for example, Bacon says that "man by the Fall fell at the same time from his state of innocency and from his dominion over Creation. Both of these losses however can even in this life be in some part repaired; the former by religion and faith, the latter by arts and sciences." In *The Great Instauration*, Bacon urges that "all trial should be made, whether that commerce between the mind of man and the nature of things... might by any means be restored to its perfect and original condition, [or at least] reduced to a better condition than that in which it now is." Bacon believed that religious reform could be accomplished through the work of others. It was his special duty to advance the reform of natural philosophy. Both were necessary for the complete instauration of man's relation to God and his dominion over nature. The complete instauration will overcome the ravages of Original Sin and restore humanity to its prelapsarian condition.

In the end, "New Atlantis" offers a multi-layered analysis of the disorder of the European sailors' society and then prescribes the necessary cures. The contrast between European nations and Bensalem points to the sources of order and disorder. Both Bensalem and Europe have the benefit of Christian religion. Bensalem's Christianity is a pure form of gospel Christianity uncorrupted by human ignorance and error. Europe's Christianity, by contrast, has been distorted and is plagued by philosophical and theological squabbling. Bensalem and Europe also have schools of natural philosophy.

Bensalem's school of natural philosophy is the House of Solomon, which investigates nature in a reverent attempt to discover the benefits placed in creation by a loving God. Europe's natural philosophy has been marginalized and corrupted by scholastic and philosophical bickering and is dominated by competing schools of thought no longer grounded in empirical investigation of nature. England, nevertheless, has at its disposal the necessary means for utopian reform: a reformed and purified religion and, through Bacon's efforts, a reformed and revitalized natural philosophy. The two are complementary and each is indispensable for the restitution of humanity to its prelapsarian condition.

The Religious Origins of Modern Science

Because Howard White and others have argued that Bacon's use of biblical images and religious themes is cynical and transforms a spiritual quest into a material hedonism, it is important to review how religious motifs actually function in the text. Contrary to White's interpretation, the transformation from the European wanderers' preoccupation with material concerns to spiritual conversion constitutes the central dramatic action of "New Atlantis." At the beginning of the story, the Europeans are concerned to be rescued from a storm, and they seek assistance for those who are ill. The Europeans quickly recognize the excellence of the island and are struck by its order and its religion.

After they have been allowed to reside in the Strangers' House, the narrator urges his companions to conduct themselves so that they can earn the respect of the Bensalemites. The more they learn about Bensalem, the more they wish to become residents there. While their initial concern was their physical rescue or well-being, their exposure to the quality of life in Bensalem makes them realise that they have been rescued from personal, social, political, and spiritual disorder and disorientation. Even White acknowledges that the European travelers "not only wish to stay but are somehow made worthy of staying."

The centrality of religious and spiritual themes is reflected not only in the transformation of the Europeans but also in the persons with whom the Europeans have contact. The Bensalemite official, who boards the European ship, offers Christian charity in the form of provisions and medicines. The first interviews are provided by the Governor of the Strangers' House, a Christian priest, who responded warmly when the first question from the Europeans concerned the island's religion. The second set of interviews is given by Joabin and centers around matters of social order and morality, including discussion of Judeo-Christian dreams of installing the Kingdom of God on earth.

The final interview is given by a Father of Solomon's House. He describes the physical and material benefits provided by Solomon's House, but he also emphasizes that their study is motivated by piety, and he stresses that the ability to discover useful information is dependent on reverence and charity. Indeed, piety and charity are the motivations for founding Solomon's House in the first place.

It is well known that Bacon repeatedly links the knowledge of nature with the ability to bring relief to man's estate. Most often this linking is associated with knowledge as power. What is often overlooked is Bacon's emphasis on charity as the motive for using the knowledge of nature for the benefit of humankind—and, more specifically, the allusion to the biblical Solomon's reward for his "large heart" and his request for knowledge that can help meet the needs of his people. It is wrong, therefore, to link Bacon to a Faustian exercise of egomaniacal power. The understanding of nature enables humanity to enjoy the blessings that God provided, not simply to conquer the natural world with impiety.

The Temple in Jerusalem was the primary symbol of religious and political order. It housed the Ark of the Covenant, which was the symbol of divine election, and represented the making of the covenant between God and the Hebrews and the giving of the law as the basis for the covenant. One of the greatest instances of Israel's defeat and humiliation was the profanation of the Temple; and one of its greatest moments of rejuvenation occurred when King Josiah was able to reestablish political independence and to rebuild the Temple. Josiah's reform did not endure; Israel was again defeated and this time taken into captivity. During the post-exilic time, the apocalyptic yearning for restoration centered on the rebuilding of the Temple, and the Temple remained an apocalyptic symbol through the New Testament period to Bacon's age. The term used in the Vulgate edition of the Bible for Josiah's reform and for other messianic or apocalyptic revivals is *instauratio*. This term is, of course, a key symbol in Bacon's writings; it signals the shape and direction of the restoration he believes it is his calling to initiate.

When examined carefully, it becomes evident that "New Atlantis" is an intricately constructed literary work permeated with religious themes, including providential deliverance (for both the Europeans and Bensalem), apocalyptic instauration of the Kingdom of God on earth, and the societal embodiment of the cardinal Christian virtues, especially charity. It is not a society of "pleasant things," as Howard White asserts, nor is it the case, as Denise Albanese claims, that "the references to crosses and oblations, to piety and Christianity, which crowd the earlier pages... virtually disappeared thereafter."

The primary religious motif of salvation and deliverance is evident from the outset. The European voyagers are tossed off course by a storm and surrounded by darkness. But then they are delivered—like Jonah—to safety. The Europeans describe the island of Bensalem as a land of angels or as the Kingdom of God on earth. The conversion of Bensalem is an act of providential deliverance, suffused with symbols of special election, including the pillar of Cloud and the Ark of the Covenant. These themes are important to understanding Bacon's real project and for the recovery of the religious origins of modern natural science. For while the hunger to restore humanity's original place in God's Creation is surely not the only spur to the modern mastery of nature, the significance of the divine for the birth of empirical science also cannot be avoided or denied.

Bibliography

- From a 1593 quote of Izaak Walton's, "The great secretary of Nature and all learning, Sir Francis Bacon."
- "The World's a bubble, and the Life of Man Less than a span" is the opening line to Bacon's poem, "Life," one of blupete's poetry picks.
- See *W. G. Thorpe's* The Hidden Lives Shakespeare & Bacon and their Business Connection; with some Revelations of Shakespeare's Early Struggles 1587-1592 (London: Chiswick Press, 1897).
- Life Letters of Francis Bacon, 7 vols., [1861-1874]; there are numerous briefer lives as for example see Bowen.
- That is not to say that Bacon did not believe that there was a God, for, as he said in "Of Atheism": "I had rather believe all the fables in the legends and the Talmud and the Alcoran, than that this universal frame is without a mind."
- Henry Hallam, Introduction to Literature..., as quoted by OED2.
- Scholars located in Christendom, in those days, wrote in Latin: the point is, that the few that read, read Latin. Latin then was to the world of thinkers what English is today to scientists an international language which facilitated free movement of thought and research.
- For what Macaulay thought of Bacon's character is set forth, in his usual brilliant fashion, by Macaulay in his 100 page essay on Bacon.

